Reappraisals of British Colonisation in Atlantic Canada, 1700–1930

Histories of the Scottish Atlantic
Series editors: S. Karly Kehoe and Chris Dalglish

Critical histories of Scotland's transatlantic connections and their influence on the development of communities and landscapes, past and present

This series showcases new research into the history of Scotland's relationship with the Atlantic World and promotes understanding of the present-day legacies of this past. An important, though not exclusive, focus is the Scottish Highlands and those areas of the Caribbean and North America (Canada and the United States) with which Highland Scots had a significant relationship. The series explores the ways in which the lives of people from one place intersected with and impacted upon the lives of people from other places. It analyses how interactions between diverse Atlantic communities influenced the development of particular landscapes and regions, both in Scotland and on the other side of the ocean. It interrogates the ways in which these past interactions and developments continue to resonate with people today, as an aspect of their identity and a factor influencing their lives and life chances. And it reveals and explores the legacies of a complex past and advances understanding of how this at once positive and negative heritage might be harnessed for the future development of communities on both sides of the Atlantic.

edinburghuniversitypress.com/series/hsa

Reappraisals of British Colonisation in Atlantic Canada, 1700–1930

Edited by
S. KARLY KEHOE AND MICHAEL E. VANCE

EDINBURGH
University Press

Edinburgh University Press is one of the leading university presses in the UK. We publish academic books and journals in our selected subject areas across the humanities and social sciences, combining cutting-edge scholarship with high editorial and production values to produce academic works of lasting importance. For more information visit our website: edinburghuniversitypress.com

© editorial matter and organisation S. Karly Kehoe and Michael E. Vance, 2020, 2022
© the chapters their several authors, 2020, 2022

Edinburgh University Press Ltd
The Tun – Holyrood Road
12 (2f) Jackson's Entry
Edinburgh EH8 8PJ

First published in hardback by Edinburgh University Press 2020

Typeset in 10/13 Giovanni by
Servis Filmsetting Ltd, Stockport, Cheshire

A CIP record for this book is available from the British Library

ISBN 978 1 4744 5903 7 (hardback)
ISBN 978 1 4744 5904 4 (paperback)
ISBN 978 1 4744 5905 1 (webready PDF)
ISBN 978 1 4744 5906 8 (epub)

The right of the contributors to be identified as authors of this work has been asserted in accordance with the Copyright, Designs and Patents Act 1988 and the Copyright and Related Rights Regulations 2003 (SI No. 2498).

Contents

Notes on the Contributors vii
Map of the Caribbean ix
Map of the USA x
Map of Atlantic Canada xi

INTRODUCTION

1 Colonial Legacies 3
   S. Karly Kehoe and Michael E. Vance

2 British Colonisation in an Atlantic Canadian Context 11
   John G. Reid

PART ONE Dispossession and Settlement

3 Barren Icy Rocks or a Nursery of Seamen? Debating Nova Scotia
   and Ideologies of Empire in the Era of the American Revolution 25
   Alexandra L. Montgomery

4 Leaving Nova Scotia: Sierra Leone and the Free Black People,
   1792–1800 41
   Ruma Chopra

5 New World, Old Problems? Aristocratic Influences on Colonial
   Governance and Land in Nineteenth-century Atlantic Canada 59
   Annie Tindley

PART TWO Religion and Identity

6 Catholic Highland Scots and the Colonisation of Prince Edward Island and Cape Breton Island, 1772–1830   77
   S. Karly Kehoe

7 The Church of England, Print Networks and the Book of Common Prayer in the North-Eastern Atlantic Colonies, *c.*1750–*c.*1830   93
   Joseph Hardwick

8 'For Christ and Covenant': Scottish Presbyterian Dissent and Early Political Reform in Nova Scotia, 1803–1832   113
   Holly Ritchie

PART THREE Reappraising Memory

9 Fenian Ghosts: The Spectre of Irish Republicanism in Ethnic Relations in Newfoundland   133
   Willeen G. Keough

10 Cosmopolitan Engagements: Class, Place and Diplomacy in the Gulf of St Lawrence Fisheries, 1815–1854   154
    Kurt Korneski

11 The Mi'kmaq, the Pattersons and Remembering the Scottish Colonisation of Nova Scotia   171
    Michael E. Vance

Index   190

Notes on the Contributors

Ruma Chopra is professor of history at San Jose State University in California. She has written on Atlantic slavery and war and society in the American Revolution. She is currently working on a project concerning environment and race in the early modern era.

Joseph Hardwick is senior lecturer in British history at the University of Northumbria in Newcastle. He specialises in the political, religious and environmental histories of British settler societies in Australia, southern Africa and Canada from the late eighteenth century.

S. Karly Kehoe is the Canada Research Chair in Atlantic Canada Communities at Saint Mary's University in Nova Scotia. She specialises in religion, migration and minority identities in the British Atlantic world.

Willeen G. Keough is professor of history at Simon Fraser University in British Columbia. One of her major research interests is the Irish diaspora in Newfoundland fishing communities, with special attention to gender, ethnicity, class and communal memory.

Kurt Korneski is associate professor of history at Memorial University of Newfoundland. His research focuses on the history of capitalism, colonialism, development policy and environmental history, particularly as they relate to diplomacy and the social history of fishers, the fishing industry and fishing communities in north-eastern North America.

Alexandra L. Montgomery is a PhD candidate at the University of Pennsylvania. She is interested in migration, empires and colonisation in seventeenth- and eighteenth-century north-eastern North America.

John G. Reid is professor emeritus of history and senior fellow of the Gorsebrook Research Institute for Atlantic Canada Studies at Saint Mary's University in Nova Scotia. His work has focused primarily on north-eastern North America in the seventeenth and eighteenth centuries, especially imperial–Indigenous relations, although he has also recently turned his attention to sport history.

Holly Ritchie completed her MA in history at Saint Mary's University in Nova Scotia. She currently assists with estate papers at the North Lanarkshire Archives in Motherwell, Scotland.

Annie Tindley is senior lecturer in modern British history at Newcastle University. She specialises in rural history, land management and reform, and aristocratic elites in the nineteenth and early twentieth centuries.

Michael E. Vance is professor of history at Saint Mary's University in Nova Scotia. His research focuses on nineteenth-century Scottish emigration and settlement as well as the nature of Scottish overseas identity.

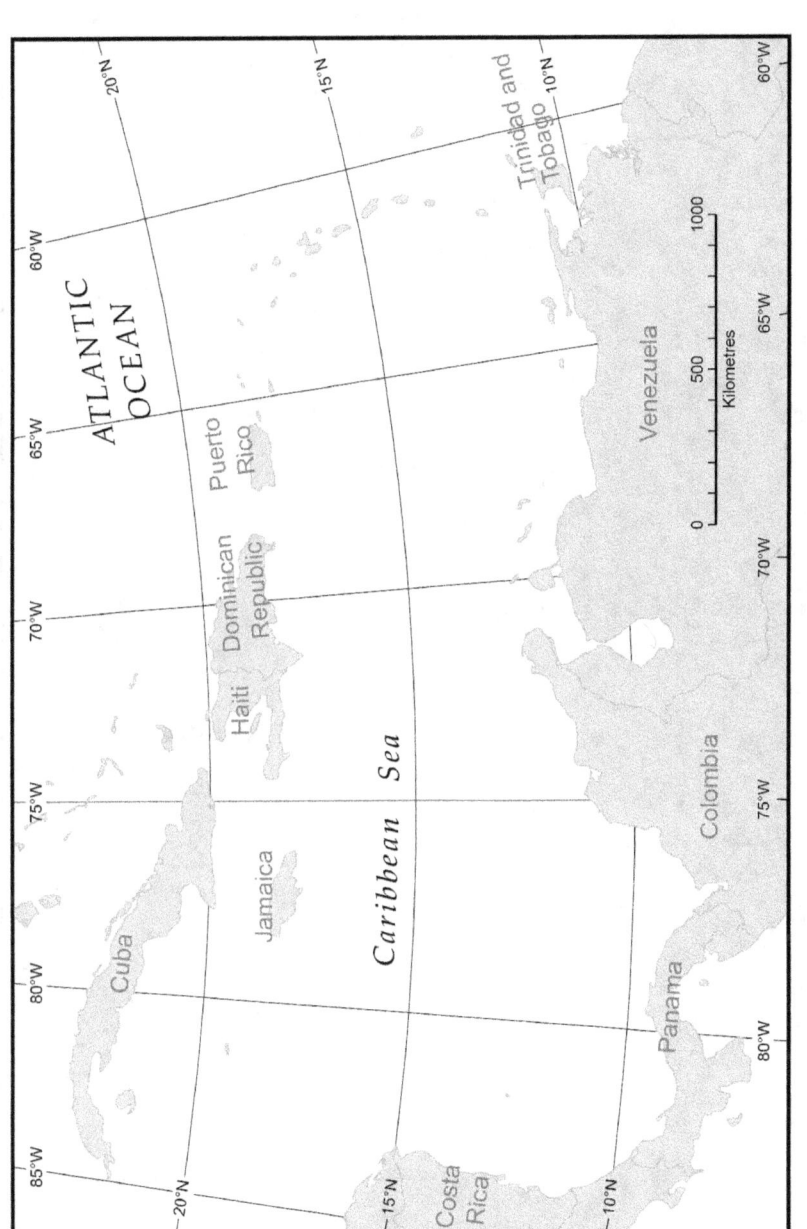

Map of the Caribbean

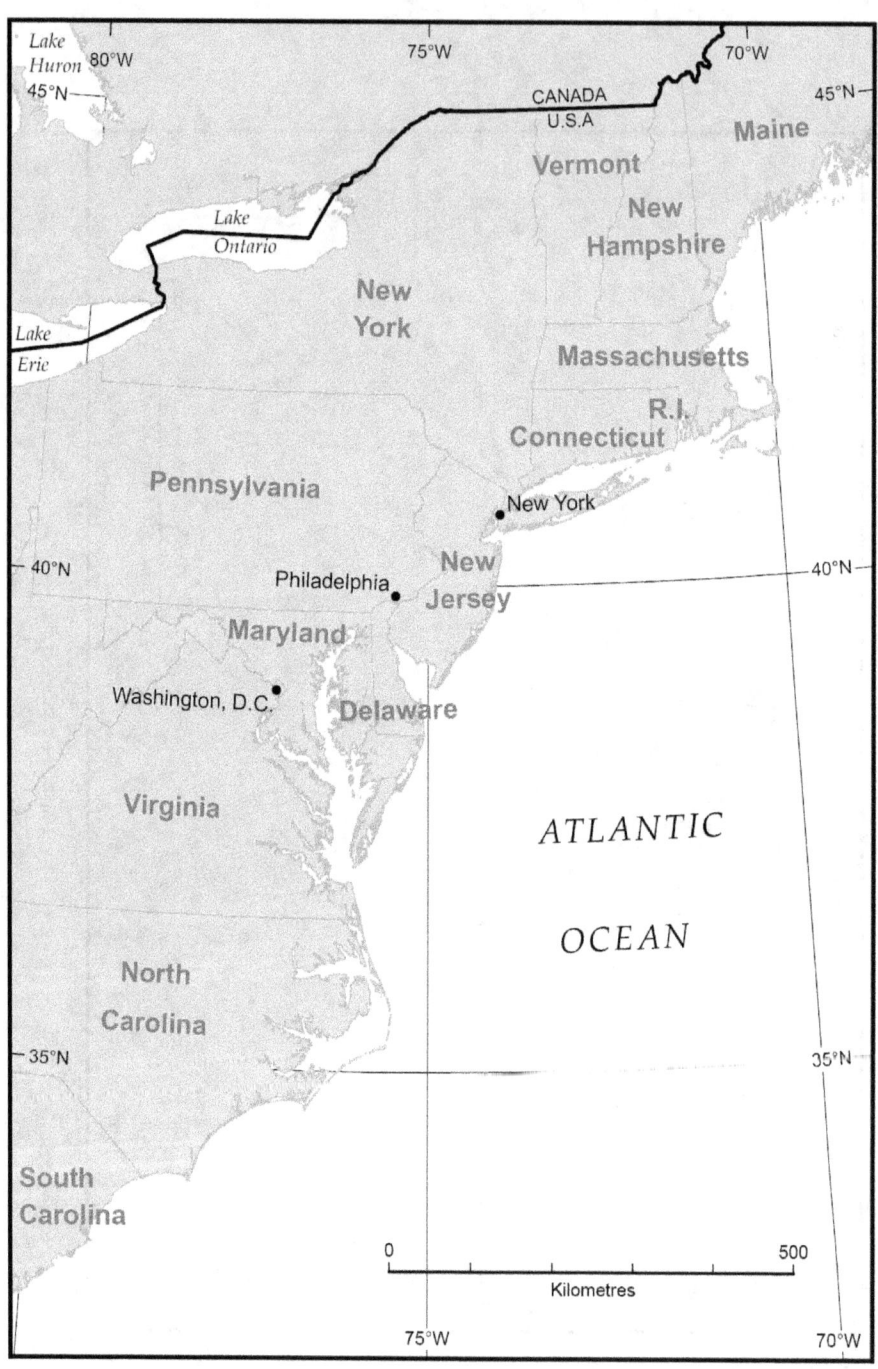

Map of the USA

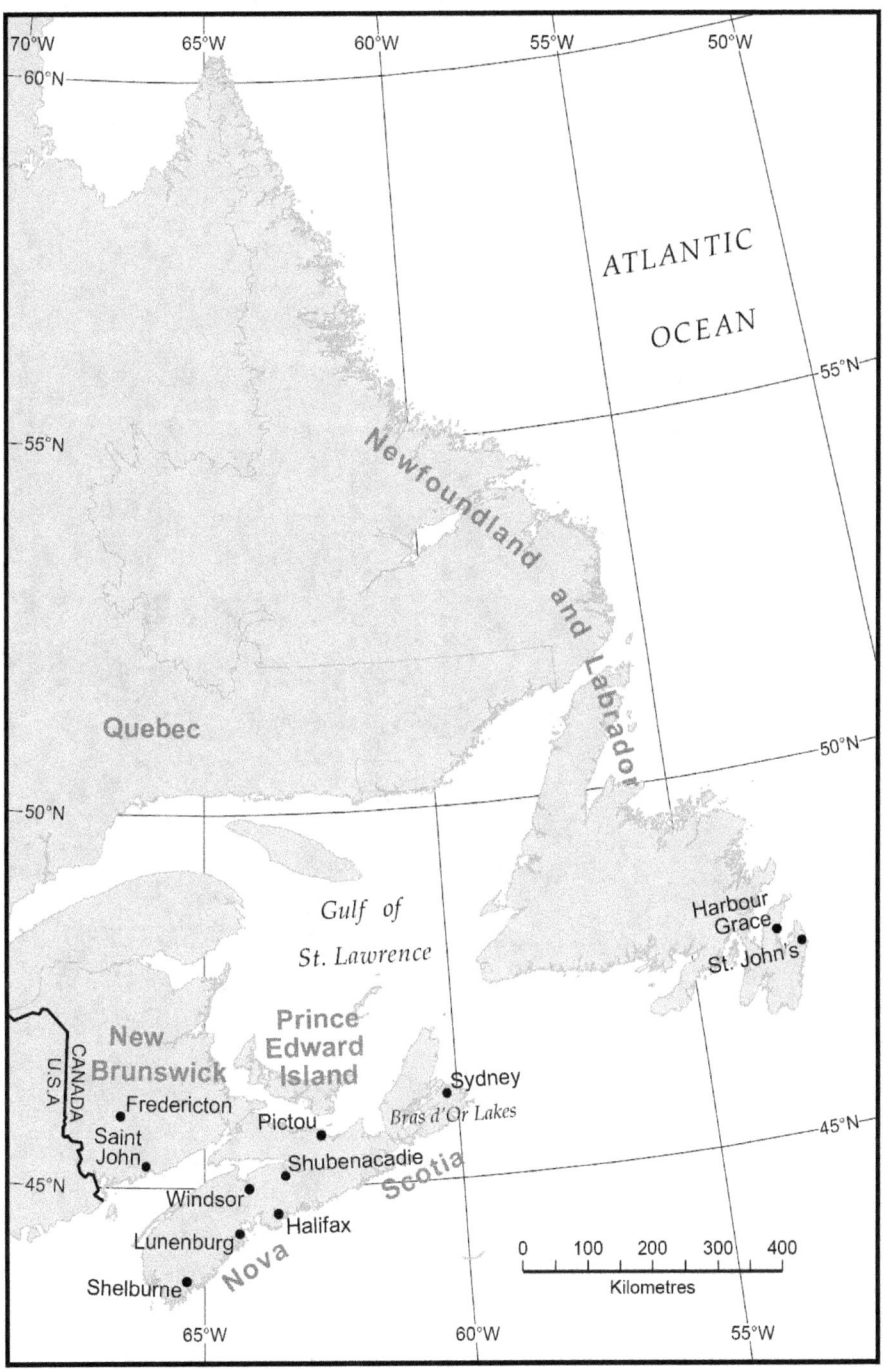

Map of Atlantic Canada

Introduction

ONE

Colonial Legacies

S. Karly Kehoe and Michael E. Vance

Before the end of January 2018, you could walk through Cornwallis Park, a small grass-covered square sitting about 500 metres, as the crow flies, from the Canadian Museum of Immigration at Pier 21 in Halifax's prosperous South End, and see a towering statue of Edward Cornwallis, Governor of Nova Scotia at the time of the city's founding in 1749. The statue, erected in 1931 by the Canadian National Railway as part of an effort to attract tourists to their new Nova Scotian Hotel directly adjacent to the park, was dismantled on 4 February 2018 and put in storage. While not drawing the violent white supremacist protest associated with the Civil War monuments in the United States, the prospect of the statue's removal had sparked a contentious debate. Some claimed that such removals were 'erasing history' whereas others, including Mi'kmaw elder Dan Paul, who had initiated the call to remove the statue, explained that the monument was an ongoing affront to Indigenous people because it stood as a reminder of Cornwallis's declared policy of extermination toward the Mi'kmaq. Halifax's city council agreed with the Mi'kmaw community and moved quickly to remove the statue, hoping to avoid any potential protest. In the end, the removal occurred peacefully as members of the Mi'kmaw community and their supporters celebrated the occasion with a traditional ceremony.[1] The significance of this event is twofold: on the one hand, it reveals that long after the official end of Empire the legacy of British colonialism continues to reverberate throughout the city, the province, the wider Atlantic region and, indeed, Canada as a whole; on the other hand, it represents an important shift in the relationship between civic authorities and Indigenous communities.

At first glance, Cornwallis was an unlikely figure to be celebrated as the 'founder of Halifax'. His military career was mired in controversy. Not only had he participated in the brutal suppression of the Scottish Highlands after Culloden, but he also faced accusations of misconduct for his behaviour in combat during the Seven Years War. His approach to the Mi'kmaq was brutal as his policy of confrontation resulted in bounties being placed on the scalps of Indigenous men, women and children. That this was in direct contradiction to the official Peace and Friendship policy did not seem to bother him, nor did the rebukes he received as a consequence from the Board of Trade. Cornwallis's elevation to the status of the city's founding figure was a late development, occurring at the end of the nineteenth century, when many Canadians and Nova Scotians were seeking ways of binding themselves more closely with the British Empire.[2] Identifying heroic figures from the imperial homeland and crediting them with pivotal roles became a preoccupation. The promotion of Edward Cornwallis as Halifax's 'founder', for example, happened at the same time that Sir John A. MacDonald was being hailed as the 'first' Canadian prime minister. It was a selective reading of the imperial past that supported the invention of an identity for an infant nation. Canadian legitimacy, it would seem, was to be defined by British men and for a long time, few people challenged that – those who did were marginalised or, in the case of the Indigenous peoples, targeted with assimilation policies. In Nova Scotia, this tailoring of the historical record was exposed during the debate over the Cornwallis statue and reflected a genuine effort to engage with the findings of Canada's landmark Truth and Reconciliation Commission (TRC). The Commission, which ran between 2008 and 2015, provided a long-overdue space for Indigenous people from across the country to talk about their experiences of the residential school system,[3] a system that John A. MacDonald had endorsed and helped to develop as a means of enforcing the assimilation of Indigenous peoples into settler society norms. In addition to documenting the countless cases of physical, emotional and sexual abuse, the commissioners called on all Canadians to recognise how systemic racism and the exclusion of Indigenous experience from the historical narratives of the nation have contributed to what has been appropriately described as cultural genocide by Cree elder, senator and the Commission's Chair, Justice Murray Sinclair, and Canada's former Supreme Court Chief Justice, Beverly McLaughlin.[4]

Among the many items listed in the TRC's Calls to Action, and highlighted in the final report, was a series of recommendations under the heading 'Education for Reconciliation' that included the development, in collaboration with Indigenous peoples, of 'curriculum on residential schools, Treaties, and Indigenous peoples' historical and contemporary contributions to Canada' to be delivered as a mandatory requirement at all levels of education from kindergarten to high school.[5] While the commissioners did not call for the removal of public monuments or the renaming of institutions, such actions have taken place across the country in the wake of the report. Indeed, Mike Savage, the current mayor of the Halifax Regional Municipality, characterised the removal of the Cornwallis statute as an act of reconciliation, and many in the Mi'kmaw community interpreted the city's actions in the same light. When asked about the broader trend, Murray Sinclair reinforced the point that what was required were monuments dedicated to, and institutions named after, Indigenous leaders in order to balance the public presentation of the past. While many Mi'kmaw advocates found the Cornwallis monument too much to tolerate, Sinclair has pointed out that such public monuments can provide the opportunity to highlight the detrimental and ongoing impact of colonisation on Indigenous peoples.[6] The onus is on educators and the research community to provide a nuanced and more complete picture of the past that aligns with the commissioners' call to 'establish a national research program . . . to advance understanding of reconciliation'.[7]

The TRC's Calls to Action necessitates a meaningful engagement with the legacy of colonisation, and it comes at a time when historians throughout the former British Empire are grappling with the impact of colonisation on both coloniser and colonised. This agenda began with the pioneering post-colonial work of Franz Fanon, Edward Said and Gayatri Spivak,[8] but it has grown to include the work of many who would not necessarily identify themselves as post-colonialist scholars. The range of approaches is perhaps best reflected in the contributions to the *Journal of Colonialism and Colonial History*, published since 2000 with a mandate to examine 'the broad range of issues that relate to imperialism and colonialism from the tenth century through modern times including the social effects on the population, the political structures under imperial rule, the transition to independence, and the lasting impact of living under colonial rule'. The re-evaluation of Britain's colonial legacy is part of a wider global reassessment of colonisation and is connected with a fundamental desire to de-colonise former imperial societies.[9] Not all of the chapters in this volume highlight the Indigenous dimension, but a number do, and this is important because it reveals the diversity of the colonial experience.

In addition to contributions to specialised academic journals, over the last few decades the complex and varied nature of British colonisation has been explored by numerous studies examining Britain's imperial past. Academic presses have supported series dedicated to the topic (including the Edinburgh University Press series in which this volume sits) and have produced a growing number of specialised monographs and edited collections that either directly or indirectly engage with all aspects of British colonisation. Among some of the more recent studies of the lasting consequences of the encounter with the Indigenous peoples throughout the Empire are Amanda Nettelbeck's monograph, *Indigenous Rights and Colonial Subjecthood: Protection and Reform in the Nineteenth-Century British Empire*, Martin Daunton and Rick Halpern's edited *Empire and Others: British Encounters with Indigenous People, 1600–1850* and Alan Lester and Zoë Laidlaw's edited collection, *Indigenous Communities and Settler Colonialism: Land Holding, Loss and Survival in an Interconnected World*. These are joined by Kathleen Wilson's edited volume, *A New Imperial History: Culture, Identity and Modernity in Britain and the Empire, 1600–1840*, Fariha

Shaikh's examination of the influence of overseas settlement on British literary culture, *Nineteenth-Century Settler Emigration in British Literature and Art*, and Charles Reed's study of the impact of royal tours on settler society and Indigenous relations, *Royal Tourists, Colonial Subjects and the Making of a British World, 1860–1911*. Recent enquiries also extend to the role of religion in forwarding the colonial project, with Hilary M. Carey's *God's Empire: Religion and Colonialism in the British World, c.1801–1908*, and to the impact of the practice of Black enslavement on both the colonies and the imperial centre as reflected in the contributions to *Emancipation and the Remaking of the British Imperial World* and Catherine Hall, Keith McClelland, Nick Draper, Kate Donington and Rachel Lang's *Legacies of British Slave-Ownership: Colonial Slavery and the Formation of Victorian Britain*. Much of the existing research is synthesised in Cecilia Morgan's *Building Better Britains?: Settler Societies in the British World, 1783–1920*, and the themes of her book – the relations with Indigenous peoples, the processes of migration and settlement, the creation of settler economies and the manufacture of colonial identity and imperial culture – helpfully summarise our current understanding of the various manifestations of British colonisation throughout the former Empire.[10]

The legacy of British colonisation in what is now Atlantic Canada – the four eastern provinces of Nova Scotia, New Brunswick, Prince Edward Island, and Newfoundland and Labrador – has not been ignored by scholars, but until relatively recently it has usually been discussed within the framework of the advent of Canadian Confederation. This teleological approach is revealed in the titles of the two-volume history of the region, intended to be the standard work in the field, *Atlantic Region to Confederation: A History* and *The Atlantic Provinces in Confederation*, and it is also apparent in the more recent, most commonly used university level textbook, *Atlantic Canada: A History*.[11] Transatlantic and transnational historiography has also had an influence on the study of the region. Among the earliest examples is John G. Reid's *Acadia, Maine, and New Scotland: Marginal Colonies in the Seventeenth Century*. More recently, this influence has extended to studies that expressly acknowledge the Indigenous experience, such as Lennox Jeffers' *Homelands and Empires: Indigenous Spaces, Imperial Fictions, and the Competition for Territory in North Eastern North America, 1690–1763*.[12] Indeed, Reid, whose chapter in this volume outlines the context for British colonisation in Atlantic Canada, has been at the forefront of the effort to understand the historical Indigenous experience in the region, and his work has been followed by important studies such as William Wicken's *The Colonization of Mi'kmaw Memory and History, 1794–1928* and Marie Battiste's edited collection, *Living Treaties: Narrating Mi'kmaw Treaty Relations* – which examines the topic from a contemporary Indigenous perspective.[13] This scholarship reveals that the treaties were understood very differently by the coloniser and the colonised: the Mi'kmaq saw them as being a formal recognition of Peace and Friendship and a means to live together with settler society, while the British ultimately understood them as 'instruments of submission'. The identification of this fundamental difference must be the starting point for understanding the legacy of British colonisation in the region.

The wider development of the historiography on colonisation has begun broadening the perspective on the experience in Atlantic Canada. Another contributor to this volume, Kurt Korneski, summarises the approach:

> [H]istorians of settler colonialism have posited that such societies are best understood as animated by the interlinked, mutually determining interplay of four distinct kinds of relations: those between indigenous peoples and a settler collective; those between the settler group and exogenous subaltern groups (for example, migrants of Asian and African descent in North America); the relations between indigenous and exogenous subaltern groups; and the overlap between settler states and the imperial metropoles that spawned them.[14]

Korneski explores these overlapping relations in his own work on Newfoundland, and other scholars have examined one or more of them elsewhere in Atlantic Canada. For example, the essays in *The Loyal Atlantic: Remaking the British Atlantic in the Revolutionary Era* place the Indigenous and settler experience in Atlantic Canada within the imperial context of ongoing African enslavement, political arguments surrounding loyalism and the development of transatlantic print culture. Contributors to *Britain's Oceanic Empire: Atlantic and Indian Ocean Worlds, c. 1550–1850* outline the role of 'orientalism', as well as commercial exchanges with non-European peoples elsewhere in the empire, on relations with the Indigenous peoples in region.[15] While this scholarship builds on work that has explored such topics as the persistence of slavery in Atlantic Canada, the legacy of the establishment of Scottish and Irish settler communities in the region and the economic ties with the mother country, the connections being made to the broader histories of British colonisation are relatively recent developments – but the fact that they are happening is encouraging.[16]

As the Cornwallis statue controversy has revealed, the impact of British colonisation is not restricted to the era before Confederation. As an important destination for settlers from the British Isles as well as the former American colonies, particularly after the American Revolution and for much of the first half of the nineteenth century, Atlantic Canada experienced all the aspects of settler colonialisation found elsewhere in the British Empire. Scottish people feature prominently in this volume and this is for two reasons: firstly, this book is the first in the Histories of the Scottish Atlantic series from Edinburgh University Press, and this required a Scottish emphasis; and secondly, there is an urgent need to understand the complexities of Scottish migration to the colonies that would become Atlantic Canada, because the tendency to perceive Scots as the victims of colonisation rather than its perpetrators has created a number of socio-economic challenges for future generations.

The erection of the Cornwallis statute in 1931 reflected the continuing cultural importance of the British connection to the region long after the period of initial settlement, while its dismantling revealed how such commemoration was linked to Indigenous dispossession – a central feature of settler colonialism. The purpose of this volume is to contribute to the broader understanding that is emerging about the nature of British colonisation. The focus on Atlantic Canada enables the contributing authors to present case studies that illuminate specific features from a variety of contexts from the eighteenth century to the twentieth. In pursuing this goal we have brought together senior and emerging scholars who are actively engaged in the study of British colonisation in the region. Their contributions are gathered together under three main themes – settlement and dispossession; religion and identity; and the construction of memory – which reflect the broader approaches to the British colonial experience and to the study of settler colonialism. By taking this approach, we have been able to reveal the multiplicity of actors, from American colonists, free persons of colour, aristocrats, labourers, Catholics, Anglicans and Presbyterians to English, Scots, Irish and Indigenous peoples, and speak to the fact that many of them often held multiple identities. Collectively, the chapters demonstrate how British colonisation in Atlantic Canada was supported and enabled by myriad groups, how it involved the creation of structures that mediated religion, language and perceptions of race, and how it was inextricably linked with a global system that placed Britain at the centre of an expansive web during the imperial age and beyond.

Notes

1. John G. Reid, 'The Three Lives of Edward corn Wallis', *Journal of the Royal Nova Scotia Historical Society*, 16 (2013), pp. 19–45; Aboriginal Peoples Television Network Report, <http://aptnnews.ca/2018/02/16/history-decolonized-a-closer-look-at-edward-cornwallis-and-why-his-statue-toppled/> (last accessed 20 October 2019).
2. Reid, 'The Three Lives'.
3. Truth and Reconciliation Commission of Canada, *Honouring the Truth and Reconciling for the Future: Summary of the Final Report of the Truth and Reconciliation Commission of Canada* (Ottawa, 2015), <http://nctr.ca/assets/reports/Final%20Reports/Executive_Summary_English_Web.pdf> (last accessed 20 October 2019).
4. Dale Eisler, 'First Nations and Public Policy: A Legacy of Failure with Blame All Around', *Policy Magazine*, 3:4 (July/August 2015), pp. 28–30.
5. Truth and Reconciliation Commission of Canada, *Calls to Action* (Ottawa, 2015), #63.1. <http://trc.ca/assets/pdf/Calls_to_Action_English2.pdf> (last accessed 20 October 2019).
6. 'Honouring Indigenous Heroes Better than Debating Macdonald: Sinclair', *Globe & Mail*, 29 August 2017.
7. Truth and Reconciliation Commission, *Calls to Action*, #66.

8. Among key works are Franz Fannon, *Black Skins, White Masks* (1952); Edward W. Said, *Culture and Imperialism* (1993); and Gayatri Chakravorty Spivak, 'Can the Subaltern Speak?' (1988).
9. See for example the contributions to *Settler Colonial Studies* published since 2011.
10. Amanda Nettelbeck, *Indigenous Rights and Colonial Subjecthood: Protection and Reform in the Nineteenth-Century British Empire* (Cambridge: Cambridge University Press, 2019); Alan Lester and Zoë Laidlaw (eds), *'Indigenous Sites', Indigenous Communities and Settler Colonialism: Land Holding, Loss and Survival in an Interconnected World* (Basingstoke: Palgrave Macmillan, 2015); Fariha Shaikh, *Nineteenth-Century Settler Emigration in British Literature and Art* (Edinburgh: Edinburgh University Press, 2018); Charles V. Reed, *Royal Tourists, Colonial Subjects and the Making of a British World, 1860–1911* (Manchester: Manchester University Press, 2017) – part of the influential 'Studies in Imperialism' series; Hilary M. Carey, *God's Empire: Religion and Colonialism in the British World, c.1801–1908* (Cambridge: Cambridge University Press, 2013); Catherine Hall, Nicholas Draper and Keith McClelland (eds), *Emancipation and the Remaking of the British Imperial World* (Manchester: Manchester University Press, 2014); Cecilia Morgan, *Building Better Britains?: Settler Societies in the British World, 1783–1920* (Toronto: University of Toronto Press, 2017).
11. Philip Buckner and John G. Reid (eds), *Atlantic Region to Confederation: A History* (Toronto: University of Toronto Press, 1994); E. R. Forbes and D. A. Muise (eds), *The Atlantic Provinces in Confederation* (Toronto: University of Toronto Press, 1993); Margaret R. Conrad and James K. Hiller, *Atlantic Canada: A History*, 3rd edn (Don Mills, ON: Oxford University Press, 2015) – first published as *Atlantic Canada: Region in the Making* (2001) – this volume is divided into two sections by Confederation.
12. John G. Reid, *Acadia, Maine, and New Scotland: Marginal Colonies in the Seventeenth Century* (Toronto: University of Toronto Press, 1981); Lennox Jeffers, *Homelands and Empires: Indigenous Spaces, Imperial Fictions, and the Competition for Territory in North Eastern North America, 1690–1763* (Toronto: University of Toronto Press, 2017) – the first title in the new series Studies in Atlantic Canada History, edited by John Reid and Peter L. Twohig.
13. See John G. Reid, 'Pax Britannica or Pax Indigena? Planter Nova Scotia (1760–1782) and Competing Strategies of Pacification', *Canadian Historical Review*, 85 (2004), pp. 669–92; 'Empire, the Maritime Colonies, and the Supplanting of Mi'kma'ki/Wulstukwik, 1780–1820', *Acadiensis*, 38:2 (Summer/Autumn 2009), pp. 78–97; and, with Thomas Peace, 'Colonies of Settlement and Settler Colonialism in Northeastern North America, 1450–1850', in Edward Cavanagh and Lorenzo Veracini (eds), *The Routledge Handbook of the History of Settler Colonialism* (Abingdon: Routledge, 2017), pp. 79–94; William Wicken, *The Colonization of Mi'kmaw Memory and History, 1794–1928: The King v. Gabriel Sylliboy* (Toronto: University of Toronto Press, 2012); Marie Battiste (ed.), *Living Treaties: Narrating Mi'kmaw Treaty Relation* (Sydney: Cape Breton University Press, 2016).
14. Kurt Korneski, '"A great want of loyalty to themselves": The Franco-Newfoundland Trade, Informal Empire, and Settler Colonialism in the Nineteenth Century', *Journal of World History*, 29:2 (June 2018), p. 149.
15. *The Loyal Atlantic: Remaking the British Atlantic in the Revolutionary Era*, edited by Jerry Bannister and Liam Riordan (Toronto: University of Toronto, 2012); *Britain's Oceanic Empire: Atlantic and Indian Ocean Worlds, c.1550–1850*, edited by H. V. Bowen, Elizabeth Mancke and John G. Reid (Cambridge: Cambridge University Press, 2012).
16. See for example James W. St G. Walker, *The Black Loyalists: The Search for a Promised Land in Nova Scotia and Sierra Leone, 1783–1870* (Toronto: University of Toronto Press, 1992); S. Karly Kehoe, 'Historical Perspectives on Migrant Integration in Atlantic Canada, 1812–1825', in S. Karly Kehoe, Jan-Christoph Heilinger and Eva Alisic (eds), *Responsibility for Refugee and Migrant Integration* (Berlin: De Gruyter Publishers, 2019), pp. 65–80; Michael E. Vance and Marjory Harper (eds), *Myth, Migration and the Making of Memory: Scotia and Nova Scotia, c.1700–1990* (Halifax, NS: Fernwood Publishers and John Donald Publishers, 1999);

S. Karly Kehoe, 'Catholic Relief and the Political Awakening of Irish Catholics in Nova Scotia, 1780–1830', *Journal of Imperial and Commonwealth History*, 46:1 (2018), pp. 1–20; Willeen G. Keough, *The Slender Thread: Irish Women on the Southern Avalon, 1750–1860* (New York: Columbia University Press, 2009); Julian Gwyn, *Excessive Expectations: Maritime Commerce and the Economic Development of Nova Scotia, 1740–1870* (Montreal: McGill-Queen's University Press, 1998).

TWO

British Colonisation in an Atlantic Canadian Context

John G. Reid

Beginning upwards of half a millennium ago, European sojourners and their settler colonialist inheritors sought to acquire resource assets and eventually the land itself in Mi'kma'ki and the neighbouring homelands of the Wolastoqiyik and the Beothuk/Innu. This area, corresponding broadly in settler terms to Atlantic Canada, has seen a process of European expansion premised on appropriating the wealth, the resources and the bodies of non-European peoples. Historically, it was a process of unique antiquity, beginning with fisheries that predated the turn of the sixteenth century, and one in which Scots took an early and influential role. This volume, focusing primarily on eras following the onset of colonial settlement, offers a series of reappraisals of key developments not only in settler societies themselves but also in relation to African and Indigenous inhabitants. Insofar as the geographical frame of reference is Atlantic Canada, there is of course a sense in which the term is anachronistic. Only with the joining of Newfoundland (formally known from 2001 as Newfoundland and Labrador) to Canada in 1949 did Atlantic Canada become a regional designation for what had previously been distinguished respectively as the Dominion of Newfoundland and the Maritime provinces of the Dominion of Canada. Yet for analytical purposes, the term Atlantic Canada represents a justifiable shorthand for a portion of north-eastern North America that – despite variations in environment and in economic trajectories – shared important elements of both Indigenous and settlement histories.

In nineteenth- and twentieth-century historiographies, influenced by the 'British and settler scholars' clustered notably in the institutions described by Tamson Pietsch as 'settler universities', imperial expansion and colonial settlement were attributed central roles throughout the post-contact era.[1] Yet Indigenous societies in this part of North America, which had evolved over a period of at least some ten thousand years, were not in reality so easily overshadowed. Contact with non-Indigenous commercial voyagers – English, French, Basque and others – from approximately 1500 onwards did make a difference, but not necessarily an unmanageable difference. Prior to that time, continuity and change were underwritten by factors operating within North America and, generally speaking, within north-eastern North America. Environmental change took forms ranging from the gradual but transformative process of warming that followed the last Ice Age to shorter-term variations that influenced transportation patterns and seasonal characteristics. Relationships among Indigenous neighbours proceeded according to shifting norms of diplomacy, alliance and hostility. Economies depended on cyclical resource harvesting, while leaderships followed established protocols of consensual decision-making. Then, at some indefinable point during the late fifteenth century, European contact began. Fisheries brought vessels from a variety of European Atlantic ports, whether the incidental and tangential visits that came from the offshore, banks-based 'green' fishery – so named because the catch was salted and stored while still wet – or the seasonal presence of the 'dry' fishery, with its shore installations and drying flakes for the less perishable dried salt cod. The early fisheries took in an extended Atlantic coastline from Labrador to what became northern New England, and were followed several decades later by the development of fur trading in some areas – primarily in the Mi'kmaw and Wolastoqiyik territories – and subsequently by the launch of competing claims to swaths of territory derived from the crowns of France, England and Scotland.

All through the sixteenth century, these processes represented a form of imperial outreach but were unaccompanied by colonial settlement, and as the seventeenth century opened the distinction changed only in some localities. In places such as Cupid's Cove in Newfoundland, and Port Royal in what the French crown claimed as its colony of Acadie and the Scottish crown conversely claimed as its colony of New Scotland, small colonial populations existed precariously during the initial decades of the seventeenth century. Even where thriving Acadian French communities grew up as the century advanced, primarily on the marshlands of the Bay of Fundy, the spatial impact on Indigenous neighbours was minimal. Without underestimating either the ravages of disease or the economic and cultural impact of European commodification of resources, neither Indigenous territorial integrity nor the integrity of the Indigenous polities had been seriously challenged by the time a tenuous French colonial administration was ousted in 1710 by the British conquest of Acadie and replaced by an equally tenuous British regime. The European presence in Mi'kma'ki was then divided for a time, as the Treaty of Utrecht (1713) designated the two Gulf islands of Cape Breton and Île Saint-Jean to France while leaving the rest of Acadie (with undefined boundaries) to Great Britain. The Wolastoqiyik territory further west lay within a continuing area of notional French–British dispute. Still the small colonial population was highly circumscribed everywhere, with even the French fortified town of Louisbourg and its later British counterpart of Halifax representing areas of dense rather than extensive settlement. The island of Newfoundland, meanwhile, saw incremental growth of a primarily English population in south-western areas that were utilised for the inshore fishery. A smaller French colony centred at the port of Plaisance was abandoned when at Utrecht the French claim to Newfoundland was surrendered, and the French colonists removed largely to Louisbourg. Thus, up until this time, and in a broadly defined north-eastern North American context, Indigenous interactions with empire were interactions with colonial settlement only in limited enclaves. Disruptions by disease and trade had proved insufficient to disturb the assurance with which Indigenous leaderships dealt with the non-Indigenous presence that existed on their periphery. Continuity from pre-contact eras remained powerful despite the changes that contact had brought. Indigenous centrality prevailed.

More far-reaching changes, however, gradually took effect. As the historian Jerry Bannister has shown, European warfare exerted a key influence in the form of 'the Forty Years' War'.[2] Beginning in 1744 and encompassing the French–British phase of the War of the Austrian Succession, the Seven Years' War and the War of the American Revolution, these years of near-continuous tension and conflict yielded a series of developments that drastically altered the relationships among Indigenous nations, European empires and colonial settlements. In Newfoundland, the uncertainties of the Atlantic passage in wartime tended to favour the growth of a resident population of fishers in preference to the previous predominance of seasonal fishing vessels over a relatively small resident presence. Along with the resulting settlement, despite some continuing uncertainties over the legality of settler landholding, came two important related developments. One was the embryonic growth of urban society, especially in St John's, while the other was the spread of residents along the main coastlines of the island. Both of these trends contributed to the diversification of the settler population through the addition of Irish migrants, even though the main era of intensive Irish settlement would come in the later eighteenth and early nineteenth centuries. Another impact was the critical intensification of environmental pressures on the Beothuk. While settler claims regarding the extinction of the Beothuk people have been challenged by recent scholars in the context of the close affinity between the Beothuk and the Innu, and of Beothuk-Mi'kmaw neighbourhood, the Indigenous presence in the principal areas of settlement declined substantially, as the non-Indigenous population approached 20,000 by the end of the 1780s.[3]

In the Mi'kmaw and Wolastoqiyik territories, treaty-making had emerged from the mid-1720s onwards as the basis for a relationship of peace and friendship with the British crown. The relationship persisted in a recognisable form for some six decades, even though friendship entailed complex political linkages, while British encroachments seriously endangered the peace at times.[4]

Following the inconclusive ending of British–French conflict in the War of the Austrian Succession, a British expedition ignited conflict when it established the fortified town of Halifax in 1749 without Mi'kmaw agreement. Plans for further expansion of settlement failed for the time being, and a broader reduction of the non-Indigenous presence came about through the British expulsion of the great majority of the approximately 14,000 Acadians between 1755 and 1762. Nevertheless, a new equilibrium was reached during the early 1760s, when a comprehensive round of treaties was concluded between the British crown and both Mi'kmaq and Wolastoqiyik in 1760–1, while some 7,000 new settlers from New England – known as the Planters – formed communities on the coasts of Mi'kma'ki and on the Wolastoq River. Bringing the settler population of Nova Scotia to some 17,000 by the eve of the American Revolution, this migration still did not impinge significantly on Indigenous territorial control, but the influx of some 35,000 Loyalist refugees and other migrants immediately after the American Revolution had a much more destructive demographic and environmental impact. Large-scale Scottish migration, both Highland and Lowland, also characterised the late eighteenth and early nineteenth centuries, as did Irish migration that was primarily pre-Famine but also reached into the 1840s and beyond. The Scots were clustered largely though not exclusively in Nova Scotia and Prince Edward Island, while the Irish – though, again, not exclusively – had the greatest impact on Newfoundland and New Brunswick. By now, as these provincial names imply, changes had taken place in the governance of the British colonies. In 1769, the Island of St John (known from 1799 as Prince Edward Island) had been detached from Nova Scotia, and in 1784 Nova Scotia was further reduced by a division to form the additional colonies of New Brunswick and Cape Breton. With Cape Breton subsequently reintegrated with Nova Scotia in 1821, the future Atlantic Canada now consisted of Newfoundland and three Maritime colonies. By the time the Maritime provinces entered the Canadian Confederation between 1867 and 1873, their collective settler population had reached some 770,000, while Newfoundland's population when it rejected Confederation in 1869 – it would finally join in 1949 – was just short of 150,000.[5]

From the mid-eighteenth to the mid-nineteenth century, a process of evolution changed Newfoundland and the Maritime colonies from areas that from an imperial perspective had only small outposts of settlement in predominantly Indigenous territory, to areas that had more in common with the settler colonial societies of New England and, increasingly, the more westerly parts of post-revolutionary British North America. Understandably, there were accompanying debates regarding the frameworks – legal, land-related, religious – within which settler communities should develop. As early as during the Planter migrations of the 1760s, as Alexandra Montgomery demonstrates in this volume, a division arose between advocates of small-scale landholdings based on freehold tenure such as the colonial promoter Alexander McNutt, and the more 'lordly' approach of the 'Nova Scotian government insiders and members of the British aristocracy' who favoured tenant-populated estates of the kind that most famously and tenaciously characterised the Prince Edward Island land system until the immediate post-Confederation era. Although there had existed a conjuncture when 'colonials and British officials . . . [had a] shared belief that their social and economic goals could be met by bringing white Protestants into the province at the expense of First Nations and Acadian people', the specifics of land tenure long remained divisive.

Newfoundland, meanwhile, had land questions of its own, deriving in part from efforts of the imperial state – long influenced by the interests of the declining but still powerful merchant families that operated the seasonal as opposed to the residential fishery – but also from uncertainties in land ownership along the west coast of the island and in the northern peninsula that proceeded from the reservation (from 1783 in its ultimate form) of the 'French Shore' for the use of seasonal French fishing vessels. Not until the conclusion of the Entente Cordiale between France and Great Britain in 1904 was the matter finally set to rest. Prince Edward Island's land question was also persistent, reaching its resolution with the post-Confederation agreement of the Government of Canada to buy out the land proprietors in accordance with the new province's Land Purchase Act of 1875. However, the settlement of the mid-1870s was not reached without illustrating the durability of the arguments that had first emerged more than a century before. Annie Tindley shows, through examining the question in the context of Canada in the post-Confederation era, that as 'a settlement colony . . . part of its attraction to European emigrants was that it offered the opportunity to own land outright', but she also highlights the personal role of Governor General Lord Dufferin. An Irish landowner himself, Dufferin, 'alongside many of his class, thought about land issues transnationally and was therefore concerned about the potential impact that reform in PEI might have on developments in Ireland, Britain, or elsewhere in the empire'. He eventually reached a position of reluctant acceptance of the Prince Edward Island land purchase, but as Tindley notes, a transnational approach to analysis of such issues reveals that the influence of 'the landed and aristocratic elite' was still capable of being exerted 'from Ottawa to Bengal, or Dublin to Canberra'.

As the growth of settler colonial populations coexisted, moreover, with the ongoing development of the eighteenth-century Atlantic World as an arena not only of multiple economic and cultural exchanges but also of forced migrations and settler pressures on Indigenous populations, so these influences inevitably impinged on the Maritime colonies and Newfoundland. The displacement of the Indigenous population in Newfoundland from key coastal resources was one illustration. Another, discussed by Ruma Chopra, was the movement of African-descended people in the Atlantic World. While the origins of such movements lay in the wider reality of enslavement, the two examples explored by Chopra – the successive migrations from Nova Scotia to Sierra Leone of a significant proportion of the free Black Loyalists (1792) and of the Jamaican Maroons (1800) – illustrate the delicate balance between forced migration and agency. While both migrant groups had their own reasons for leaving marginalised circumstances in Nova Scotia, they received support from such sources as the Sierra Leone Company and imperial anti-slavery advocates. The Black Loyalists were seen as well placed to exert a 'civilising' influence on indigenous Africans, while climatic theory also took a role in the encouragement of Maroons to move to Sierra Leone, which possessed a climate deemed to be well suited to their physical needs. In demonstrating the interconnection between imperial interests and African migration, Chopra also offers a contrast with the emerging clash of imperial priorities with Indigenous commitments to homeland and kinship, in that in an age of colonial settlement Indigenous dispossession became central to imperial goals in a sense that – in Mi'kma'ki and its neighbouring territories – had not been the case when peace and friendship had been shared aspirations.

The coexistence of imposed migration with assertive self-direction is also a major theme of Karly Kehoe's examination of Catholic identity among Highland migrants to Prince Edward Island and Cape Breton Island. Following the collapse of the Stuart insurgency in 1746, pressures on Highland Catholics became intense and combined with increasing commercialisation of land to make out-migration a workable response to adversity long before it became, as for some in the early nineteenth century, a matter of outright coercion. Funded in part by the Church itself, but also by funds originating from Caribbean slavery, early migrations led to the establishment in the Maritime colonies of a distinctive form of Catholicism characterised by a Scottish-derived experience of resisting Protestant antagonism but also by the need to coexist with other variants of Catholicism elsewhere in British North America. Ironically, however, Highlanders, who brought with them a deep cultural awareness of their own deprivations, now became leading agents of Indigenous dispossession, principally in Mi'kma'ki. Despite Mi'kmaw efforts to assert a shared Christianity, the demographic and environmental impacts of the Scots proceeded from 'rapid and largely uncontrolled settler growth'.

Religious tensions were central also to the wider settler society. As Joseph Hardwick points out, the early role of the Church of England in the Maritime colonies and in Newfoundland has received limited historiographical attention, despite the existence of substantial studies that have linked it with the Loyalist elite and more generally and questionably with the difficulties supposedly associated with 'a conservative and cumbersome institution'. Hardwick illustrates, instead, the more diverse roles of 'a dispersed and cosmopolitan Anglican communion'. Beginning with the introduction of missionaries supplied by the

Society for the Propagation of the Gospel (SPG) – which, in a further Atlantic World interconnection, drew significant revenue from enslaved labour on its own Codrington Plantations in Barbados – the Church of England exerted its Newfoundland influence during the mid-eighteenth century in places such as Trinity, Harbour Grace, and St John's, as well as the provision of bilingual missionaries to German-speaking 'Foreign Protestants' in Nova Scotia. Despite the development of a more focused Anglicanism in the Loyalist era, and the largely uniform character of the religious literature that was distributed, Hardwick notes that 'Atlantic Canada in the age of revolution was ... a region where the authority of bishops tended to press lightly, and where congregations and churches had freedom to develop peculiar characters and features.' Even as more intrusive episcopal influence subsequently increased, along with its symbols such as Gothic architecture, the early legacy was never wholly abandoned.

Not that these early characteristics could erase or even eclipse the identification of the Church of England with the colonial state that in Nova Scotia emerged from the Loyalist era. As Holly Ritchie shows in examining the religious and political implications of Thomas McCulloch's efforts on behalf of Pictou Academy, which reached their political height in the late 1820s and early 1830s, the Church of England establishment and its college – King's College, in Windsor – were powerful representations of privilege and of the insulation of the state against dissidence in any form. McCulloch, a Secessionist minister moulded intellectually by Covenanting ideology as well by commitment to a Scottish-influenced academy curriculum extending beyond classical education to embrace philosophy and science in an Enlightenment context, opened the academy to admission on a non-sectarian basis. As Ritchie points out, the Church of Scotland had its own stake in the empire that cast it in Nova Scotia as, in effect, a supporter of the notion that Pictou Academy was a subversive institution. McCulloch's challenge ultimately fell short, and in 1838 he resigned from Pictou to begin a troubled five-year spell as president of the nascent Dalhousie College in Halifax. Yet the historical significance of McCulloch's lengthy campaign on behalf of Pictou Academy lay in its illustration of 'concentric loyalties' and of 'how dissenting Presbyterians navigated the demands of the colony' as political critics who remained loyal subjects.

Religious and political loyalties took different forms in Newfoundland, in ways that were evident from the influence of Ribbonism in the Conception Bay of the 1830s through to the responses of Irish Newfoundlanders during the era of the Irish Civil War. As Willeen Keough points out, 'a historical collective memory of grievance among the Newfoundland Irish' had its origins in the hostility of British naval and then colonial authorities to any concentration of Irish fishers or settlers who were deemed because of their ethnic and religious character to be potentially seditious. Related fears that developed among Protestant settlers, notably in St John's and Conception Bay South, led in turn to the rapid spread of the Orange Order after its introduction in 1863, and thereafter not only the perceived Fenian threat of the later 1860s but also the news of every successive crisis over English rule of Ireland brought renewed tensions in Newfoundland that had both ethnic and religious overtones. Fenianism did not take formal root in Newfoundland, and explicit support for the Friends of Irish Freedom – founded in Ireland in 1916 – was short-lived, and yet Keough shows that republicanism was a historically revealing force in Newfoundland. Despite the role of an organisation such as the Benevolent Irish Society in encouraging imperial loyalty, and although most Irish Newfoundlanders were not republican in any explicit sense, 'it is important to recognise that not all . . . were supporters of the British Empire'. The desire for 'an acknowledgment of their right to share power and resources in Newfoundland' animated a continuing accord with, at least, 'the shade of Fenianism'.

Newfoundland, in the meantime, was also one important element in the geographical and economic composition of the mid-nineteenth-century Gulf of St Lawrence. The fisheries of the Gulf were critically important not only to the trade patterns of north-eastern North America but also to the lives and livelihoods of the fishers themselves, and of workers in related occupations. As Kurt Korneski demonstrates, international stresses were characteristic of an arena in which French and US interests competed with those from Newfoundland, the Maritime colonies and Lower Canada/Canada East. In the complex political economy that emerged, disputes played out at the level of colonial and even imperial levels were inseparable at more localised levels from the operation of the 'truck system' of merchant-fisher clientage or the mobility of labour in a borderland context. Thus, Korneski notes, 'when it appeared that colonial governments might become effective in asserting control of the spheres technically under their control, working people would, and did, defend alternative ideas about how spaces, resources, and transactions should be governed, sometimes violently'. By prioritising what they perceived as independent action essential to Britishness in a broad sense over the petty assertions of the colonial state, 'working people in the Gulf region not only inhabited what was an indeterminate space in the first decades of the nineteenth century, [but also] they were important architects of it'.

In delineating the creative importance of settler populations in political, religious, ethnic and social-class terms, many of the chapters in this volume combine to substantiate the point rightly made by Keough that an emphasis on the general impact of settler colonialism must not obscure the existence of 'considerable diversity among white settlers, and unequal access to power even among those who came from the "British Isles" – itself, a loaded term that requires intersectional analysis on the bases of gender, class, religion, ethnicity and region'. Nevertheless, Indigenous persistence is also an important theme. The era of imperial-Indigenous friendship in Mi'kma'ki and the Wolastoqiyik territory that commenced with the treaty-making of 1725 – uneasy as it had frequently been – began in the Loyalist era to give way to dispossession through demographic and environmental pressures. The consequences were frequently abrupt, an example being the wholesale appropriation of the Wolastoq valley, and everywhere settlers encroached and irrevocably changed the physical environment through clearance, depletion of faunal and sylvan resources and obstruction of Indigenous transportation routes. Peter Paul of the Pictou-area Mi'kmaq was three years old when the Loyalist-era migration reached its most intense phase, and he was aged eighty-six when in 1865 he described in detail to 'An Amanuensis' the environmental effects of settlement. Despite recalling instances of friendships he had shared with some of the settlers, Paul – to whom the amanuensis attributed stereotyped speech patterns – recalled pointedly that 'one time this [was] Micmac country . . . now white people say this [their] country, take 'em from Indian and never pay 'em. Indian speak 'em 'bout that good many times.'[6] By this time also, environmental and other destructive impacts on the Beothuk had led to the casting of the death of Shanawdithit in 1829 as representing the extinction of those deemed to be the island of Newfoundland's earliest Indigenous population. However, recent reappraisals ranging – among other authors – from the archaeological analysis of Lisa Rankin to the cultural and ethnomusicological portrayal of the later Indigenous woman Santu Toney by Beverley Diamond have problematised the assumptions underpinning the notion of extinction and raised the possibility of a more complex and continuing Indigenous presence on the island.[7]

The continuing existence of Mi'kma'ki, moreover, was and remained self-evident, and nowhere more so than in the area in which Peter Paul had described Mi'kmaw conversations focusing on the results of colonial settlement. In the final chapter of this volume, Michael Vance reflects both on the 'naturalisation' of Scottish settlement and on Mi'kmaw persistence by focusing on the *Hector* celebrations of July 1923, which commemorated the arrival 150 years earlier of the vessel carrying Scottish migrants sometimes extravagantly portrayed as 'the *Mayflower* of Canada'. Vance begins with an analysis of a posed photograph of some forty Mi'kmaw men, women and children who attended the festivities. Including chiefs and captains, the group was a gathering of distinction. Its purpose in a settler context, and notably for Judge George Geddie Patterson as chair of the celebration committee, was to lend additional credence to the normality of Scottish occupation of this portion of Mi'kma'ki. However, Patterson's father – Rev. George Patterson, who had studied with McCulloch at Pictou Academy and later at Dalhousie University – had been an amateur archaeologist, who as well as collecting Mi'kmaw artefacts had also consulted Mi'kmaw informants for the county history that he published in 1877.[8] Accordingly, Vance draws a careful distinction between father and son, noting too that Judge Patterson's verdict in the important Sylliboy hunting case of 1928 would supply 'a precedent that would be used as a model to deny Indigenous treaty rights up to the establishment of the Canadian Charter of Rights and Freedoms in 1982'. And yet, it remained true also that the Mi'kmaq photographed in 1923 had their own reasons for attending the ceremonies, in reasserting the treaty-based Mi'kmaw relationship with the crown. In doing so, they were in a symbolic sense looking ahead to the Charter era, when the treaties would be repeatedly upheld by the Supreme Court of Canada and Patterson's 1928 verdict decisively set aside.

Thus, in Scottish and other related contexts, this volume effectively brings together at least three broad and overlapping areas of historiography. One of them is the historiography of the Atlantic World, as an arena of exchanges that were economic, political and cultural, as well as recurrent debates over the shape of empire and settlement. It was also a world characterised from the seventeenth century into the nineteenth by enslavement, displacement of populations and the imperial exploitation of non-European peoples, even though their agency was not necessarily extinguished. The historiography of the British World is a second area to which the volume contributes notably, recognising that the weight of that sphere of influence could be felt acutely by non-British peoples as well as being experienced in distinctive ways by migrants from the British Isles who were distinguished by ethnicity, religion or social class. Thirdly, the historiography of settler colonialism – with its associated implication of the acknowledged or unacknowledged objective of normalising settlement through Indigenous erasure – is also central to the contributions powerfully made in the volume. Settler societies were diverse and complex, and to understand the phenomenon of settler colonialism as well as to measure its cost to Indigenous populations requires that these variations be fully explored. Thus, while chapters might be categorised as falling more fully within one or other of these broad areas of interpretation, it is no stretch to assert that the work of each and every author can be seen as having a significant bearing on all three. The history of what became Atlantic Canada yields crucial insights that have importance both within the region and far beyond, as this volume amply demonstrates.

Notes

1. Tamson Pietsch, *Empire of Scholars: Universities, Networks and the British Academic World, 1850–1939* (Manchester: Manchester University Press, 2013), p. 8 and passim.
2. Jerry Bannister, 'Atlantic Canada in an Atlantic World? Northeastern North America in the Long 18th Century', *Acadiensis*, 43:2 (Summer/Autumn 2014), p. 4.
3. See Fiona Polack (ed.), *Tracing Ochre: Changing Perspectives on the Beothuk* (Toronto: University of Toronto Press, 2018); Shannon Ryan, 'Fishery to Colony: A Newfoundland Watershed, 1793–1815', *Acadiensis*, 12:2 (Spring 1983), p. 38.
4. This relationship is more fully defined in John G. Reid, 'Imperial–Aboriginal Friendship in Eighteenth-century Mi'ma'ki/Wulstukwik', in Jerry Bannister and Liam Riordan (eds), *The Loyal*

Atlantic: Remaking the British Atlantic in the Revolutionary Era (Toronto: University of Toronto Press, 2012), pp. 75–102.
5. Margaret R. Conrad and James K. Hiller, *Atlantic Canada: A History*, 3rd edn (Don Mills, ON: Oxford University Press, 2015), p. 142.
6. 'Biography of Peter Paul – Written February 16th, 1865, from his own Statement by an Amanuensis', Nova Scotia Archives, MG9, vol. 5, 'Scrapbook of Dr George Patterson on Indians'.
7. Lisa Rankin, 'Towards a Beothuk Archaeology: Understanding Indigenous Agency in the Material Record', in Polack, *Tracing Ochre*, pp. 177–98; Beverley Diamond, 'Santu Toney, a Transnational Beothuk Woman', in Polack, *Tracing Ochre*, pp. 247–68.
8. George Patterson, *A History of the County of Pictou, Nova Scotia* (Montreal: Dawson Brothers, 1877). It is also possible that Patterson was the 'amanuensis' for the statement of Peter Paul, quoted above, a newspaper copy of which Patterson placed carefully in his own scrapbook on 'Indians'.

Part One

Dispossession and Settlement

THREE

Barren Icy Rocks or a Nursery of Seamen? Debating Nova Scotia and Ideologies of Empire in the Era of the American Revolution

Alexandra L. Montgomery

In late May 1765, a very young Anthony Wayne sat hunched over pen and paper on the deck of a ship. For three weeks, he had been surveying the southwest coast of Nova Scotia. What he found exceeded all his expectations. Eager to report back to his employers in Philadelphia – a group of well-connected men that included Benjamin Franklin – he had flagged down a Halifax-bound sloop and was scribbling out a letter. The land he saw in Nova Scotia, he wrote, was 'equal to any [in] Pennsylvania', even 'equal to any [he had] ever seen'.[1] Anticipating that what was at that moment undeveloped coastal and riverine meadowland would 'be a place of great importance in a very short time', he instructed his employers to apply for lots in the city he was about to help survey. Modestly, it was to be called Jerusalem.[2] 'I do assure you the land exceeds any idea I ever could have formed of it before I saw it,' Wayne wrote.[3]

Wayne was not alone in Nova Scotia that summer. The warm months of 1765 unleashed a mob of so-called 'land jobbers' onto the province's shores, culminating in a frenzy of land granting in late fall timed to avoid the implementation of the Stamp Act.[4] In a little over two weeks, the Nova Scotian government, acting on instructions from the Board of Trade, granted more than 2.5 million acres of land to companies and individuals from both sides of the Atlantic. Wayne and others like him were key players in the attempt by British imperial officials to transform Nova Scotia from a place of Native and French dominance which, in many ways, shared more in common with the trans-Appalachian west into a profitable Protestant settler colony like its neighbours to the south. Philadelphia's plantations, if successful, would have led to the arrival of an unprecedented number of new Protestant settlers and drastically undermined the land base and power of the Mi'kmaq and Wulstukwiuk who still dominated the province. The enthusiastic colonial response to the project of developing Nova Scotia was a rare moment during the 1760s when colonial elites and British imperial planners could agree on a common goal widely seen as beneficial – both socially and financially – to both sides: the dispossession of Indigenous people in the name of commercial and imperial development in the coastal periphery.

Yet just three years later, another Philadelphian took direct aim at the attempts to develop Nova Scotia in *Letters from a Farmer in Pennsylvania*.[5] In the eighth *Letter*, John Dickinson dismissed Nova Scotia and the new gains of the post-1763 Empire as, at best, drains on the public pocketbook and, at worst, actively detrimental to the development of the older settler colonies by threatening to siphon off populations that would be put to better use in the near colonial west. 'The icy rocks of *Canada* and *Nova-Scotia*', Dickinson finally declared, 'never will return to us one farthing that we send to them.'[6] Dickinson's harsh words reflected the fact that the Nova Scotian land boom was, for the vast majority of speculators, a complete failure. It ultimately resulted in barely a handful of new settlers and only one successful new town, Pictou, originally named Philadelphia Plantation. Indeed, the boom's primary legacy was to create a temporary legal roadblock to Loyalist resettlement: in the 1780s, the majority of the land granted in the middle 1760s was escheated and re-granted to refugees.[7] The site of Jerusalem, never developed, was transformed practically overnight into the boom town of Shelburne.

This chapter will chart the transformation of Nova Scotia in the Anglo colonial imaginary from Wayne's fertile land of great economic promise to Dickinson's barren waste. Although Nova Scotia and the region which became the Canadian Atlantic Provinces have been generally ignored in modern discussions of the run-up to the American Revolution, this was emphatically not the case for contemporaries. As a laboratory of empire newly open to investment, Nova Scotia attracted a representative sample of would-be imperial planners during a crucial period when the very meaning of empire was being debated. As such, rather than a peripheral or marginal space, Nova Scotia lay at the very centre of an ideological battle over what the post-Seven Years' War territory would look like, and who it would serve.

Because it did not result in a significant settler migration, this period in Nova Scotia's history has often been dismissed or glossed over in larger histories of the region. It is generally characterised as a time of wanton land speculation in which government corruption led to the transfer of thousands of acres of land to insiders with little interest in development or settlement.[8] Marcus Hansen memorably referred to the period as 'a veritable carnival of land-grabbing', a description which has been much quoted elsewhere.[9] Fred Anderson describes it as 'a decade of feverish speculation' characterised by 'wild schemes, conflicting claims, and unfulfillable promises that actually hindered the colony's recovery from the devastations of war and depopulation'.[10] Bernard Bailyn has given the period its most thorough modern account, writing of the era as a 'wild land boom' during which 'speculation in Nova Scotia lands swept like an epidemic throughout the British world'.[11] Although dismissive, these assessments nevertheless point to the unprecedented amount of attention directed at Nova Scotia during these years, as moneyed gentlemen from across the Empire jockeyed for the chance to stake a claim in an expanded imperial world.

Taking a more expansive view of Atlantic Canadian colonisation, however, the 1760s boom appears far more in keeping with the broader history of the region. As the target of centuries of imperial dreaming and scheming, much of greater Nova Scotia's eighteenth-century history took place within the bewigged heads of imperial planners, colonial governors and would-be land barons, some of whom never even visited the region. In the years between the fall of French Canada and the outbreak of the American Revolution, it was this imaginary of Nova Scotia that took centre stage in debates about what the British Empire should be and who it should serve, driving both the land boom and its ultimate collapse. While Wayne and Dickinson saw Nova Scotia as a potential new addition to an older colonial order based on smallholding farm families and a relatively horizontal political structure, other interested parties, including speculators as well as government officials, saw it as an opportunity to enforce a vision of empire based on hierarchy and deference.[12] The clash between these two visions brought a swift end to this fleeting moment of shared interest, as Nova Scotia, along with the rest of the continent, was engulfed in the American Revolution.

By 1765, there was nothing new about imagining Nova Scotia as a place of particular imperial control. The province, which then included the modern provinces of Prince Edward Island (PEI) and New Brunswick, already had a decades-old history of central management of settlement. Following the indecisive American end of the War of Austrian Succession in 1748, the British colony of Nova Scotia became a kind of laboratory of empire largely through the impetus of George Montagu-Dunk, 2nd Earl of Halifax.[13] Nova Scotia at that time was a struggling colony, if it could even be called that. Although it had been 'conquered' from the French in 1710, two generations later the British establishment was little more than a single garrison surrounded by a sea of French and Indigenous inhabitants.[14] Halifax, then first Lord of Trade, proposed an ambitious plan to transform the province into a model colony populated by loyal Protestants. The set piece of this plan was the founding, in June 1749, of the city that still bears his name. In stark contrast to the overwhelmingly private ventures that had characterised British expansion up to that point, Halifax was founded using parliamentary money under the direction of the British government.[15]

Halifax's reformed vision for Nova Scotia was sketched out almost entirely within London, with some limited input from colonial officials like Massachusetts governor William Shirley.[16] Perhaps unsurprisingly given that the plan was meant in no small part to reduce Indigenous power, First Nations people were not consulted, and the accomplishment of the Board of Trade's full vision was stymied by Mi'kmaw resistance and the outbreak of the Seven Years' War. By the time of the fall of Louisbourg in 1758, Protestant Nova Scotia had only expanded by one small community: the German town of Lunenburg, peopled by government-recruited 'foreign Protestants' who survived only on government rations.[17] In fact, in terms of overall European population it had in fact contracted due to the deportation of the French Acadian inhabitants at the start of the war.

Following the collapse of French power in North America, the plan continued along the lines Halifax had envisioned, as more settlers were attracted by offers of free land and government provisions and transportation. About 8,000 New Englanders were brought into the province by this scheme, and repopulated the prime agricultural lands painstakingly carved out by the deported Acadian population.[18] But turnover in the London administration and strict instructions to cut costs in the wake of an expensive war soon ended the experiment. Nova Scotia still received a stipend from Parliament in order to keep the province running, but Whitehall would no longer pay for experiments in directly sponsored settlement. Instead, between 1761 and the end of large private land grants in the early 1770s, the Nova Scotian government turned to private individuals to settle the province for them.[19] Individuals and companies were provided with tracts of land up to 100,000 acres, given a brief timeline to fill the tract with a set number of Protestant families and obligated to pay a royal quitrent; other than that, the new proprietors were free to manage their lands however they saw fit. The result was an explosion of settlement schemes which reflected a multitude of different perspectives on land tenure, economics and political organisation, all circulating within the same period and the same 130,000 square kilometres.

Nova Scotia attracted so much attention in these years in part due to its particular geographic position as an Atlantic colony which was also perceived to be an open 'frontier'. On the one hand, developing Nova Scotia buttressed a notion of an empire centred on the ocean, the navy and transatlantic trade. This model of empire, which David Armitage memorably summed up as 'Protestant, commercial, maritime, and free', carried with it a political and economic logic that favoured developing European settlements on coastlines and securing important sea-lanes.[20] Within certain forms of this framework, Anglo-American movement into the western interior could be deeply disturbing. Though far from the only vision of the Empire's future, this coast-centric, interior-phobic view was widely held within the post-Treaty of Paris administration. Henry Ellis, sometime absentee governor of Georgia and Nova Scotia, expressed a common concern when he argued that by 'planting themselves in the Heart of America' Anglo-Americans would lose their ties to the mother country and be more prone to such sins as domestic manufactures, smuggling and not engaging in trade with Britain.[21]

As the Board of Trade grew increasingly hostile toward the creation of interior colonies, Nova Scotia – as well as Georgia and the Floridas to the south – were proposed as the alternative, new colonies waiting to be developed which still fit seamlessly into a blue water notion of empire. In particular, adding new Protestant bodies to Nova Scotia would mean better access to the fisheries and a host of spin-off benefits that would promote and sustain the British naval apparatus. The fishery, for example, was often understood through the ancient trope of the 'nursery for seamen', where valuable sailors could be trained up and drawn upon in times of war.[22]

This understanding of the nature of the English-speaking part of the British Empire translated into policy. The Royal Proclamation of 1763, for example, was passed as much to keep Anglo-American settlers from disappearing into the interior and out of imperial control as it was to prevent war with the powerful Indigenous coalitions of the Ohio country. A 1768 report by the Board of Trade to George III laid this out explicitly in relation to the efforts to settle Nova Scotia as a British province. It claimed that the proclamation's restriction of British settlement in the American interior was done to pin settlement colonies to the coast as much as possible, suggesting that opening the core of the continent to British settlement by creating interior colonies would depopulate the northern and southern coasts, i.e. Nova Scotia, Georgia and the Floridas, as whatever settlers had been diverted there since 1763 would flee 'the opposite extremes of Heat & Cold' for 'a moderate Climate'. Going on to discuss the efforts made in Nova Scotia since 1749 in glowing terms, the Board concluded that 'encouraging settlements upon the sea coast of North America is founded in the true principles of commercial policy'.[23]

Philadelphian speculators, on the other hand, do not appear to have shared this vision, but were – at least for a time – just as interested in the economic and political opportunities Nova Scotia could provide. Benjamin Franklin, for example, who was heavily involved in the Nova Scotian boom, certainly disagreed that the Anglo-American population should be kept within relatively easy access to the sea. Rejecting the notion of checks on Anglo-American settlement to the west, Franklin argued in the 1750s and early 1760s that through the process of territorial expansion across the North American continent, wealth based on colonial consumption was practically limitless. Settler expansion into the west should therefore be encouraged as much as possible.[24] The many ties that he and his fellow Philadelphian speculators had to other land projects in the west and beyond the Appalachian Mountains suggests that a great many of them also shared Franklin's opinions. To these men, an increase in the colonial consumption of British manufactures, rather than the production of naval stores, was the primary economic justification for settling Nova Scotia. Specifically, they argued that access to Nova Scotia's plentiful raw materials would facilitate Philadelphia's ever-increasing consumption of British-made goods.²⁵ As the battles of the Imperial Crisis would show, these men also tended to favour much less direct imperial intervention in questions of land and economy than the Board of Trade and many in the British government hoped for.

Historians such as Steven Pincus and others have argued that divergent views of empire and the imperial relationship such as these are to blame for the tensions that fuelled the imperial crisis and, later, the American Revolution itself.²⁶ But while these two perspectives on the political economy of empire and the role of Anglo-American settlers within it led to clashes, when it came to westward settlement and taxation in the older colonies, in Nova Scotia both positions roughly agreed that the future needed to include white settler expansion, the export of raw materials and the importation of British manufactures. This overlapping goes a long way towards explaining the shared enthusiasm for the project in the very years that the colonial–imperial relationship was worsening elsewhere on the continent.

And yet, crucial differences between the goals and even basic assumptions of British and colonial speculators quickly became evident. One area where this was most obvious was around the question of land tenure. While holding land as a tenant was the norm in the British Isles and in Europe throughout the eighteenth century, the British American colonies were often understood as the special domain of the independent yeoman freeholder. In truth, land ownership was hardly universal even among free whites. However, the relatively free availability of land for white settlement, pried from the hands of a kaleidoscope of First Nations, remains perhaps *the* central fact of North American colonial history.²⁷ Furthermore, as Franklin's 1750s work demonstrates, the concept of an empire of freeholding small households expanding across the continent was ideologically potent in the late eighteenth-century colonies. It was these pre-Revolutionary ideas about settlement and expansion that were later revised by men like Thomas Jefferson into the so-called 'Empire of Liberty' that would define the early national United States.²⁸

All of the schemes of the 1760s involved at least the temporary transfer of large amounts of land to a small number of people. However, the assumption that the freeholding farm family as opposed to an aristocratic landlord was the ideal base unit of empire is clearly evident in the majority of schemes dreamed up by investors from Philadelphia and other colonial centres. Perhaps no individual better represents this settler-colonial approach to expansion than the controversial figure of Alexander McNutt. McNutt was born in Ulster, grew up in rural Virginia and gained notoriety in the 1760s as a promoter and land agent working in and around Nova Scotia. In memorials and meetings, McNutt claimed to have contacts throughout North America and northern Europe and contracts with thousands of prospective settlers. More than any other person, McNutt was responsible for bringing the craze for Nova Scotian land to the middle colonies through his contacts in Philadelphia. Indeed, at the height of his influence, on one day in 1765 his name was included on grants making up over one million acres of land.

McNutt, when historians have paid attention to him at all, has not come across particularly well. Bailyn refers to him as 'frenetic and unscrupulous'.[29] Others have characterised him as 'utterly unreliable' and 'distinctly untrustworthy', while one early biographer stated that as many of McNutt's statements were 'so grossly at variance with facts' that the author 'hesitate[d] to believe that a person who could so boldly make them can properly be regarded as sane'.[30] He was a man who had no compunction about overstating his achievements or credentials: for example, he claimed at one point to have brought more people to Nova Scotia than currently lived in the province, and, in the 1780s, he insisted to the Continental Congress that he had an official contract to settle the entirety of the Ohio River Valley, the Susquehanna and most of what is now upstate New York.[31] During the American Revolution, he took it upon himself to declare Nova Scotia an independent republic, which he called New Ireland, and wrote several pamphlets laying out a detailed plan of government.

It is difficult to avoid the conclusion that McNutt had a rather fluid relationship with the truth. But in his consistent articulation of a land policy and imperial vision based on the absolute rights of Protestant settler families, McNutt represents the effort to incorporate the Canadian Maritimes into a colonial order more reminiscent of the Pennsylvania and Virginia Backcountry than anything the Board of Trade had in mind.[32] It was an ideology that placed working settler families at its heart, demanding a wide latitude of independence and freedom for some while simultaneously rejecting dealings with non-Protestants and non-whites.

The large number of grants made in McNutt's name, the fact that few of them were ultimately settled, and his habitual self-aggrandisement have led many historians to portray him as a ruthless land speculator. But examining his many memorials suggests quite the opposite: McNutt espoused an ideology of empire which placed the smallholding agricultural settler family at the forefront. Drawing on a discourse that hearkened back to the plantation of Ulster, he saw himself as the champion and facilitator of hard-working Protestants everywhere who simply needed (in the words of a memorial to him written by Benjamin Franklin and others) 'a little encouragement to transport themselves'.[33] As he put it in a memorial to the Continental Congress in the late years of the American Revolution:

> ... his undertaking [was] wholly calculated for the relief of the distressed of the human species on both sides of the Atlantic, not confined to seats or parties, party views or party plans, but wholly for the public good, and for the benefit of all those of fair moral character who may embrace the opportunity'.[34]

The Crown and government were needed to encourage promoters like McNutt, who saw himself, rightly or wrongly, as directly deputised by the royal authority to settle Nova Scotian lands. Imperial authority was also needed to protect settlers from forms of land granting which McNutt saw as predatory, and to ensure their civil and religious liberties so that they might 'take their own way to happiness'.[35] In short, in the eyes of McNutt, the heart of the Empire was a network of independent small householders, and the correct role of imperial authority was to facilitate an orderly transfer of lands to white settler families who would work them. Although few were as explicit as McNutt, the colonial speculators he attracted broadly shared his vision of an empire of smallholding Protestant families. They uniformly framed their role as that of middlemen facilitating – and profiting from – the sale to white families, with some limited proprietary rights centred mostly on the control of saw- and gristmills built for the use of settlers.

Nova Scotia, however, proved to be very attractive to individuals, including several members of the British peerage, who saw the future of the American British Empire as one of increasing hierarchy. Many other potential grantees instead approached their projects more like a traditional English manor, with tenants and a significant amount of reserved proprietary rights. Unlike township grants, which were 100,000 acres and typically granted to companies, these manorial grants were made to individuals and tended to be somewhat smaller, although at 20,000 acres, they were far from modest.

Manorial schemes, in contrast to the freehold townships imagined by McNutt and the Philadelphians, were especially attractive to Nova Scotian government insiders and members of the British aristocracy. For example, Michael Francklin, one of the most important political figures in 1760s Nova Scotia, obtained a grant on the southern side of Chignecto Bay. Clearly signalling his intentions, he named this tract Francklin Manor, and was seeking tenants for his property in Germany as early as 1765.[36] A number of proposals written by Francklin between 1765 and 1768 show that he was experimenting with terms and his role as landlord. In 1765 he drafted a sample agreement with German tenants, which laid out rents of £10 per year and disallowed tenants from selling their lands or moving without his permission. Later, he also experimented with rents paid by turning in one third of their merchantable produce and half of the 'increase of their stock' on a yearly basis.[37]

Francklin was far from alone. Other Nova Scotian officials, such as J. F. W. DesBarres, also adopted a manorial model, and similar grants were made to others close to the government. In 1767, for example, William Owen, a close friend and sometime employee of Governor William Campbell, received a large grant in Passamaquoddy Bay, then considered part of Nova Scotia. Owen's claim included the largest island in the bay, which he renamed Campobello in honour of his patron.[38] Owen arrived in Passamaquoddy Bay in June 1770 with thirty-eight indentured servants to found a settlement he called New

Warrington, after the town in England where the voyage had been fitted out.[39] Owen's plan was to develop Campobello as an English estate. He planned to grant ninety-nine-year leases to his tenants in return for a tax on livestock and half of any profits or produce, including grain and slaughtered animals.[40] As the region's sole justice of the peace, he was also responsible for meting out justice for his tenants, most of whom were his own indentured servants.[41]

Other would-be landlords were already members of the British aristocracy. The most notorious of these was John Perceval, 2nd Earl of Egmont. In late 1763, he petitioned for a grant of all of St John's Island, the modern province of PEI.[42] Owen, who of course had his own manorial schemes for Nova Scotia, wrote of the Earl's plans:

> He proposed dividing it into certain Lordships, lots, or divisions, to be held under him by Feudatories, upon a system somewhat similar to the old feudal tenures in England; and that it should be governed by a new Code of laws calculated upon that principle. Thus would his Lordship, like the duke of Athol in the Isle of Man, have been King in St John's; acknowledging the sovereignty of the King of England, but not subject to any acts or ordinances of the Legislature. His patent was absolutely made out; but before it passed the Seals, the eyes of the Ministry were opened and it was cancelled.[43]

His initial plans thwarted, Egmont scaled down the acreage of his request, but not his vision. In 1768, Egmont received a 22,000-acre grant stretching from Jeddore Harbour on Nova Scotia's eastern shore to the Shubenacadie River.[44] By the following year he had drawn up detailed plans, which called for a 'Mansion House, Park, Castle, &c' held in demesne located in what is now Head of Jeddore, Nova Scotia.[45] He was also interested in perhaps getting a second grant for Isle Madame, a small island that sits off the south-east coast of Cape Breton, and additional lots along the Shubenacadie River.[46]

In a series of closely written annotations on a map of his new lands, Egmont laid out his distinctly feudal vision. For example, he singled out such details as a blockhouse to be built next to the mansion house where settlers could flee in time of war, an arrangement combining a medieval castle with modern frontier defence tactics. He also sketched out six perfectly square three-mile by three-mile settlements, divided into individual square miles in an even checkerboard pattern. In a marginal note written in October 1769, Egmont wrote that within each of the square settlements he intended settle the central squares himself; the four 'angular' squares in each were to be 'granted away in Fee to any 4 Gentlemen who will plant each 4 Families of 5 to a Family on his Respective Square Miles' or to a set of sixteen families.[47] Egmont explained the importance of the mile divisions by reference to William the Conqueror, who, according to Egmont, granted square mile fiefs to the men who had assisted him in the conquest.[48]

Egmont's scheme was warmly supported by both Governor Campbell and significant members of government like Francklin and Joseph Gerrish. Indeed, Gerrish, who acted as one of Egmont's agents, proclaimed that Egmont Harbour would be 'a great & valuable Setlement [sic], so necessary for the well Being of this Colony'.[49] Eventually, Egmont's original vision of turning St John's Island into a manorial holding also came to pass, in modified form, in 1767, when the island was erected into a separate colony and divided up between a handful of English absentee landlords.

The flurry of land grants in the 1760s, then, can be divided into two broad approaches: a colonial one that imagined a settler-driven landscape of small-hold farms and limited imperial involvement, and a more aristocratic one that looked to English manors for inspiration. Unsurprisingly, these two different visions of what a white, Protestant Nova Scotia should be clashed. For example, the Board of Trade, looking to preserve potential mast trees for the British navy, attempted to insert a clause into grants barring settlers from cutting trees above a certain size on their own lands.[50] This clause caused deep consternation among colonial speculators, and several threatened to abandon their grants. McNutt in particular was deeply dismayed by this new provision, writing a memorial to the Board in early 1766 which characterised it as an attack on property rights. He also drew on a Patriot Whig understanding of manufactures as the heart of the imperial economy, and objected to the implicit economic calculus of the provision. 'The several Companys', he wrote,

> had principally in view the carrying on an extensive Fishery in order to enoble [sic] them to make remittances to Britain for their manufactures ... One Hundred Thousand pounds sent to Britain for her manufactures wou'd its presumed be of more value than any imaginary advantage arising from the reservation of timber.[51]

In miniature, McNutt's objections to the tree reservation provision replayed the clashes over the nature of the Empire which characterised the era as one of imperial crisis. It pitted a vision of empire, which placed a premium on colonial consumption and unfettered settler access to and use of land, against that of the Board of Trade, which desired more controls over both land and trade.

McNutt also emerged as a highly vocal critic of the spread of manorial schemes like Francklin, Owen and Egmont's. In 1763 he accused the grantees of several large patents of using their influence with the government to deny grants of land to his settlers, thereby forcing them to become tenants on their land.[52] A few years later he repeated his accusations, claiming that the tenants on these properties 'cannot properly be called by any other name than slaves'.[53]

In 1766, the Nova Scotia Council and acting governor, Francklin, wrote a scathing report to the Board of Trade on McNutt's claims which seems to have decisively turned the imperial government against him.[54] Yet McNutt's populist tendencies only became more pronounced after his fall from grace. In 1767, for instance, he was censured by the Nova Scotia Council for parcelling out land to settlers in New Dublin township that had not been granted to him, claiming that he had a right from the crown to redistribute all Nova Scotian lands to settlers. Some of this land was likely owned by Attorney General William Nesbitt, who brought the complaint against him and whose land he had singled out in a memorial to the Board of Trade.[55]

Most of the Philadelphia companies, including Franklin's, declined rapidly around the same time, and the escheating of American lands in Nova Scotia began in 1770, when two of Alexander McNutt's township grants were revoked.[56] As the imperial crisis raged, critiques of both Nova Scotia's peculiar settlement history and its growing reputation as a money pit made their way into political discourse. The pro-colonial merchant Dennys deBerdt, for instance, wrote suspiciously of parliamentary support of Nova Scotia, Georgia and the Floridas. He drew a clear line between these colonies and the older ones they bracketed. 'All the Colonies but Georgia & Nova-Scotia, were originally settled by persons drove from their native Country,' he wrote. 'If you consider the thousands that have been expended in settling Georgia & Nova-Scotia, you will better judge of the merit of the other Colonies which settled themselves without any expence [sic] to their mother Country'.[57] Franklin made a similar observation on several occasions. Barely two years after he became involved in the Nova Scotia land rush, he scribbled in the margin of a pamphlet that

> Except the late attempted Colonies of Nova Scotia and Georgia, No Colony ever received Maintenance in any Shape from Britain: And the Grants to those Colonies were mere Jobbs for the Benefit of ministerial Favourites: English or *Scotchmen*.[58]

Franklin continued this judgement on the spoils of the Nova Scotian settlement in the margins of another pamphlet sometime after 1770. First remarking that all colonies except Georgia and Nova Scotia had been founded by settlers at no expense to the Crown, he concluded that those Atlantic peripheries 'were sent wrong People who dy'd or went away'.[59] It is hard to say if he acknowledged himself as a contributor to what he now saw as an utterly failed and wasteful cause. Although it is impossible to claim direct causation between Franklin and DeBerdt's views and the failure of the Philadelphian companies, colonial perceptions of Nova Scotia's currency as a worthwhile field of action sharply declined after 1766. DeBerdt, for instance, dismissed an overture to invest in (yet another) Philadelphia Nova Scotia project by writing scornfully that 'Nova Scotia . . . is in general a bleak, barren country.'[60]

It was in this context that Dickinson wrote his *Letters*, the key document in generating a colonial resistance movement to the Townshend acts.[61] While not involved himself in the Nova Scotian land boom, he had many associates who were. Indeed, many proprietors were regulars at David Hall's stationery shop, where Dickinson purchased writing equipment while composing the *Letters*.[62] It is easy to imagine some of the bitterness over a failed land scheme, discussed casually while buying ink and quills, seeping into Dickinson's writing. Even if that was not the case, the fact remains that Nova Scotia, once a geographic space that promised imperial cooperation and a shared vision of empire, was now a symbol of everything colonists were growing to hate about their attachment to empire.

By the outbreak of hostilities between some of the mainland colonies and the Crown, then, Nova Scotia had gone from an example of the promise of the British Empire to a cautionary tale. While the landscape and geography of Nova Scotia itself had not changed, where once it had been possible for all to see 'a place of great importance', more and more now saw simply 'a bleak, barren country'.[63] For colonials and British officials, the shared belief that their social and economic goals could be met by bringing white Protestants into the province at the expense of First Nations and Acadian people created a rare moment of colonial–imperial cooperation during a time of deepening crisis. However, like other encounters during the 1760s, what had seemed like agreement proved chimerical, and the debates over an imaginary Nova Scotia only served to show just how out of step colonial and British elites had become.

Notes

1. Anthony Wayne to John Hughes, 30 May 1765, Anthony Wayne Papers, Historical Society of Pennsylvania [HSP], Collection #699, vol. 1, p. 4. Just how much Wayne had seen at this point in his life is, of course, open to question.
2. 30 April 1765, Minutes of His Majesty's Council 1757–1766, Nova Scotia Archives [NSA], Commissioner of Public Records Collection, RG 1 vol. 188; Wayne to Hughes, 30 May 1765.
3. Wayne to Hughes, 30 May 1765.
4. Bernard Bailyn and Barbara DeWolfe, *Voyagers to the West: A Passage in the Peopling of North America on the Eve of the Revolution* (New York: Vintage Books, 1988), p. 364; Michael Francklin to the Lords of Trade, 2 Sept 1766, CO 217/78, The National Archives [UKNA].
5. P. J. Marshall, *The Making and Unmaking of Empires: Britain, India, and America, c.1750–1783* (New York: Oxford University Press, 2005), pp. 311–12.
6. John Dickinson, 'Letter VIII', *Letters from a Farmer in Pennsylvania*. Quoted version was printed 8 February 1768, *The Boston Evening-Post*.
7. Margaret Ells, 'Clearing the Decks for the Loyalists', *Report of the Annual Meeting of the Canadian Historical Association/Rapports Annuels de La Société Historique du Canada* 12:1 (1933), pp. 43–58.
8. As with most things concerning 1760s Nova Scotia, the tone was set by John Brebner, who argues that 'from 1764 onward settlement and speculation were sadly allied'. John Bartlet Brebner, *The Neutral Yankees of Nova Scotia: A Marginal Colony during the Revolutionary Years* (New York: Columbia University Press, 1937), p. 94.
9. Marcus Lee Hansen, *The Mingling of the Canadian and American Peoples*, vol. 1 (New Haven: Yale University Press, 1940); quoted for example in Fred Anderson, *The Crucible of War: The Seven Years' War and the Fate of Empire in North America, 1754–1766* (New York: Vintage

Books, 2001), p. 523; David Jaffee, *People of the Wachusett: Greater New England in History and Memory, 1630–1860* (Ithaca: Cornell University Press, 1999), p. 179; Bailyn and DeWolfe, *Voyagers to the West*, p. 364.
10. Anderson, *The Crucible of War*, p. 523.
11. Bailyn and DeWolfe, *Voyagers to the West*, p. 364.
12. This argument is indebted to Elizabeth Mancke's work on Nova Scotia as a post-1713 colony beholden to both the crown and parliament and thus subject to greater imperial control, as well as John Murrin and Rowland Berthoff's work on the 1760s as a moment of 'feudal revival' in the colonies: Elizabeth Mancke, *The Fault Lines of Empire: Political Differentiation in Massachusetts and Nova Scotia, ca. 1760–1830*, New World in the Atlantic World (New York: Routledge, 2005); John Murrin and Rowland Berthoff, 'Feudalism, Communalism, and the Yeoman Freeholder: The American Revolution Considered as a Social Accident', in John Murrin, *Rethinking America: From Empire to Republic* (Oxford: Oxford University Press, 2018), pp. 131–60.
13. See in particular Andrew D. M. Beaumont, *Colonial America and the Earl of Halifax, 1748–1761* (Oxford: Oxford University Press, 2015).
14. For this, and for Nova Scotia's central place in the 'imperial fictions' of the French and British empires in the pre-Seven Years' War era, see in particular Jeffers Lennox, *Homelands and Empires: Indigenous Spaces, Imperial Fictions, and Competition for Territory in Northeastern North America, 1690–1763* (Toronto: University of Toronto Press, 2017).
15. Jeffers Lennox, 'An Empire on Paper: The Founding of Halifax and Conceptions of Imperial Space, 1744–55', *Canadian Historical Review*, 88:3 (September 2007), pp. 373–412.
16. Shirley's level of input is unclear, but the final plan mirrored in many ways his 1748 plan for the future of the province, as well as a tract by New Englander Otis Little written the same year: William Shirley, 'General heads of a Plan of a Civil Government propos'd for his Majesty's Province of Nova Scotia', 18 Feb 1748, CO 5/45, f.145–8; Otis Little, *A State of the Trade in the Northern Colonies Considered, with an Account of the Produce, and a particular Description of Nova Scotia* (London: G. Woodfall, 1748).
17. Winthrop Pickard Bell, *The 'Foreign Protestants' and the Settlement of Nova Scotia: The History of a Piece of Arrested British Colonial Policy in the Eighteenth Century* (Toronto: University of Toronto Press, 1961).
18. For Planter use of Acadian infrastructure, see Jonathan Fowler, 'From Acadians to Planters in the Grand-Pré Area: An Archaeological Perspective', in Wendy G. Robicheau and T. Stephen Henderson (eds), *The Nova Scotia Planters in the Atlantic World, 1759–1830* (Fredericton, NB: Acadiensis Press, 2012), pp. 37–61.
19. See for example Jonathan Belcher to the Board of Trade, 3 Nov 1761, CO 217, UKNA.
20. David Armitage, *The Ideological Origins of the British Empire* (Cambridge: Cambridge University Press, 2000), p. 173.
21. 'Hints relative to the Division and Government of the Conquered and Newly Acquired Countries in America', n.d., CO 323/16, UKNA.
22. In the British context, this trope dates from at least the late medieval/Tudor era. Maryanne Kowaleski, 'The Expansion of the South-Western Fisheries in Late Medieval England', *Economic History Review*, 53:3 (August 2000), pp. 452.
23. Report of the Board of Trade to George III, 7 March 1768, CO 324/18, UKNA, pp. 213–65.
24. See especially Benjamin Franklin, *Observations Concerning the Increase of Mankind* (Boston, 1751); Franklin, *The Interest of Great Britain Considered* (London: 1760). Franklin also repeated this belief in direct relation to his involvement in Nova Scotia in a letter to Jonathan Shipley: Benjamin Franklin to Jonathan Shipley, 10 March 1774, in Willcox (ed.), *The Papers of Benjamin Franklin*, vol. 21 (New Haven: Yale University Press, 1978), p. 138.
25. See Montagu Wilmot to the Board of Trade, 30 April 1765, CO 217, UKNA; Alexander McNutt, 'Memorial against the Reservation of Trees', 16 May 1766, CO 217, UKNA. For the

middle colonies' and New England's struggles to find things to export in exchange for British manufactures, see T. H. Breen, 'An Empire of Goods: The Anglicization of Colonial America, 1690–1776', *Journal of British Studies*, 25:4 (1986), p. 487.

26. Pincus, *The Heart of the Declaration: The Founders' Case for an Activist Government* (New Haven: Yale University Press, 2016). For roughly compatible but somewhat different explanations of the crisis hingeing on different notions of the imperial relationship, see T. H. Breen, 'Ideology and Nationalism on the Eve of the American Revolution: Revisions Once More in Need of Revising', *The Journal of American History*, 84:1 (1 June 1997), pp. 13–39; Anderson, *The Crucible of War*.
27. Daniel K. Richter, *Trade, Land, Power: The Struggle for Eastern North America* (Philadelphia: University of Pennsylvania Press, 2013), p. 5.
28. Thomas Jefferson to George Rogers Clark, 25 December 1780, *The Papers of Thomas Jefferson: Digital Edition*, ed. James P. McClure and J. Jefferson Looney (Charlottesville: University of Virginia Press, Rotunda, 2008–19).
29. Bailyn and DeWolfe, *Voyagers to the West*, p. 364.
30. Bell, *The 'Foreign Protestants'*, p. 111; Brebner, *Neutral Yankees*, p. 37; Arthur Wentworth Hamilton Eaton, 'Alexander McNutt, The Colonizer', *Americana*, 8:2 (1913), p. 1078.
31. Memorial of Alexander McNutt to the Board of Trade, 18 March 1763, CO 217, UKNA; Memorial of Alexander McNutt to the President and Congress, 15 June 1781, Remonstrances and Addresses pp. 172–6, Papers of the Continental Congress [PCC], National Archives and Records Administration [NARA].
32. On Nova Scotia as kind of laboratory for imperial policy, see Mancke, *The Fault Lines of Empire*, passim; Beaumont, *Colonial America and the Earl of Halifax, 1748–1761*, pp. 51–2; Geoffrey Plank, *An Unsettled Conquest: The British Campaign against the Peoples of Acadia*, Early American Studies (Philadelphia: University of Pennsylvania Press, 2001), p. 7. For contemporary judgements on the seeming artificiality and exceptional nature of Nova Scotia and its settlers, see Dennys deBerdt to Lord Dartmouth, 5 Sept 1765, in *Letters of Dennys deBerdt*, pp. 434–8; John Dickinson, 'Letter VIII', *Letters from a Farmer in Pennsylvania*, 1768; Franklin Marginalia in a Pamphlet by Matthew Wheelock, 1770, franklinpapers.org; Franklin's notes on *Intended Vindication and Offer from Congress to Parliament*, in 1775, franklinpapers.org. For frontier notions of political power and empire, see especially Peter Silver, *Our Savage Neighbors: How Indian War Transformed Early America* (New York: W. W. Norton & Company, 2009).
33. Benjamin Franklin, John Foxcraft and John Hughes to Alexander McNutt, 10 July 1764, Hughes Papers, HSP.
34. Memorial of Alexander McNutt to the President and Congress, 15 June 1781.
35. Alexander McNutt Memorial to the Board of Trade, 16 April 1763, CO 217, UKNA.
36. Settlement Agreement, c.1765, enclosed in Michael Francklin to the Earl of Egmont, 29 Aug 1769, Nova Scotia Materials, Add. MSS 47054A, Egmont Papers, British Library, ff. 23–4.
37. These proposals are all held together as 'Francklin Proposals for Settling Francklin Manor', Townshend Papers vol. XVI, Add. MSS 38507, British Library.
38. Victor Hugo Paltsits (ed.), 'Narrative of American Voyages and Travels of Captain William Owen, R.N., and the Settlement of the Island of Campobello in the Bay of Fundy, 1766–1771 (Part 5)', *Bulletin of the New York Public Library*, 35:10 (October 1931), p. 714.
39. Paltsits, p. 715. Owen's settlers – only seven of whom were women – seem to have come from Montgomeryshire or Warwickshire, where Owen lived and owned land.
40. William Owen Advertisement for Settlers, 20 February 1772, reproduced in Paltsits, bet. 754–5. Campobello ultimately was run in such a fashion, but not successfully until after the Revolution, and caused a great deal of tension between the Owen family and their tenants. See Paltsits, p. 758.
41. Owen's plans fell apart even faster than most. After less than a year in Passamaquoddy, Owen

sailed back to England with all of his servants, and his claim was not taken up again until after the Revolution: Paltsits, pp. 753–8.
42. Earl of Halifax to the Board of Trade, 18 Jan 1764, CO 217, UKNA.
43. Paltsits, pp. 94–5.
44. Egmont Group Grant, 7 June 1768, Nova Scotia Materials, Egmont Papers Add. MSS 47054A, British Library. After the township boom of 1765, the governor was restricted to grants no larger than 20,000 acres; William Campbell expressed regret that he could not grant Egmont the full 100,000 acres. William Campbell to the Earl of Egmont, 15 March 1769, Nova Scotia Materials, Add. MSS 47054A, Egmont Papers, British Library, ff. 8–9.
45. Joseph Gerrish to the Earl of Egmont, 15 March 1769, Nova Scotia Materials, Add. MSS 47054A, Egmont Papers, British Library, ff. 6–7.
46. Joseph Gerrish to the Earl of Egmont, 15 March 1769, Nova Scotia Materials, Add. MSS 47054A, Egmont Papers, British Library, ff. 6–7; Joseph Gerrish to the Earl of Egmont, 10 April 1769, Nova Scotia Materials, Add. MSS 47054A, Egmont Papers, British Library, ff. 14–15; Joseph Woodmass to the Earl of Egmont, 15 December 1769, Add. MSS 47054A, Egmont Papers, British Library, ff. 25–30. Egmont was able to purchase about 1,000 acres from councilman John Newton in July 1770: Shubenacadie Grant, 2 July 1770, Nova Scotia Materials, Add. MSS 47054A, Egmont Papers, British Library, ff. 35–6. Notably, both Isle Madam and the Shubenacadie River were crucial geographies of Mi'kmaw power and political organising.
47. Map of Egmont Holdings with Annotations, Add. MSS 47054B, Egmont Papers, British Library.
48. Egmont also indicated that he wanted divisions of these square mile plots to be referenced using medieval names, i.e. carucates, virgates and furlongs – although in true Enlightenment fashion Egmont standardises these divisions, rather than using their original subjective measures (which referred to how efficiently a specific plot of land could be worked by oxen).
49. Joseph Gerrish to the Earl of Egmont, 10 April 1769, Nova Scotia Materials, Add. MSS 47054A, Egmont Papers, British Library, ff. 14–15.
50. Report of the Board of Trade, 15 May 1766, CO 217, UKNA.
51. McNutt, 'Memorial against the Reservation of Trees'.
52. Alexander McNutt Memorial to the Board of Trade, 16 April 1763.
53. Alexander McNutt Memorial to the Board of Trade, 17 April 1766.
54. Committee to the Board of Trade, 30 Aug 1766.
55. Minutes of Legislative Council, 27 June 1767, RG 1 vol. 188, Nova Scotia Archives [NSA]. Despite conventional narratives that argue McNutt was delusional and unliked, he seems to have continued to find common cause with Nova Scotia's everyday settlers. In 1771, for instance, the leaders of Cornwallis Township recorded that they planned to apply to him 'on the Matter of applying to His Majesty for a Charter of Privileges Both Sivil & Relidgeous', a prospect that no doubt would have delighted McNutt. Cornwallis Township records, in *Nova Scotia Township Records*, microfilm, New England Historic Genealogical Society.
56. Minutes of the Legislative Council, 14 April 1770, NSARM; William Campbell to Hillsborough, 9 October 1770, CO 217, UKNA.
57. Dennys DeBerdt to Lord Dartmouth, rec. 5 September 1765, Dennys De Berdt, *Letters of Dennys de Berdt, 1757–1770*, ed. Albert Matthews (Cambridge, MA: J. Wilson and Son, 1911), p. 437.
58. MS notations in the margins of a copy in the Historical Society of Pennsylvania of [Josiah Tucker], *A Letter from a Merchant in London to His Nephew in North America* (London, 1766).
59. Marginalia in a pamphlet by Matthew Wheelock.
60. Dennys De Berdt to Joseph Reed, 18 March 1766, De Berdt, *Letters of Dennys de Berdt, 1757–1770*, p. 443.
61. Marshall, *The Making and Unmaking of Empires*, pp. 311–12.

62. Based on a sampling of David Hall's account book for the years 1764–8. The account book is found in Series II, David Hall Papers, Mss B-H124, American Philosophical Society, Philadelphia, PA. Hall's customers included members of the Pictou, Philadelphia Township, and Monckton companies; many Halls, including a David Hall, were also involved; they may or may not have been relatives of David Hall the stationer and partner of Franklin.
63. Dennys De Berdt to Joseph Reed, 18 March 1766, De Berdt, *Letters of Dennys de Berdt, 1757–1770*, p. 443.

FOUR

Leaving Nova Scotia: Sierra Leone and the Free Black People, 1792–1800

Ruma Chopra

Shuttling dependent people within imperial zones became essential to preserving and consolidating British interests in the Atlantic during the late eighteenth century. Free black people proved no exception. This chapter offers a close study of two migrations of black people from Nova Scotia to West Africa during this period to illuminate the enduring logic of an expansionist empire during the age of slavery.

In the last two decades of the eighteenth century, two communities of free black people reached Nova Scotia by sea, and they were known as the Black Loyalists from the Thirteen Colonies and a community of Jamaican Maroons. Both groups were of the Americas in that each was formed through various accommodations and encounters with slavery, Indigenous people and white settlers. Many of the approximately 3,000 Black Loyalists, who arrived between 1782 and 1783, were former slaves, who had fled agricultural slavery in the southern colonies to join the British military; others left the urban slavery of New York and New England. The 549 Maroons, who entered Halifax in July 1796, came from the northern mountains of Trelawney Town in Jamaica. A single military community of fugitive slaves and their descendants, the Maroons had remained a free people for generations. Unlike the Black Loyalists, they had not voluntarily arrived in Nova Scotia; these 150 families were deported to the peninsula as punishment after a seven-month rebellion against the Jamaican plantocracy. The Maroons were united by their experience as a free community in a slave society, whereas the Black Loyalists shared a range of individual experiences with slavery in the white societies of the thirteen colonies.[1]

Both groups of black exiles had the potential to be useful to Nova Scotia, a northern colony that had been in desperate need of settlers and labourers since the founding of its capital, Halifax, in 1749. Prevailing racial hierarchies meant that black people were viewed as less desirable settlers than the white Protestants, who came from Germany in the 1750s, or the planters, who came from New England in the 1760s. However, they could be assimilated, not as neighbours or marriage partners, but rather as permanent housekeepers, construction workers and servants, with little chance for advancement as landowners. Nova Scotia would follow the pattern of racism already established in non-agricultural settlements such as New England. Yet unexpectedly, these two groups of free black people decided to relocate again. They imagined a second migration from a cosmopolitan perspective that was likely unavailable to other former enslaved people, since their first exile broadened their awareness of imperial alternatives.

In the late eighteenth century, these once-displaced people became valuable to the British Empire for their allegiance as much as their labour. The Black Loyalists, many of whom were Protestant, shared the values, aspirations and language (English) of the colonial authorities. The Maroons too, although only nominally Christian, had sworn loyalty to the British monarch for decades. Unlike the Acadians and the Mi'kmaq of north-eastern British North America, over whom the British assumed control on account of the Treaty of Utrecht in 1713, the Black Loyalists and the Maroons were long-time members of the British Empire. Yet, in spite of their proven attachment to British norms, which even included naming their children after respected British officers, they were deemed unworthy of the rights and protections granted to white settlers. The Black Loyalists, it was felt, could be transplanted to regions in need of settlers, to places considered unsuitable for whites but crucial to British aims of expanding into West Africa.

The Black Loyalists seized upon British Sierra Leone as a surer alternative to Nova Scotia since it was felt that, there, they could imagine owning land and living under anti-authoritarian laws that would secure the future of their families. Supported by rising anti-slavery sentiments in Britain, they successfully petitioned to start anew and, in 1792, nine years after reaching the Maritimes, 1,196 of the 3,000 Black Loyalists left Nova Scotia.[2] Their precedent set the course for the Maroons, who, in 1800, just four years after their arrival to Halifax, followed the Black Loyalists to Freetown, Sierra Leone. The Maroons had gained autonomy and regard in Jamaica through their formidable military skills and they were determined to re-establish this niche in Sierra Leone. In the end, the maritime colonies of north-eastern British North America could not compete with the Maroons' and Loyalists' vision of Sierra Leone as a one-time opportunity for advancement. Studied together, these two relocations reveal British Nova Scotia as being in competition for trusted settlers in the peripheries of an expanding British Empire; they highlight the selective effects of British humanitarianism in the Maritimes, revolutionary for blacks but not the Mi'kmaq; and they illuminate how climate theories played an influential role in the relocations of blacks within the empire.

The Black Loyalists

The Black Loyalists were unfortunate because they accompanied a group more than ten times their size – over 30,000 White Loyalists.[3] John G. Reid has argued that the influx of White Loyalists to the Maritimes, after Britain's loss of the thirteen colonies, created a permanent alteration in Imperial–Aboriginal relationships in the region. Prior to the 1780s, the First Nations had maintained some autonomy because the British settlers were not powerful enough to impose their rules and did not have the demographic strength to plant settlements within traditional hunting, fishing and gathering grounds: 'the territorial basis for regeneration remained intact'.[4] This changed with the Loyalist migration. Along with their aspirations for land without 'Indian' neighbours, White Loyalists brought with them the racial prejudices of American society. They viewed the Indigenous peoples as enemies and the black people as competitors and subordinates. Aspiring to become farmers and landholders, the White Loyalists seized any chance for status and security in a region with only a limited quantity of productive agricultural land. By monopolising the most accessible coastlines and river frontage for farms, fisheries and sawmills, they undermined the chances for Indigenous and Black Loyalist families to have any kind of security.[5]

From 1782 to 1783, the black migrants to Nova Scotia included the Black Loyalists as well as 1,500 to 2,000 slaves brought north by their Loyalist masters.[6] These slaves joined black people already in bondage in the Maritimes – a few hundred slaves had been present in Cape Breton since the early eighteenth century, slaves owned by British military officers and merchants settled in Halifax after 1749, and possibly 200 slaves who accompanied New England migrant planters from 1759 to 1774.[7] These slaves washed clothes, cut firewood, repaired fences, moved hay and piled firewood. As Harvey A. Whitfield writes, this was not a slave society of the Caribbean mould, but a society that freely made use of slaves as 'multi-occupational labourers'.[8]

Although no slave code legitimated slavery in Nova Scotia or New Brunswick (though Prince Edward Island did have a statute that recognised slaveholding), slavery remained protected. Slave ads in newspapers and wills reveal the wide acceptance of the institution. Most slaves toiled side by side with their owners in farms and shops or on the docks. White settlers used slaves to clear stumps, cultivate fields, fell trees and build homes and barns; slave women did domestic chores and minded white children. As in the United States, slavery established deeply ingrained racial prejudices and precluded black people's chances of integrating into Nova Scotia's civic society. Slaves as well as free black people received harsh indications of their servile place: public whippings for small offences were the most visible and painful reminders. Slavery only disappeared in the 1820s.[9]

The circumstances of Black Loyalists were more comparable to those of the poorer White Loyalists in the Maritimes than they were to the circumstances of enslaved people in the region. The majority of the latter came from modest circumstances, and also struggled to establish farms on rocky soil with long periods of sub-zero temperatures. Although many were generally treated better than those who remained enslaved, they expressed dismay at the short agricultural season and the weaker economic potential of Nova Scotia when compared to their former colonies.[10] Many White Loyalists lived a miserable existence on meagre rations with little promise of prosperity, and competed with Indigenous peoples and Black Loyalists to keep their position in the growing hierarchy. Indeed, some White loyalists maintained close ties with family members and neighbours in the new United States and grabbed any chance to return to their previous lives.[11] Black Loyalists, however, could not return to the former thirteen colonies and continued to endure extreme poverty as well as the constant threat of re-enslavement.[12]

As with the White Loyalists, the British had promised the free black people land in Nova Scotia in return for their loyalty and for their part, the Black Loyalists also expected to be treated as politically equal to white people. Instead, for eight years, between 1783 and 1791, they faced the hostility of White Loyalists, the impossibility of sustaining themselves on infertile land, and for many who never received land, a lifetime of servitude as servants. Accustomed to the legal processes of empire, Black Loyalist leaders petitioned to leave the Maritimes. Their 1790 petition summarised the Black Loyalists' distress: they had not received their 'promised allotments of land', and were 'refused the rights and privileges of the other inhabitants, not being permitted to vote'. Moreover, they lived in a colony that not only tolerated slavery, and practiced a 'degrading and unjust prejudice against People of Colour', but 'shot and maimed' runaway slaves.[13]

John Clarkson, brother of the evangelical abolitionist Thomas Clarkson, sent to supervise the Black Loyalists' relocation to Sierra Leone, made note of their desperate circumstances in a tiny notebook. They were forced to work as day labourers, sharecroppers, indentured servants and, in the case of children, apprentices. Black Loyalists told Clarkson that 'whites seldom or ever pay for work done'. The black people feared that their former masters would kidnap them and return them to the United States. Others never received land and were tired of living on 'white men's property'. Some received lower wages than promised for their work: 'It is a common custom in this country', they said, 'to promise a black so much per day and in evening when his work is finished' to renege on the commitment. Their children received no pay when they worked in white households because white people insisted they obliged black parents by providing children with lodging and food.[14]

The British need for black colony builders in West Africa coincided with the predicament of the Black Loyalists in the Maritimes. During the mid-1780s, when the evangelical lawyer Granville Sharp, who had earlier become deeply invested in abolitionism through the Somerset Case, seized the opportunity to establish a free community in Sierra Leone, black emigration became irrevocably linked to British humanitarianism. In 1787, the first candidates for the Sierra Leone settlement came from amongst the thousands of free black poor in London, numbered to be over 14,000. The 439 settlers included the black poor and some white people, among whom were seventy women.[15] In addition to domestic slaves, the influx of black people in England after the War of American Independence had further expanded the indigent black population. Sharp, along with other Christian reformers, saw a chance to reduce England's burden and to launch the anti-slavery experiment in West Africa.[16]

Humanitarian goals intersected perfectly with imperial aims. People with commercial vision and philanthropic friends hoped that new colonies in West Africa would replace the thirteen American colonies lost in 1783 by exporting raw materials and becoming a new market for British manufactured items. Thomas Clarkson celebrated the benefits of colonising West Africa and noted the many items that could be procured: palm oil, ivory, gold, wood including mahogany, cocoa and tulip, spices such as nutmeg, clove, cinnamon, black pepper and cardamom, and staples such as rice, cotton, indigo and sugar.[17]

The founders of the Sierra Leone Company also highlighted the stability that would result from 'civilising' Africans who would be socialised according to British culture and values. The evangelical abolitionist, William Wilberforce, noted that the colony would work best if 'American settlers' would board and lodge with a few natives to teach them 'language and religion, the habits of industry, the mode of cultivating lands, and the mechanical arts'. This was echoed by Thomas Clarkson, who explained that 'civilization can only take place by the natives living near a community of civilized settlers, and observing their government, customs, laws, & c.'.[18] The Company would also benefit from African chiefs sending their children to England for instruction.[19] The children would be taught the 'actual practice of cultivating land, making bricks, building houses', and trades such as blacksmithing.[20]

African-descended migrants in the Maritimes were perceived as potential civilisers of Sierra Leone. The settlement saw the value of acquiring 'free black colonists, acquainted with the English language, and accustomed to labour in hot climates'.[21] Nova Scotia's black people, it was felt, could inhabit regions where British interests exceeded Britain's ability to populate with white settlers, thereby extending its imperial claims in tropical zones deemed too dangerous for the latter. In comparison with West African communities, Black Loyalists' complexion mattered less than their availability, their familiarity with British customs and laws and their readiness to advance within and not outside the British Empire. Moreover, and despite the high mortality rates among the black people who went to Sierra Leone in 1787, the belief persisted that blackness would protect the Loyalists from the diseases of tropical climate.[22]

In 1791, Henry Thornton, Director of the Sierra Leone Company, outlined the primary reason for choosing black people: few Englishmen would 'work in the sun'.[23] Thornton stressed that the Company's first object was 'to procure labourers' without which the 'expense of our establishment must otherwise devour us'. In addition to cultivating crops, the black people from Nova Scotia would 'converse with the natives and draw them to work for us'.[24] Ultimately, it was believed that the Sierra Leone colony would flourish because of the labour of Africans. The perception was that grateful American-born loyal black people would serve as middlemen and overseers and create plantations that would then benefit from thousands of African 'servants' whose labour cost less than slaves in the West Indies.[25]

Curiously, John Clarkson was asked by William Wilberforce to stay clear of the anti-slavery agenda in Nova Scotia. Wilberforce told him not to 'tather about the abolition of the slave trade except when you are sure of your company' and recommended that he avoid a conversation with the Governor on the 'ill-usage the blacks had received' as it would 'nettle' him.[26] Clarkson also explained that the distribution of printed information promoting Sierra Leone was not intended to 'spread discontent' in the colony.[27] Eager to avoid sowing anti-slavery sentiments in Nova Scotia, Wilberforce and Clarkson sought only to remove one segment of a valuable group of free black people for their experiment in West Africa. A free Sierra Leone coexisted with the slave society of Jamaica as much as with the Nova Scotian society of slaves.

In 1791–2, unhappy Black Loyalists confronted a second choice outside of Nova Scotia: they could serve in the British army in the West Indies as an alternative to relocating to Sierra Leone. Serving under British officers, black men were entitled to the same bounty, clothing, and provisions as white soldiers. Free black people, who had already proven their allegiance in the last American war, were an ideal reserve for the war instigated by slaves in San Domingue. But since only sixty of those in Nova Scotia accepted a military assignment in the West Indies it suggests that for the majority of the uprooted Black Loyalists from the American colonies, military service was a means to secure freedom and did not mean a lifelong commitment to the British imperial establishment.[28]

The black migrants from Nova Scotia who arrived in Sierra Leone in March 1792 confronted the same heavy casualties experienced by London's poor black population in 1787.[29] In May 1792, the botanist Adam Afzelius reported the high mortality and sickness among this group, referred to as 'Nova Scotians': 'I found then a great confusion and want, particularly of houses and fresh provisions ... The evils have since that time daily increased ... about 500 persons over the half colony is now sick and about 200 are already dead, and we have no Medical or Chirurgical assistance, but from a very young surgeon who is ill himself.'³⁰ Of the 1,196 Nova Scotians who reached Sierra Leone, less than 1,000 remained, supervised by thirty to forty white Company servants.³¹

The Maroons

Four years after the Black Loyalists left for Sierra Leone, the Maroons arrived in Halifax. They entered a society where other black people, including enslaved people and over 2,000 Black Loyalists who had not abandoned the region for Sierra Leone, endured various degrees of racism and humiliation. As James St Walker has noted, the migrants who left for Sierra Leone represented teachers, preachers and leaders, those who were the more prosperous among the Black Loyalists. The people who remained included the elderly and the unskilled as well as 'indentured servants and debtors, including many sharecroppers who had borrowed seed from their white landlords and were not allowed to leave'.³² Their wages or treatment did not improve after their brethren's migration to Sierra Leone since their labour had never become an integral component in Nova Scotia's growth. When the Maroons arrived, about fifty black Loyalist families lived near Halifax as servants and apprentices in the mid-1790s.³³

Like the Black Loyalists, the Trelawney Town Maroons arrived in Nova Scotia after a war. In 1738–9, the Trelawney Town Maroons, along with the other five Maroon communities of Jamaica, had signed peace treaties with the colonial government and in exchange for their own freedom in isolated pockets in the mountains, they agreed to align themselves with the British against attacks from other European powers and to protect Jamaican slave owners from internal insurrections.³⁴ The established Maroons captured runaway slaves for sugar planters and prevented the emergence of new Maroon communities. The Maroons' peace with the plantocracy, maintained for over five decades, was shattered when a sudden war with the slaveholders erupted in 1795–6 and resulted in their deportation. This was indicative of the fact that treaties signed between Europeans and non-Europeans in the Americas carried no weight.³⁵

When the Trelawney Town Maroons arrived in Halifax in July 1796, the lieutenant governor and long-time settler of Nova Scotia, John Wentworth, welcomed the chance to use Jamaican funds to acquire and support settlers. The Maroons' military experience made them valuable from the start. During a time of intense British–French rivalry in places like Saint Domingue and the North Atlantic, Wentworth was impressed by this group's hostility to the French.³⁶ In need of military reinforcements to counter a potential French attack, and eager to boost population numbers in an effort to balance the threat posed by an expanding United States to the south, Wentworth viewed the Maroons as a useful people.³⁷ Moreover, he had regretted the loss of labour of the Black Loyalists caused by their exodus to Sierra Leone. The Maroons represented another opportunity to secure a reservoir of temporary but necessary labour near Halifax.[38]

The Maroons' reputation for military bravery even meant an audience with royalty. In Halifax, they were greeted not only by the lieutenant governor, but also by the son of King George III, Edward, Duke of Kent, who was commander-in-chief of the British forces in Canada. The Maritimes became the first place where a group of free blacks met British royalty. The Maroons immediately and eagerly offered their military services to the Prince. As the Prince reported, they 'want to merit His Majesty's favour and forgiveness'.[39] Although Nova Scotia did not make use of their military experience and the Prince was aloof with them, the Maroons sustained a lifetime attachment to the monarch. Wentworth plotted a future for the Maroons. On one hand, his design for them resembled the Sierra Leone Company's vision of civilising Africans. Indeed, the British had become renowned for their single-minded efforts to 'elevate' colonised people around the world. Administrators such as Sierra Leone's governor Zachary Macaulay showed themselves to be ideologically invested in this mission, and stood ready to boast their own refinement by launching civilising campaigns. In Nova Scotia, Wentworth set out to instruct the Maroons in the habits of industry and to persuade them to view agricultural labour as natural to their situation. He hired schoolteachers and clergymen to socialise the unchurched Maroons to Protestantism, literacy and monogamy. At least nineteen Maroon boys attended the makeshift school, copying phrases such as, 'Good Manners always procure respect' and 'God gives us the greatest encouragement to be good'. John Morgan, a boy of twelve, learned to write in seven months.[40]

Yet, on the other hand, Wentworth's vision for the Maroons echoed the long-held hope of the French and British empires for managing non-European peoples. In an effort to alleviate worries about loyalty and to allow for their close supervision, these powers sought ways of concentrating Indigenous and other groups in one place that was within convenient proximity to colonial authorities. In emergencies, these people could serve in the militia or undertake other forms of labour required to advance a frontier settlement. Confronted with a shortage of British Army regulars, Wentworth regarded both the Maroons and the Mi'kmaq as dangerous collectives, who needed to be wooed and conciliated, as well as potential allies, who could protect the colony from French attack.[41]

The Maroons, who had their own ideas, undoubtedly drew inspiration from the example of the Black Loyalists when they sent their first petition to England on 23 April 1797, requesting help in escaping their 'miserable situation' in Nova Scotia.[42] This petition was addressed to General Walpole, the British officer who had protested their deportation to Nova Scotia but to no avail. Remarkably, Walpole remained a friend to the Maroons and accused the Jamaican government of criminal injustice in the British Parliament.[43] In June 1797, the Maroon Captain Andrew Smith remained optimistic about leaving the colony: 'The governor [of Nova Scotia] has promised to write a good word to the King for our removal next year.'[44] Wentworth did not keep his promise and for three years, despite Maroon resistance and British reformers' concerns, he secretly conspired to keep the Maroons in the Maritimes.[45]

From the beginning, the Maroons rejected becoming the black peasantry that Wentworth had envisioned. They equated a life of agricultural cultivation with enslavement and exploitation. They suspected that the lands they cleared and cultivated 'would not be theirs but given to white people'.[46] They protested field work by feigning stomach pains, and they attributed any sickness to the cold climate and the want of West Indian fruits.[47] Eager to earn money by doing other tasks such as loading ships, the Maroons resolutely evaded work that paid by the day like picking stones and clearing land, and they boycotted jobs 'without pay equal to a whiteman'.[48] Six months after their arrival, in January 1797, an unsigned letter from a well-wisher in Nova Scotia recounted the Maroons' inward turn. The Trelawney Town Maroons never left their houses, they sat close 'around their stoves', and lived 'a most melancholy and pitiable existence'. Their misery, his report stated, counted no less than the abuses borne by slaves.[49]

Despite his best efforts, Wentworth lost his battle to keep the Maroons in Nova Scotia. In discussions about the Maroons' stay in Nova Scotia and their possible removal to another zone, winter factored prominently. Both sides – British reformers, who worried about their plight away from tropical Jamaica, and Nova Scotia's leaders, who dismissed the travails of winter to retain them – hit upon the cold winters of Nova Scotia to make their case.[50] From the time the Maroons stepped ashore in Halifax, anti-slavery British sympathisers regarded Maroons' rescue from the cold as akin to freeing slaves from tyrannical masters. They insisted that the Maroons could not endure such a cold climate because they were not suited to it and that the only kind of climate they would thrive in was one that was tropical like Jamaica's or that of Sierra Leone. As one correspondent lamented, 'Conceive if you can the feelings of a West India constitution, in such a climate.' Other essays in London's newspapers noted that the cold climate was 'uncongenial' to the Maroons' 'constitution'.[51]

Remarkably, in their preoccupation with climate, London humanitarians treated the Maroons as victims uprooted from the tropics rather than as dangerous enemies of the British state who had fought with and killed white settlers in Jamaica. These humanitarians likened them to voluntary immigrants, and protested that the deported Maroons could not simply be dropped into the Nova Scotia climate without being acclimatised. These arguments drew from the prevalent discourse on climate which emphasised the positive correlation between successful settlement and a temperate climate. It was believed that newcomers fared best in a land when the climate matched the environment of their place of origin. One contemporary noted, for example, that 'English' emigrants should, when settling in the United States, avoid the heat of the southern states and settle only in the northern regions. 'A sudden and violent change should if possible be avoided,' Thomas Cooper wrote, and 'newcomers should be exposed to no great excess of heat or cold, beyond what they have been accustomed to bear'. In the most sentimental tone, British sympathisers argued that the Maroons, because they came from a tropical climate, could never survive in Nova Scotia and that transplanting them from their homes would see them would wilt and die.[52] The Maroons also stressed that they would 'never thrive in a climate where the Pine Apple does not'.[53]

United States' newspapers shared in this preoccupation: Black bodies could never fit in cold climates. In December 1797, a Boston newspaper, *The Columbia Centinel*, noted the 'painful' cold the Maroons must surely endure. The following month, *The New-York Commercial Advertiser* alleged that two Maroons died upon drinking cold water. The essayist cautioned, 'Persons from warm latitudes should be cautious of taking large draughts of water in northern climates.'[54] Concerns about the climate also troubled Imperial decision-makers at the highest level. The British politician who became responsible for Maroon affairs in London, the Duke of Portland, immediately requested specifics about the Maroons' survival in a severe climate. Portland assumed that exiles from a tropical climate should naturally be repatriated to a region with a similar climate – in this case, to Sierra Leone. The knowledge of black fatalities of the first two groups of black exiles in Sierra Leone – London's black poor population in 1787, and the Black Loyalists in 1792 – did not dampen enthusiasm for sending the Maroons to Sierra Leone.

The concern with Nova Scotia's climate did not originate with the Maroons' arrival. Questions about black people's intolerance for Nova Scotia's winters had emerged at least a decade earlier. In 1786, when English reformers like Granville Sharp considered destinations for relocating poor black people from England (refugees of the War for American Independence), Nova Scotia emerged as a possibility. These reformers knew that Black Loyalists had emigrated there after the American Revolution, but they explicitly rejected Nova Scotia for this purpose. A handbill from 17 May 1786 announced that 'It has been mediated to send blacks to Nova Scotia but this plan is laid aside, as that country is unfit and improper for the said blacks.' Curiously, the philanthropists who proposed to resettle poor blacks never discussed the winter in England – only Nova Scotia stood symbolic of frozen possibilities.[55]

Sensing the general unease about the Maroons' ability to live in cold temperatures, Wentworth was compelled to offer a rationale for keeping people of African ancestry in Nova Scotia. He dismissed the cold as deleterious to black health and addressed the climate directly: '[If] well fed, warmly clothed, and comfortably lodged, I have always found negroes directly from the hottest coasts of Africa have grown strong and lusty in the winter and that they

Figure 4.1 A clear representation of 'Herculean bodies', this image has been reproduced many times but first appeared in *The Proceedings of the Governor and Assembly of Jamaica in Regard to the Maroon Negroes . . .* (London, 1796). [Public domain.]

did not suffer by it.'⁵⁶ His careful ministrations eclipsed any disadvantages of climate. The lieutenant governor lamented the long preoccupation with the theme of cold climate and black bodies and recalled that in 1792, when over 1,000 Black Loyalists had arrived in Sierra Leone, many had perished within months from terrible disease. At least in Nova Scotia, black people 'were still healthy, although poor and almost naked'. The winters, he observed, 'excited apprehensions and universal competition' among all inhabitants, and led to misery for whites and blacks alike. Exaggerated 'zeal and affection' expressed for the Maroons' plight would lead only to the worst of consequences. Black constitutions were 'Herculean', he argued; the Maroons could thrive even better in Nova Scotia than whites. Indeed, from his observations, the 'constitution of the Black species are stronger than the whites and better calculated to endure labours and hardships'.⁵⁷

Whereas Wentworth's racist focus on the 'Herculean' body emerged from Atlantic slavery, Maroon supporters adopted another British tradition to elevate the Maroons, one which saw 'primitive' societies possessing virtues which modern societies had lost. Wilberforce and Walpole were not unique in their high regard for the Maroons. Despite the fact that the latter were considered alien and racially inferior, they were a group who remained standard-bearers for long-held beliefs about the martial virtues of an 'untamed' people. Romantic sensibilities found aesthetic beauty in so-called 'untamed' people of 'untamed' lands.[58] This mindset influenced widely held British conceptualisations of the Maroons as distinct from slaves. The contemporary historian Robert Dallas observed that the Maroons maintained themselves in a state of 'savage freedom'.[59] Nevertheless, they merited praise. As Edwards put it, their savagery 'strengthened their frame and served to exalt them to great bodily perfection'. His description of the dignity of their bearing is striking:

> Their demeanour is lofty, their walk firm, and their persons erect. Every motion displays a combination of strength and agility. Their muscles (neither hidden nor depressed by clothing) are very prominent, and strongly marked. Their sight withal is wonderfully acute, and their hearing remarkably quick.[60]

In the British Parliament, too, Maroon sympathisers represented them as 'brave men' who had made a 'noble resistance'; exterminating them would 'fix an indelible stain on the British character'.[61]

That the Maroons made their home in a mountainous region also figured in British sensibility. The eighteenth-century production of multi-volume universal geographies gave a special esteem to mountains, regarded as dynamic, turbulent and powerful.[62] This was an age which invested mountains – especially the tops of mountains – with power and strength.[63] The Maroons in their mountains hence were extended to a realm of myth, a set of ideologically laden signs and images associated with masculine fearsomeness. The hidden, almost primordial difficulties of the mountains supposedly created dauntless warriors worthy of esteem – and British sentimentality. The Maroons' social qualities were seen to derive from their physical environment, which geared them to be warlike.[64] It is possible that the Maroons exploited this branding to present themselves as naturally brave and most suited as military warriors.

Anti-slavery evangelicals in Britain drew from these associations of soft emotions and bold actions to portray the Maroons as tropical warriors who were betrayed by the brutal nabobs of the Caribbean.[65] Influential abolitionists such as Wilberforce expressed sympathy for the Maroons' plight in the British Parliament.[66] The Maroons, Wilberforce argued, were not 'robbers and murderers' but freedmen foremost, and had claim to humanity and to protection; they did not deserve to suffer under the hands of British 'sportsmen'. Indeed, he accused Britain of violating the treaties which stipulated that the Maroons could only be punished for a crime by their own community.[67] Ironically, in an age of anti-slavery and humanitarianism, the dangerous enemies of Jamaica transformed into 'helpless & injured' warriors in need of rescue and resettlement. Their petitions to relocate to the 'warmer climate' of Sierra Leone met with approval and the British government began making arrangements to relocate them in 1799.[68]

The Maroons arrived in Sierra Leone in September 1800. In 1796, the Sierra Leone government had refused to take the Jamaican rebels, rejecting them as too dangerous and a likely contaminant to the colony. Four years later, as the West African colony struggled to remain viable and to find ways to be profitable, the Maroons – a climate-suitable and militarily formidable people – appeared perfect colony builders. Coincidentally, the Maroons arrived just in time to quell the Black Loyalist uprising against the local British government. As they had in Nova Scotia, these Black Loyalists demanded more secure title to their lands and a greater degree of self-governance, as they had been promised by the promoters of the Sierra Leone colonisation scheme.[69] The Maroons, more prepared to ally with the British Empire than with a small group of Black Loyalist rebels, demonstrated their loyalty by suppressing the uprising. In a recent essay, S. Karly Kehoe makes a case for considering how migrants themselves participated in new communities, specifically, how they 'chose to respond to circumstances'.[70] Maroon leaders *decided* to take a stance against Nova Scotia's Black Loyalists and thereby tied their advancement, status and security to the prosperity of the Empire. Over the long run, the Maroons were more influenced by Black Loyalists' religious evangelicalism than their politics. Among those Black Loyalists who fled Nova Scotia were David George's Baptist congregation and Moses Wilkinson's Methodist church members.[71] In time, the Maroons and Black Loyalists intermarried and integrated as the 'Creole' class. They built Christian churches, monopolised prestigious clerical positions and set themselves as superior to nearby African groups. Their attachment and aspirations served the needs of expansive politics and strengthened British colonialism.

Conclusion

Both the Black Loyalists and Maroons merited Atlantic-wide attention during an era in which British reformists associated the imperial programme with benevolence and during a time when a ready solution – a second transplantation – served imperial interests. The relocations highlight the Maritimes' full integration in the British Empire by the end of the eighteenth century. They also serve as a reminder of the selectivity of British humanitarianism in the late eighteenth century, which focused almost exclusively on black bodies and neglected the growing poverty of Indigenous nations. These black migrations extended empire; Aboriginal claims threatened to restrict it. The words of the Mi'kmaq elders, who protested the British establishment of Halifax in 1749, capture one key difference between Aboriginal nations and black exiles of the Maritimes, and show why the black diaspora remained beholden to the Empire. Translated into the first-person voice, the elders stated, 'This land, over which you now wish to make yourself the absolute master, this land belongs to me, just as surely as I have grown out of it like the grass, this is my place of birth and my home, this is my native soil; yes, I believe that it was God that gave it to me to be my country forever.'[72] After centuries of French and British incursions, the Mi'kmaq continued to protect their kinship networks and their home.[73] For free blacks who had no 'country', the British Empire was their best chance at home. As a sign of their gratitude, a marker of their attachment and a final testimony to British power, both the Black Loyalists and Maroons named Freetown streets in Sierra Leone after trusted British military officers: Tarleton, Rawdon, Howe and Walpole.

Notes

1. Ruma Chopra, *Almost Home: Maroons between Freedom and Slavery in Jamaica, Nova Scotia, and Sierra Leone* (New Haven: Yale University Press, 2018). Any treatment of Black Loyalists must start with James W. St G. Walker, *The Black Loyalists: The Search for a Promised Land in Nova Scotia and Sierra Leone, 1783–1870* (New York: Africana Publishing Company, 1976) and Harvey A. Whitfield, 'Black Loyalists and Black Slaves in Maritime Canada', *History Compass*, 52:10 (2007).
2. According to Julian Gwyn, the total population of Nova Scotia in 1791 was 45,000. It would grow to 66,000 by 1801. See Julian Gwyn, *Excessive Expectations: Maritime Commerce and the Economic Development of Nova Scotia, 1740–1870* (Montreal: McGill-Queen's University Press, 1998), p. 26.
3. The expansion of the British settlement led to the division of Nova Scotia into separate political units. Nova Scotia was partitioned in 1784, with the mainland side of the Bay of Fundy becoming the colony of New Brunswick. Cape Breton was a separate colony until 1821. Finally, the third jurisdiction, St John's Island (shortly to be Prince Edward Island), kept its own government, which it had established since 1769. See L. F. S. Upton, *Micmacs and Colonists: Indian–White Relations in the Maritime Provinces, 1713–1867* (Vancouver: University of British Columbia, 1979), p. 81.
4. John G. Reid, 'Pax Brittanica or Pax Indegena? Planter Nova Scotia (1760–1782) and Competing Strategies of Pacification', *Canadian Historical Review*, 85:4 (2004), p. 678.
5. As Julian Gwyn notes, there was an 'almost total absence of fertile land suitable for profitable agriculture'. The land available was 'distributed in widely scattered and discontinuous settlements with severely limited wealth-forming potential'. See Gwyn, *Excessive Expectations*, p. 5; Upton notes that the 'indented coastline and numerous rivers of the province ensured that this white settlement intruded almost simultaneously into every part of the land, and as a result, the Indian, in moving from forest to river to coast, inevitably encountered the newcomers'. See Upton, *Micmas and Colonists*, p. 82.
6. As Whitfield has noted, the status of these black slaves remains uncertain. Some slaves may actually have been servants and some servants may have been slaves. See Harvey A. Whitfield, *North to Bondage: Loyalist Slavery in the Maritimes* (Vancouver: University of British Columbia Press, 2016), p. 106.
7. Harvey A. Whitfield, *Black Slavery in the Maritimes: A History in Documents* (Halifax, NS: Broadview Sources Series, 2018), p. 2.
8. Whitfield, *Black Slavery in the Maritimes*, p. 2.

9. Whitfield notes that slavery gradually ended because of 'black agency, growing numbers of anti-slavery whites, and sympathetic judges'. See *Black Slavery in the Maritimes*, p. 11.
10. Graeme Wynn observes that Newfoundland produced more dried cod than New Brunswick and Nova Scotia combined. See Graeme Wynn, 'A Region of Scattered Settlements and Bounded Possibilities: Northeastern North America, 1775–1800', *The Canadian Geographer*, 31:4 (1987), p. 326; Cole Harris, *Reluctant Land: Society, Space, and Environment in Canada before Confederation* (Vancouver: UBC Press, 2009), pp. 162–3; Julian Gwyn, *Excessive Expectations*, pp. 5–7; Graeme Wynn, '1800–1810: Turning the Century', in Phillip A. Buckner and John G. Reid (eds), *The Atlantic Region to Confederation: A History* (Toronto: University of Toronto Press, 1994), pp. 212–15.
11. Robin W. Winks, *The Blacks in Canada: A History* (New Haven: McGill-Queens University Press, 1971), pp. 28–36; John N. Grant, 'Black Immigrants into Nova Scotia, 1776–1815', in *The Journal of Negro History*, 58:3 (July 1973), pp. 253–70 (253–6).
12. The US constitution had not abolished slavery. For the intense poverty experienced in Black Loyalist communities see the groundbreaking archaeological study of Birchtown, Nova Scotia by Laird Niven and Stephen A. Davis in John W. Pulis (ed.), *Moving On: Black Loyalists in the Afro-Atlantic World* (New York: Garland Publishing, 1999). For re-enslavement, see Carole Watterson Troxler, 'Re-enslavement of Black Loyalists: Mary Postell in South Carolina, East Florida and Nova Scotia', *Acadiensis*, 37:2 (Summer/Fall 2008), pp. 70–85; Whitfield, *Black Slavery in the Maritimes*, pp. 81–5, 107–11, 128; and Whitfield, *North to Bondage*, pp. 13–16.
13. Whitfield, *Black Slavery in the Maritimes*, p. 80.
14. Notebook of John Clarkson, British Library, AD MS 41262B, 29 October 1791 (other dates also possible).
15. R. R. Kuczynski, *Demographic Survey of the British Colonial Empire, Volume 1: West Africa* (London: Oxford University Press, 1948), p. 43. Importantly, in 1787, the black poor were not sent to Botany Bay, which was reserved for convicts. Granville Sharp to Dr Lehsom, Clarkson Papers, 13 October 1788, Huntington Library. Initially, seven hundred people had volunteered to go to the settlement; they left on 8 April 1787 and arrived on 9 May 1787. Eveline C. Martin, *The British West African Settlements, 1750–1821* (New York: Longmans, Green, 1927), p. 106.
16. Also see important essays by Gretchen H. Gerzina and Wallace Brown in *Moving On: Black Loyalists in the Afro-Atlantic World* as well as Stephen J. Braidwood's, *Black Poor and White Philanthropists: London's Blacks and the Foundation of the Sierra Leone Settlement 1786–1791* (Liverpool: Liverpool University Press, 1994).
17. Clarkson Papers, 1792, Report on Sierra Leone, Huntington Library.
18. Thomas Clarkson to John Clarkson, 17 July 1792, Add. MS 41262A, British Library.
19. Wilberforce to John Clarkson, London, 27 April 1792, Library and Archives Canada (Ottawa).
20. Carl Bernhard Wadstrom, 'An Essay on Colonization' (1794), vol. 1, p. 94, Huntington Library.
21. Eveline C. Martin, *The British West African Settlements, 1750–1821* (New York: Longmans, Green, and Co, 1927), p. 115.
22. Henry Smeathman, the unscrupulous original promoter of Sierra Leone as a colony suited for black people, had stated that it was 'a country congenial to their constitutions'. Braidwood, *Black Poor and White Philanthropists*, p. 85.
23. To J. Clarkson, from Henry Thornton, 30 December 1791, A-1981 microfilm, Library and Archives Canada.
24. Ibid.
25. *Report from the Committee on the Petition of the Court of Directors of the Sierra Leone Company*, 1802 (Boston College, Williams Collection).
26. From Wilberforce, 8 July 1791, Rothley Temple near Leicester (to Lieutenant Clarkson?), A-1981 microfilm, Library and Archives Canada.

27. For anti-slavery in Nova Scotia see Barry Cahill, 'Mediating a Scottish Enlightenment Ideal: The Presbyterian Dissenter Attack on Slavery in Late Eighteenth-Century Nova Scotia', in Marjory Harper and Michael E. Vance (eds), *Myth, Migration and the Making of Memory: Scotia and Nova Scotia c.1700–1990* (Halifax, NS and Edinburgh: Fernwood and John Donald Publishers Ltd, 1999), pp. 189–201; and Whitfield, *North to Bondage*, pp. 92–5.
28. Jennifer K. Snyder, 'Black Flight: Tracing Black Refugees throughout the Revolutionary Atlantic World, 1775–1812', PhD dissertation (University of Florida, 2013), p. 187. When the black refugees of 1812 were provided this option, they refused unanimously. See S. Karly Kehoe, 'Historical Perspectives in the Integration of Black Refugees in Atlantic Canada, 1812–1830', in S. Karly Kehoe, Jan-Christoph Heilinger and Eva Alisic (eds), *Responsibility for Refugee and Migrant Integration* (Berlin: De Gruyter Publishers, 2019), pp. 65–80.
29. They left Halifax on 15 January 1792 and arrived 6 March 1792. See Kuczynski, *Demographic Survey*, 66.
30. Adam Afzelius, *Sierra Leone Journal, 1795–96*, ed. and trans. Alexander Peter Kup (Uppsala: Studia Ethnographica Upsaliensia, 1967), p. 2.
31. Kuczynski, *Demographic Survey*, pp. 58, 65; James W. St G. Walker, 'The Establishment of a Free Black Community in Nova Scotia, 1783–1840', in Martin L. Kilson and Robert I. Rotberg (eds), *The African Diaspora: Interpretive Essays* (Cambridge, MA: Harvard University Press, 1976), p. 221.
32. Walker, 'The Establishment of a Free Black Community', quote from p. 221.
33. Ibid. pp. 224–5.
34. The treaties the British officials in Nova Scotia signed with nine Mi'kmaq villages in 1760–1 may be a useful point of comparison. Wicken notes that these treaties constituted an end of the treaty-making period in British–Mi'kmaq relations. William C. Wicken, *Mi'kmaq Treaties on Trial: History, Land and Donald Marshall Junior* (Toronto: University of Toronto Press, 2002), p. 191. Like the 1760–1 treaties, the 1738–9 treaties forged personal relationships with the Maroons and helped to keep the peace that allowed Jamaica's settlement.
35. Eliga H. Gould, *Among the Powers of the Earth: The American Revolution and the Making of a New World Empire* (Cambridge, MA: Harvard University Press, 2014), p. 30.
36. As Julian Gwyn notes, warfare was central to Nova Scotia's development. Gwyn, 'Economic Fluctuations in Wartime Nova Scotia, 1755–1815', in Margaret Conrad (ed.), *Making Adjustments: Change and Continuity in Planter Nova Scotia, 1759–1800* (Fredericton: Acadiensis Press, 1991), p. 61.
37. Chopra, *Almost Home*, chapter 4.
38. Within weeks, he moved the entire community of Trelawney Town Maroons to Preston, across the harbour from Halifax and some six miles to the north-east.
39. Prince Edward to Duke of Portland, 15 August 1796, Colonial Office Papers, January to August, 1796, MG II N.S., 'A', vol. 123, Nova Scotia Public Archives (Halifax).
40. Specimen of handwriting, 15 August 1799, C9138, Colonial Office, Nova Scotia, 'A', July–December, 1799, vol. 130), Library and Archives Canada.
41. The idea of settling Aboriginal people in one consolidated village was, John G. Reid notes, 'an ancient preoccupation' and could not be fulfilled. Reid, 'Pax Brittanica or Pax Indegena?', p. 687; also see Ruma Chopra, 'Maroons and Mi'kmaq in Nova Scotia, 1796–1800', *Acadiensis*, 46:1 (Winter/Spring 2017).
42. Maroons to General Walpole, 23 April 1797, C9137, MG II N.S. 'A' vol. 125, Nova Scotia Public Archives.
43. Chopra, *Almost Home*, chapter 3; Heather Street, *Martial Races: The Military Race and Masculinity in British Imperial Culture, 1857–1914* (Manchester: Manchester University Press, 2004), pp. 1, 7.
44. Andrew Smith, from Nova Scotia, 3 June 1797, in Colonial Office Papers, 1798, MG II N.S. 'A' vol. 127, Nova Scotia Public Archives.

45. Mavis C. Campbell, *Nova Scotia and the Fighting Maroons: A Documentary History* (Williamsburg: College of William and Mary Press, 1990).
46. John Wentworth to J. King, 30 May 1799, 'A', January–June, 1799, vol. 129 (166), Library and Archives Canada.
47. Maroon Petition to the Duke of Portland, 4 January 1799, Colonial Office Papers, Nova Scotia Public Archives, January to June, 1799, MG II, N.S. 'A', vol. 129.
48. Alexander Howe to Wentworth, 8 June 1798, MG II N.S. 'A', vol. 127, Library and Archives Canada; T. Chamberlain, 20 June 1798, MG II N.S. 'A', vol. 127, Library and Archives Canada; *Journals of the Assembly of Jamaica*, 18 December 1798, JCB; Wentworth to John King (Private), 23 May 1799, CO 217/37, Library and Archives Canada; T. Chamberlain, 20 June 1798, MG II N.S. 'A', vol. 127.
49. Précis of letters from His Royal Highness Prince Edward and John Wentworth, 21 April to 24 May 1797, CO 218/23, Library and Archives Canada; précis of letters from His Royal Highness Prince Edward and John Wentworth, 21 April to 24 May 1797, CO 218/23, Library and Archives Canada; extract of letter to Walpole, 10 January 1797, *Committee of Correspondence Out-Letter Book*, 1B/5/14/2, Jamaican Archives and Records Department (Spanish Town, Jamaica).
50. Thomas Peters' petition on behalf of the Black Loyalists also mentioned that 'the cold was less congenial to whites than blacks'. Whitfield, *Slavery in the Maritimes*, p. 80.
51. Quote from *Telegraph* (London, England), Monday, 15 August 1796; Also see: *London Packet or New Lloyd's Evening Post* (London, England), 5 April 1797; *True Briton* (London, England), Friday, 7 April 1797.
52. Thomas Cooper, 'Extract of Letter from Gentleman in America to a Friend in England – Emigration, July 2014, 1798', in Sabin, 16611, E187 Box, Massachusetts Historical Society.
53. Jeffrey A. Fortrin, '"Blackened Beyond Our Native Hue": Removal, Identity and the Trelawney Maroons on the Margins of the Atlantic World, 1796–1800', *Citizenship Studies*, 10:1 (February 2006), p. 5.
54. *The Columbia Centinel*, 16 December 1797, Boston; *The New-York Commercial Advertiser*, 2 January 1798, New York City.
55. Robin W. Winks, *The Blacks in Canada*, p. 62.
56. John Wentworth to Duke of Portland, 13 August 1796, Colonial Office Papers, Nova Scotia Public Archives, January to August, 1796, MG II N.S., 'A', vol. 123.
57. John Wentworth to John King (Private), 23 May 1799, CO 217/37.
58. Streets, *Martial Races*, p. 59.
59. R. C. Dallas, *The History of the Maroons, from their origin to the establishment of their chief tribe at Sierra Leone, including the expedition to Cuba for the purpose of procuring Spanish chasseurs and the state of the island of Jamaica for the last ten years with a succinct history of the island previous to that period*, vol. 1 (London: Frank Cass, [1803] 1968), p. 45.
60. Bryan Edwards, 'Observations on the Maroon Negroes of the Island of Jamaica', in Richard Price (ed.), *Maroon Societies: Rebel Slave Communities in the Americas* (Garden City, NY: Anchor Books, [1774] 1973), p. 244.
61. *The Parliamentary History of England from the Earliest Period to the Year 1803*, vol. 32, from 27 May 1795 to 2 March 1797 (London: Hansard, 1818), p. 929. This quote comes from the debates on 21 March 1796.
62. Charles W. J. Withers, 'Towards a Historical Geography of Enlightenment in Scotland', in Paul Wood (ed.), *The Scottish Enlightenment* (Rochester: University of Rochester Press, 2000), p. 68.
63. Charles W. J. Withers, 'The Historical Creation of the Scottish Highlands', in Ian Donnachie and Christopher Whatley (eds), *The Manufacture of Scottish History* (Edinburgh: Polygon, 1992), p. 145.
64. Withers, 'The Historical Creation', p. 145; John R. Gold and Margaret M. Gold, *Imagining*

Scotland: Tradition, Representation, and Promotion in Scottish Tourism since 1750 (Aldershot: Scholar Press, 1995), p. 62.

65. Padraic X. Scanlan, *Freedom's Debtors: British Antislavery in Sierra Leone in the Age of Revolution* (New Haven: Yale University Press, 2017), p. 7. Scanlan notes that British anti-slavery was 'imperial in its geography and its ambitions'.

66. W. A. Green, 'Was British Emancipation a Success? The Abolitionist Perspective', in David Richardson (ed.), *Abolition and Its Aftermath: The Historical Context, 1790–1916* (London: Frank Cass, 1985), p. 184.

67. *Parliamentary History of England*, vol. 32, pp. 924, 926, 928. This quote comes from the debates on 21 March 1796.

68. Chopra, *Almost Home*, chapter 5.

69. For the circumstances that led to the Black Loyalist revolt see Cassandra Pybus, *Epic Journeys of Freedom: Runaway Slaves of the American Revolution and Their Global Quest for Liberty* (Boston: Beacon Press, 2006).

70. Kehoe, 'Historical Perspectives in the Integration of Black Refugees.'

71. Sylvia Frey, *Water from the Rock: Black Resistance in a Revolutionary Age* (Princeton: Princeton University Press, 1991), p. 196.

72. Mi'kmaq elders to Cornwallis, 24 September 1749 – translated from Mi'kmaw into French by Abbe Peter Millard. Upton, *Micmacs and Colonists*, pp. 201–2. Wicken, *Mi'kmaq Treaties*, pp. 179–80.

73. Susan Sleeper-Smith, 'Furs and Female Kin Networks: The World of Marie Madeleine Reaume L'archeveque Chevalier', in Susan Sleeper-Smith, Jo-Anne Fiske and William Wicken (eds), *New Faces of the Fur Trade: Selected Papers of the Seventh North American Fur Trade Conference, Halifax, Nova Scotia* (East Lansing: Michigan State University Press, 1998). Sleeper-Smith observes that kin networks 'transcend and confuse the questions posed by historical analysis' (p. 63); Reid notes that the Mi'kmaq lost ground only after 1815, when the British conflicts with France and the United States came to an end and Aboriginal neutrality became less valuable. See John G. Reid, 'Empire, the Maritime Colonies, and the Supplanting of Mi'kma'ki/Wulstukwik, 1782–1820', *Acadiensis*, 38:2 (2009), p. 80. The Mi'kmaq, on the other hand, continued to use names that tied the community's identity with the surrounding landscape. As Wicken writes, 'culture and place were inextricably linked together' (Wicken, *Mi'kmaq Treaties*, p. 37).

FIVE

New World, Old Problems? Aristocratic Influences on Colonial Governance and Land in Nineteenth-century Atlantic Canada

Annie Tindley

'Proprietorial rights, in the sense in which they exist in England, are very unsuitable to the atmosphere of this country [Canada], and I imagine a perpetual agitation will prevail in the island [Prince Edward Island] until its land tenures are assimilated to those of neighbouring provinces.'[1]

Introduction

In the nineteenth-century British and Irish rural imagination, Atlantic Canada was regarded as a place of refuge from the abuses and injustices of the old feudal world; an escape, where a family might settle and cultivate land free from the dead hand of landlordism. It was the vanguard of one of the most popular settlement colonies of the British Empire, a land of promise and opportunity, and many hundreds of thousands were drawn across the Atlantic by these attractive qualities.[2] Anti-landlordism as a political as well as an economic and cultural movement increased in nineteenth-century Britain and Ireland, paralleling the great European exodus to North America.[3] But this was not the only story of British colonisation. Atlantic Canada was a location of escape, not just for the rural poor, but for many of Britain and Ireland's landed elite. Although much smaller numerically, in terms of influence, governance and policy – constitutional and in relation to land tenure and ownership – they more than held their own.[4]

This chapter will examine aristocratic influence on colonial governance and land in Atlantic Canada in the nineteenth century, using the governor-generalship of Frederick Temple Hamilton Temple Blackwood, Lord Dufferin (1872–8) as its key exemplar.[5] It has three aims in view: first, it will seek to explore landed and aristocratic understandings of Atlantic Canada as a place in its own right, but also as part of the wider web of the British Empire. What purpose did Atlantic Canada serve, in their view, and what kind of impact did it have on them directly? Second, it will consider the direct influence that landed elites had on the Atlantic provinces. Using Prince Edward Island (PEI) as a case study, this chapter explores the ways and means by which both agitation and its intellectual underpinnings were communicated, challenged and incorporated in Atlantic Canada, in the context of the wider British World.[6] Lastly, the chapter will put Atlantic Canada into its wider governmental context by unpacking the complex relationship between provincial, national and imperial power structures and how they influenced land policies and with what results.

This chapter will emphasise the fluid, transnational nature of ideas of land, class and governance. As transnational historians have highlighted, it is not helpful to think of these in binary terms of metropole and periphery, but instead track the circuits of communication and feedback loops.[7] This wider perspective needs to be rooted in the specificity of locality as well as changes over time and geographies. Much of the historiography around the movement of people, goods and ideas between Britain, Ireland and Atlantic Canada tends to focus on the mass movement of people.[8] This chapter, by focusing on the tiny numbers of the governing classes, allows us to consider elite definitions of 'universal truths' regarding property and contract as well as their understandings of how these should be maintained and enforced in challenging imperial contexts.[9] This allows us to consider the self-perception of the landed classes and their mental frameworks. To take a somewhat facetious example, privately to Lord Kimberley, a fellow peer and landowner, Dufferin described PEI as 'a pretty little place, about 130 miles long by 16 broad and would make a snug estate'.[10] This example highlights, in a light-hearted way, how conceptions of land and power developed through landed inheritance were applied in the imperial context. Lastly, the nature of 'good' governance – meaning aristocratic governance, or 'rule by the best' – and how this was constructed by the British and Irish landed elite and perceived by Canadians will be discussed.[11] By using the governor-generalship of Lord Dufferin, covering the early years of the confederation and the period of PEI's accession to it and turmoil over land reform, these themes can be unpacked.

Section I: Will to rule

Although one of the more popular governor generals, Lord Dufferin struggled politically with the limits of the role, coming into sharp conflict with Canada's federal and provincial governments and public opinion as to the extent of his – and by extension, Britain's – influence over them.[12] Essentially, Dufferin was confronted with the limits of exporting the British deferential aristocratic framework into the colonial context, challenging his aristocratic and landed conceptions of the nature and future of Atlantic Canada. As a peer and landowner, Dufferin was firmly convinced that he possessed the requisite skills to handle responsibility, the proper education and, generally, the accepted understandings of aristocratic leadership.[13] His real problem was failing to recognise that his role 'was not to save Canadians from themselves'.[14] It was worth the trouble, however, at least financially; one of the key attractions of the post was the salary and cheap living that came with the role.[15] The Canadian governor-generalship offered a salary of £10,000 per year, plus expenses, two properties and other perks.[16] Although the financial opportunities were not Dufferin's primary reason for taking up the post – it was a prestigious, secure and not too challenging role, in line with his status – they are worth highlighting to demonstrate the mix of pressures and objectives in the appointment of aristocratic and landed governors.[17] As Dufferin argued when his Colonial Office superior and old friend, Lord Kimberley, warned him about his escalating living costs in the Dominion:

> By dint of a great deal of bodily exertion and I admit by a considerable amount of expenditure at the chief cities of the Dominion I have succeeded in making the GG a personage who fills the public eye, and whose social influence is recognised and regarded . . . but in order to effect anything of this kind the Governor General must be something more than a *nominis umbra* registering Minutes of Council in Rideau Hall.[18]

This was a very aristocratic framing of the nature and purpose of the role.[19] As he pointed out to Lord Lorne, his successor as governor general, 'When I first drove up to the door of "Rideau Hall", as it used to be called, I was very nearly driving straight back to the steamer . . . for at that time it was nothing more than a very small villa, such as would suit the needs of some country banker.'[20] Clearly, standards were initially not what they should have been in his view, and he worked hard to build up the status and visibility of the role. This also related to longstanding conventions as to personal fitness to rule in British and Irish politics, where an independent income was regarded as the surest guard against corruption. In imperial terms, this had been a long-standing convention, from what was regarded as the high-water mark of corruption under the British in India, when nabobs of humble origins, such as Robert Clive and Warren Hastings, exploited imperial positions for personal financial gain on a staggering scale.[21]

Dufferin was an assiduous promoter of Canada and the wider empire, both to Canadians and the British, and he was a strong advocate of the British connection for both sides.[22] In doing so, he was making a deliberate effort to counteract the growing political view in 1850s and 1860s Britain that the overseas empire should be reduced as a wasteful distraction, particularly its self-governing territories, which should be supported to full independence.[23] These debates had had a damaging effect in Canada, and so Dufferin set out to promote a vision of a secure British World.[24] He did this primarily by being a highly visible governor, working alongside his wife to run an ambitious programme of public events, travels and speech-making. In these speeches, he was always keen to press home a number of points; firstly, the positive future of Canada, blessed with space and natural resources; secondly, Canada's loyalty to Queen and empire and how this loyalty was supported, not undermined, by its political autonomy. Lastly, he promoted the continuing flow of European migration into Canada as the best support for the bright future he predicted for the dominion.[25] Dufferin was driven in part by his wider desire to ensure that Canadian institutions and norms differed as far as possible from those of the United States, for the purposes of both British foreign policy and Canadian loyalty: 'it has been my object to lose no opportunity of stamping upon all our [i.e. Canadian] institutions, whether social or political, such a character as would most tend to remove them from the American and approximate them to the English type'.[26] Having watched with concern Queen Victoria's retreat into private life after the death of the Prince Consort in 1861, he understood the importance of visibility, particularly in an overseas and self-governing polity.[27] Part of the bright future Dufferin predicted for the dominion was the consolidation and extension of the confederation, and during his tenure the focus was on Prince Edward Island, which joined in 1873.[28] This was not a simple process, however; tension between notions of British governance and rule of law on the one hand and local conditions, expectations and demands on the other changed the shape and substance of property rights and law as well as conditions for joining the confederation in PEI.[29] Linking the constitutional to the political through an examination of the contested issue of land on the island is a useful way of exposing the underlying assumptions of elite landed men such as Dufferin, and of seeing how they were challenged in Atlantic Canada.[30]

Section II: Land questions

As with any discussion about land issues – economic, political or cultural – in any geographical context, multiple layers of meaning and consequence created the combustible conditions for disagreement.[31] This was in evidence globally during the nineteenth century. Dufferin was no stranger to controversies over land tenure reform and landownership and use; indeed, his entire perspective on land in the dominions and colonies was framed by his ownership of land in Ireland and the existential challenges made to it during his lifetime. While in Canada, he was horrified to see some of the same issues emerge in the maritime provinces, and he was quick to identify international links between land reform movements.[32] Witness his outrage when first made aware of a potential land act for Prince Edward Island: his language was certainly not that of compromise, but spoke of a growing paranoia about the international threat to landed power: 'There has also come up from the Local Legislature of Prince Edward Island a Bill expropriating land owners in the Island under very unfair conditions. I have told my Government that I could not consent to it becoming law.'[33] He went on, in the same private letter, to discuss Irish land reform measures then being debated at Westminster, explicitly linking the two land questions.[34] But Dufferin's views were not shared by Canadian politicians or the Canadian public. Canada was a settlement colony, and part of its attraction to European emigrants was that it offered the opportunity to own land outright, allowing escape from the life of a tenant who was subject to the whims of Old World feudal landlordism, in a territory protected by British military power.[35] As such, definitions of landownership, tenure and land use are central to understandings of nineteenth-century Canada, and when those conceptions came into conflict, as in PEI, controversy followed.

There were really a number of different issues at stake during this period in the island province. The land lottery held in eighteenth-century London had left large portions of the island's 1.4 million acres of excellent arable land in the ownership of about 100 mainly absentee private individuals and families.[36] The history of their ownership was not a happy one, being characterised by one historian as 'frustration on one side and unaccountability on the other'.[37] A royal commission had been appointed in 1860 to investigate the issue and make recommendations, which condemned the original settlement of the lots and recommended the application of a Land Purchase Act to all the original holdings.[38] The commissioners suggested that the British government guarantee a loan of £100,000 to fund this policy, but this recommendation was rejected by the Colonial Office.[39] A period of tenant agitation, including rent strikes, ensued as no action was taken at all.[40]

But there were also constitutional issues to consider: in 1873, after extensive and at times acrimonious negotiations, PEI came into the confederation, an occasion Dufferin marked by visiting the island to celebrate. 'Nothing could have been more joyous or exuberant than our reception,' Dufferin wrote to Kimberley, 'the whole population are unanimous in their delight at Confederation, but regard it as the annexation of the Dominion to the Island.'[41] It was not all celebration, however; the costs of that confederation, set out in the terms agreed between PEI and the federal government, are what link the two issues of land and constitution.[42] In an attempt to demonstrate the benefits of confederation to good governance at the provincial level two key proposals were made. First, economic support was demanded to subsidise a failed railway-building project on the island. Second, the possibility of a legislative solution to the PEI land question was held out to encourage confederation. This was in the form of both legislative and financial support for a Land Purchase Act, by which the island government proposed to buy out the large absentee landlords, who were regarded as holding back economic development. The issue was kept hot by the continuing tenant agitation on the island, organised by the Tenant League, including mass meetings, petitions and rent strikes. Having been failed by Canadian politicians on both ends of the political spectrum and by the imperial government, PEI tenants took matters into their own hands and founded a Tenant League in May 1864, with a programme of rent strikes, resisting sheriff officers and enticing soldiers to desert.[43] The League and the PEI government had been arguing for a land purchase act since the early 1860s but the imperial government had refused to approve any such measure, until 1869 when they suggested that if PEI joined the confederation they would reconsider the land question.[44] This pressure was eventually successful in persuading the major landowners to sell, in part because the tenant movement had led them to conclude that this was more in their interests than hanging onto depreciating (both politically and economically) assets.[45]

In taking this view, PEI's landowners behaved in almost exactly the same fashion as Irish landlords such as Dufferin in the same period. Tenant agitation had long been part of Irish rural life, and in the 1840s and 1850s Dufferin had experienced stiff turbulence during the Tenant Right agitation, which was especially strong in Ulster, where his Clandeboye estate was located.[46] The issues at stake were in direct parallel, too: land hunger; lack of security of tenure, landowner absenteeism, compensation for improvements made by tenants and a demand for fair rents.[47] Land agitation was a global issue: extensive reforms had been made in British India by this period, for instance, and acrimonious and controversial settlements were being conducted in South Africa, New Zealand and Australia.[48] For Dufferin and his peers, their views on it were conflicted. On the one hand, their landowning instincts placed them firmly in the camp of property rights and privileges, and their defence in any place was made on both principled and practical grounds. After all, if concessions were made in PEI or Bengal, why not Ireland, Scotland or England, the home nations?[49] But on the other hand, as British imperial administrators, they were keenly aware of their responsibility to ensure good governance, including liberal and progressive reform, in order to justify a British dominion.[50] In the case of PEI, tenant agitation had a long history before the 1860s and 1870s, and resistance to landlordism had long been part of the formal politics of the island.[51] It could not be ignored, especially in the context of confederation.

The PEI land controversy is interesting on a number of different levels. It reminds us that even in Canada, regarded by many prospective European emigrants as a free, land-rich utopia where the dead hand of landlordism could be escaped, land issues were not clear-cut, with competing definitions of the rights and responsibilities of property.[52] Even Dufferin, in his many speeches encouraging migrants to Canada, would often stress as one of its advantages that of 'the prospect of independence, of a roof over his head for which he shall pay no rent, and of ripening cornfields around his homestead which own no master but himself'.[53] He admitted privately that approaches to and expectations of land rights were necessarily different in Canada to those in

Britain, eventually acknowledging that they would need to be reformed in PEI.[54] In the early 1870s, the majority of PEI's inhabitants did not recognise large-scale absentee landlordism as conducive to their interests or identity, and this posed a challenge to Dufferin – to *his* interests and identity.[55] In terms of British imperial interests, however, reforms had to be made and recurrent agitation could not simply be repressed forever while the British proclaimed liberty and progressive policies as the benefits they endowed to their empire.[56] On PEI in the 1870s, as would come to pass for Ireland in the 1900s, large-scale landlordism was a lost cause.[57]

The PEI example also allows us to examine Dufferin's responses to a major controversy over land rights outwith, but connected to, Ireland. Dufferin, alongside many of his class, thought about land issues transnationally and was therefore concerned about the potential impact that reform in PEI might have on developments in Ireland, Britain or elsewhere in the empire.[58] In the early 1870s, Dufferin was engaged in the sale of his estates at Clandeboye, County Down, and was highly sensitive to issues around land prices, conditions of sale and the darkening political context for landed privilege.[59] He had inherited his estates in 1845 when he was fifteen, already heavily burdened with debt, to which he enthusiastically added. His main expenditure consisted of relief programmes during the Great Irish Famine, estate improvements and a colourful and well-travelled social life, which included yachting, keeping up with his wealthier landed friends and being a lord-in-waiting to Queen Victoria.[60] His concern for estate improvements was part of his personal and political identity as a landlord and was directly influenced by his social circle, which was dominated by other improving landowners including the 3rd duke of Sutherland and the 8th duke of Argyll.[61] For Dufferin, a central part of the duty and identity of a landowner was improvement, and he was disappointed by the lack of zeal demonstrated by Irish landowners in general, when compared to their British counterparts.[62] Dufferin was also motivated in his desire to improve by his conception of landlordism as a mechanism for wider leadership, in this case economic, with related political and social benefits.[63] In a similar way, his view was reflected in the extensive (and expensive) public works programmes he oversaw as Indian viceroy, or the genesis of the Canadian Pacific Railway project while serving as governor general.[64] For Dufferin and most of his elite, landed and governing contemporaries, the provision and financing of infrastructure was a central mechanism for putting the theory of landed service into practice, both defining and defending landed privilege.[65]

The early 1870s represented financial Armageddon for Dufferin as he sold the bulk of the Clandeboye estates. His auditor's report for 1871–2 laid out the difficulties in stark terms: the total rental from his estate that year was £19,809.2.1, but Dufferin's debts towered over that and he was struggling to pay even the interest on them.[66] When his land agent in Ireland, Mr Thomson, totted up the total debt in 1873, it came to a heart-stopping £299,171.1.11.[67] Thomson estimated that years' income to be £21,635, but interest payments would immediately claim £14,421 of that.[68] Taking into account essential expenditure, Dufferin had only £153 free income for a whole year. The costs of borrowing were high for struggling landowners in Dufferin's position, and this, alongside the impossibility of finding anyone else to borrow from and the scale of the debt, meant that there was no other option but land sales.[69]

The sale of Irish land in a difficult market at a time of economic depression was no simple task, as Dufferin knew very well, further colouring his view of the demands of the PEI land reformers.[70] He was also keenly aware of the pressure placed on him as a man who was obliged to sell his family's patrimony; it was difficult to identify another interpretation aside from failure.[71] He recognised the importance of the symbolic, as well as the practical step he was taking, and emphasised the high stakes to Thomson: 'I need not remind you that we are now embarking upon a most momentous operation upon the successful issue of which will depend the future prospects and position not merely of myself, but of my children.'[72] As well as being a practical issue, this concern highlights again the emphasis men of Dufferin's landed position placed on the power of the heritable principle; something he applied to the PEI context as much as to his own.[73] Although the leasehold system of PEI was unpopular, most aspects of English land law were in fact broadly accepted in Canada; agrarian society in the dominion, like that in Britain and Ireland, was based and depended on family units and their preservation, so these principles were not completely irrelevant in Atlantic Canada.[74]

As with most Irish land sales in this period, the process was slow and fraught with difficulty.[75] The difficulty lay in getting the right price: Dufferin had to achieve sales of at least twenty-five years' purchase (his preference was twenty-eight years) in order to clear his debts and have something left over.[76] Dufferin calculated in 1877 that if the sales could achieve twenty-eight years' purchase he would realise £540,000 from the sale of 17,400 acres (out of a total estimated estate value of £700,500, by leaving the Clandeboye demesne in his hands).[77] Thomson took a more realistic view, noting that twenty-five years' purchase was more likely, and that from a verified rental of £12,663 per annum they would expect to make £316,550 from a sale.[78] In the end, Dufferin did not achieve a one-off sale, but piece by piece, land was sold between 1875 and 1878 and Dufferin's crushing debts were cleared, although at the future cost of a much reduced base of landed capital and financial leverage.[79]

Although direct and unsentimental in his letters to his agent, Dufferin was clearly very disappointed and anxious that he had to make the sales at all, and further worried that he would not achieve the best possible price for them and therefore cheat himself and his descendants out of their patrimony.[80] He indulged in these reflections when writing to his friend, the duke of Argyll:

The sense of bitter injustice involved in these transactions is so painful, as to render one's position intolerable nor am I required by any conceivable call of duty to undergo this species of annoyance. God knows I have done my duty by my tenantry only too liberally for my own advantage and now that they are well protected against any possible exaction at the hands of strangers, I shall make my escape. I shall have to leave something like £150,000 behind me in the shape of improvements, from which I have had no time to reap no other advantage than the ameliorated condition of the farmers themselves, but an Irish estate is like a sponge, and an Irish landlord never so rich as when he is rid of his property... In many ways it will be a great pain to part with a possession that has been for nearly 300 years in my family and which I had done so much to embellish, but there are many counteracting considerations and the interests of those who come after me, I am inclined to think that Great Britain will afford a firmer foothold than poor dear Old Ireland.[81]

This was Dufferin's immediate concern when the PEI land agitation and reforms came into focus, colouring his views of the situation there. In his embittered view, 'the [PEI] Act is one of simple confiscation under the pretence of arbitration, as it compels owners to sell and no one can believe that they will get the full value of their lands thus forced onto the market'.[82] This was an issue close to the hearts of all Irish landowners, and had been since the dark days of the Great Irish Famine. As the value of Irish land fluctuated and decreased, Dufferin and other Irish landowners became increasingly sensitive to government pressure and legislation to sell at defined times and for prices defined by state appointed arbiters, as under the Irish Encumbered Estates Court, set up to revive the Irish land market after the Famine. Dufferin was opposed to the PEI land legislation in the mid-1870s both in principle and on a practical basis because he feared that the PEI landowners would not receive the market value of their land if it were bought from them via the proposed legislation, as compared to the prices they might expect if selling freely on the open market.[83] By the early 1880s, however, when faced with the Irish Land Act of 1881, Dufferin had changed his mind and argued that land purchase was the only realistic solution for Irish landowners. This view was informed by his experiences in Canada and how the 1874 Act for PEI operated in practice, which was that the compensation the landowners received was relatively generous.[84]

The other transnational aspect of the PEI land question focused on regional economic development and who was to pay for it. There was fairly universal support on PEI, among its residents, government and rural tenants, for the view that ownership of land granted, imposed even, the power to implement economic and infrastructure development plans. Among the most important of these on PEI was the island railway, which would better facilitate the movement of agricultural and fishing produce and eventually link up (via a ferry) with the railway planned from Ontario to the Maritimes. The development of the local economy – dominated by agriculture and fishing – was tied to the development of suitable infrastructure, and to the opportunities and restrictions of the leasehold form of landlordism that had developed on the island.[85] It was also linked to questions surrounding the development of a coherent Canadian national identity. PEI was part of and contributed to the identity of confederated Canada, an identity which itself was still under construction and would remain fluid.[86] Dufferin gave considerable thought to this question and saw it as one of his most important duties as governor to promote the idea of a strong, united Canada. By contrast, Lord Kimberley, who in the early 1870s was the secretary of state for the colonies, was more cynical: 'The mess they have got into with their railways makes them feel the necessity for Confederation.'[87] The lieutenant governor of PEI made no bones about these pressures either when he wrote privately to Dufferin: 'Our railway debt . . . will not fall short of £660,000 sterling . . . Looking the question fairly in the face, my ministers see that there are only two courses open to them; either they must impose heavy additional taxes on the people . . . or seek admission into the Union, provided that Canada would thereupon make our railway debt her own.'[88] For Dufferin, it did not really matter so long as the federal government took the opportunity created by the financial travails of the island government to bring it into the confederation and further strengthen the unity of the dominion.

The other tricky question presented by the PEI land question surrounded Dufferin's navigation of his role in a system of responsible government.[89] This is illustrated by his outrage on his first reading of the PEI Bill, when he decided he could not approve its passage and assumed that the federal government would support him. He was not unaware of the problems with this approach, however:

> Of course it is always better for the Governor General to veto a measure of the kind at the instance of his responsible advisors and I still hope to succeed in inducing them to take the same view of the Bill as I do myself, but I have also intimated to them that under no circumstances, even should I be forced to differ with them, can I consent to such a measure becoming law.[90]

He was under pressure from the PEI landlords, who sent petitions arguing that land purchase legislation was at odds with the fundamental building blocks of British society, that it would be used by Irish agitators and that landlordism would not be safe anywhere.[91] The two aspects of the bill he really objected to were, first, the fact that the PEI government wanted to push through this purchase at very low values, perhaps less than sixteen years' purchase;[92] and second, due to the tenant agitation, landowners had not received the full rental income from their estates for some years, and Dufferin fought hard to ensure they were eventually paid the value of these lost rents plus interest as part of their compensation package.⁹³ An initial arbitration committee sat in 1875, resulting in the settlement of the first ten cases, totalling, '187,000 acres (out of about 310,000 intended to be purchased by the government) ... and the total of the awards is $306,550'. Although Dufferin had initially been entirely opposed to the land reform programme proposed for PEI, by the end he was able to report that 'generally I think the proprietors have got all they could expect'.⁹⁴ His eventual acceptance of PEI land reform was emblematic of a wider recognition of the changing political realities, not just in Canada, but in Ireland too. Dufferin recognised he could not fight these and so worked to ensure they were as advantageous as possible to the interests of private property instead. This was increasingly becoming the norm for landed elites in Britain and Ireland, who were losing their political, territorial and social dominance in this period, a trend clearly refracted into the imperial context in PEI.

Conclusions

From a position of total hostility in the early 1870s, land purchase was a principle Dufferin would come to support by 1880, promoting it as a more landlord-friendly alternative to the 1881 Irish Land Act. This *volte-face* came about because he saw the policy action in the colonial context, recognised the political and economic realities and sought a favourable compromise for the interests of private property. He also saw for the first time central government funds being applied to the land question, effectively nationalising land and compensating the ousted private owners. Initially he was entirely opposed to this policy because by removing their ownership of land, the government did more than remove a source of income. Land was not like other assets, in Dufferin's view; it endowed not simply a financial position, but also a social, cultural and political status. As such, he regarded its removal by compulsion as immoral confiscation and a policy that should be outside of the powers of any liberal parliamentary property-owning democracy. But, as he recognised (reluctantly) himself, he could not in practice refuse to give assent to the bill, and by the mid-1870s he regarded it as a better outcome for landlords than the model of 'dual ownership' that the British Liberals had imposed on Ireland in 1881 and on the Highlands of Scotland five years later.⁹⁵ His main concern then was to make sure that the PEI (and later, Irish) landlords received a fair price for their land.

This episode demonstrates the importance of taking a transnational perspective on imperial land issues, as personnel such as Dufferin translated, discussed, opposed and proposed different models of land reform in different places at different times, binding them up together, influencing and layering responses across the imperial world. Although making up by far the minority of those British and Irish people travelling to Atlantic Canada to live, either temporarily or permanently, the landed and aristocratic elite had a significant impact – for better or for worse – on their new home. This was primarily through thinking on governance, constitution, identity and land: the building blocks of the imperial project and issues that clearly link Atlantic Canada to its wider imperial context, from Ottawa to Bengal, or Dublin to Canberra.

Notes

1. Belfast, Public Record Office of Northern Ireland [PRONI], D1071, Dufferin papers, H/H/6/2, ff. 51, Lord Dufferin, governor general, to Holland, Colonial Office, 9 June 1874.
2. J. M. Bumsted, *Land, Settlement and Politics on Eighteenth-Century Prince Edward Island* (Kingston and Montreal: McGill-Queen's University Press, 1987), p. 195.
3. I. Ross Robertson, *The Prince Edward Island Land Commission of 1860* (Fredericton: Acadiensis, 1988), p. xiv.
4. C. Wilson, *A New Lease on Life: Landlords, Tenants and Immigrants in Ireland and Canada* (Montreal: McGill-Queen's University Press, 1994).
5. Dufferin's entry in the *Oxford Dictionary of National Biography* can be viewed at <http://www.oxforddnb.com/view/article/31914> (last accessed 20 October 2019).
6. For an example of this type of approach see Wilson, *A New Lease on Life*, pp. 3–10, 147–73.
7. N. Whelehan, 'Playing with Scales: Transnational History and Modern Ireland', in N. Whelehan (ed.), *Transnational Perspectives on Modern Irish History* (Abingdon: Routledge Publishing, 2015), pp. 7–8; C. A. Bayly, *The Birth of the Modern World, 1780–1914: Global Connections and Comparisons* (Oxford: Wiley-Blackwell, 2004), p. 2; C. Hall and S. Rose (eds), *At Home with the Empire: Metropolitan Culture and the Imperial World* (Cambridge: Cambridge University Press, 2006); C. A. Bayly, S. Beckhert, M. Connelly, I. Hoffmeyr, W. Kozol and P. Seed, 'AHR Conversation: On Transnational History', *American History Review*, 111:5 (2006), p. 1444; E. Delaney, 'Our Island Story? Towards a Transnational History of Late Modern Ireland', *Irish Historical Studies* 37 (2011), p. 603.
8. Bayly, *The Birth of the Modern World*, p. 2.
9. M. Bentley, *Lord Salisbury's World: Conservative Environments in Late-Victorian Britain* (Cambridge: Cambridge University Press, 2001), pp. 94–101.
10. PRONI, D1071, H/H/2/1b, ff. 52, Dufferin to Kimberley, 23 July 1873. He further noted: 'The climate was pronounced to be just like that of England, for everybody promptly got colds.' C. Drummond Black, *The Marquess of Dufferin and Ava: Diplomatist, Viceroy, Statesman* (London, 1903), p. 103; R. Bitterman, 'Upholding the Land Legislation of a "Communistic and Socialist Assembly": The Benefits of Confederation for Prince Edward Island' (with Dr Margaret McCallum), *Canadian Historical Review*, 87:1 (March 2006), p. 16.
11. B. Crosbie, *Irish Imperial Networks: Migration, Social Communication and Exchange in Nineteenth Century India* (Cambridge: Cambridge University Press, 2012), pp. 3–14; S. Cook, 'The Irish Raj: Social Origins and Careers of Irishmen in the Indian Civil Service, 1855–1914', *Journal of Social History*, 20:3 (1987), pp. 507–10; S. B. Cook, *Imperial Affinities: Nineteenth Century Analogies and Exchanges between India and Ireland* (Sage Publishing, 1993), pp. 9–15; Z. Laidlaw, *Colonial Connections, 1815–45: Patronage, the Information Revolution and Colonial Government* (Manchester: Manchester University Press, 2005), pp. 17–21.
12. See for example British Library, Carnarvon Papers, Add. MS 60797, vol. XLI (ff.1–141, 142–246), ff. 17, Dufferin to Lord Carnarvon, 18 January 1876; D. Cannadine, *Ornamentalism: How the British Saw Their Empire* (London: Oxford University Press, 2001), p. 38; J. Cowan, *Canada's Governors General, Lord Monck to General Vanier* (Toronto: York Publishing, 1965), pp. 15–17.

13. At least in part influenced by the Scottish Enlightenment tradition: M. E. Vance, 'Advancement, Moral Work and Freedom: The Meaning of Independence for Early Nineteenth Century Lowland Emigrants to Upper Canada', in N. C. Landsman (ed.), *Nation and Province in the First British Empire: Scotland and the Americas 1600–1800* (Lewisburg: Bucknell University Press, 2001), pp. 151–80; A. Kirk-Greene, 'The Governor-Generals of Canada, 1867–1952: A Collective Profile', *Journal of Canadian Studies* 12 (1977), p. 48; B. Messamore, *Canada's Governors General, 1847–1878: Biography and Constitutional Evolution* (Toronto: University of Toronto Press, 2006), pp. 148–9.
14. Messamore, *Canada's Governor Generals*, p. 9.
15. F. M. L. Thompson, 'English Landed Society in the Twentieth Century: III: Self-help and Outdoor Relief', *Transactions of the Royal Historical Society*, 6:2 (1992).
16. Famously, Dufferin constructed both a tobogganing rink and a tennis court at Rideau Hall, the Canadian seat of the governor general.
17. British Library, Gladstone Papers Add. MS 44151, vol. LXVI, ff. 130, Dufferin to Gladstone, 23 March 1872; PRONI, D1071, H/H/1/2, Dufferin to Carnarvon, 13 November 1874; H/H/1/4, Dufferin to Carnarvon, 9 March 1876; H/H/1/5, Dufferin to Carnarvon, 1 November 1877; B. Messamore, '"The line over which he must not pass": defining the office of Governor General, 1878', *Canadian Historical Review*, 86:3 (2005), p. 461; M. Francis, *Governor and Settlers: Images of Authority in the British Colonies, 1820–60* (Basingstoke: Palgrave Macmillan, 1992), p. 3.
18. PRONI, D1071, H/H/2/1a, ff. 9, Dufferin to Carnarvon, 21 February 1873; see also a similar explanation to the Colonial Office official, Herbert, H/H/6/4, ff. 89, Dufferin to Herbert, 11 September 1878; Kirk-Greene, 'The Governor Generals', pp. 39–40; Messamore, *Canada's Governor Generals*, p. 19; A. Lyall, *The Life of the Marquis of Dufferin and Ava* (London, 1905), p. 200; R. Gwyn, *Nation Maker: Sir John A. Macdonald: His Life, Our Times, vol. 2, 1867–1891* (Toronto: Random House Canada, 2011), pp. 218–19.
19. Francis, *Governors and Settlers*, p. 8; Kirk-Greene, 'The Governor Generals', pp. 46–7.
20. PRONI, D1071, H/H/6/4, ff. 27, Dufferin to Lord Lorne, 12 August 1878; Lyall, *Life of Lord Dufferin*, p. 213; Kirk-Greene, 'The Governor Generals', p. 41.
21. This was imperial governance conceptualised as a personal and moral task: Francis, *Governors and Settlers*, pp. 4–5.
22. Lyall, *Life of Lord Dufferin*, p. 192.
23. These attitudes were also present in the Colonial Office permanent staff until the 1870s: B. Knox, 'Conservative Imperialism 1858–1874: Bulwer Lytton, Lord Carnarvon and Canadian Confederation', *International History Review* 4 (1984), pp. 341, 354; B. Blakely, *The Colonial Office, 1868–1892* (Durham, NC: Duke University Press, 1972), p. xi; D. Creighton, 'The Victorians and Empire', *Canadian Historical Review* 19 (1938), pp. 139–41; P. J. Durrans, 'A Two-Edged Sword: The Liberal Attack on Disraelian Imperialism' *Journal of Imperial and Commonwealth History*, 10:3 (1982), p. 263.
24. Drummond Black, *The Marquess of Dufferin and Ava*, pp. 76–7, 161; J. W. Cell, *British Colonial Administration in the Mid-Nineteenth Century: The Policy-Making Process* (London: Yale University Press, 1970), p. vii; B. Knox, 'The Earl of Carnarvon, Empire and Imperialism, 1855–90', *Journal of Imperial and Commonwealth History* 26 (1998), pp. 48–9, 52, 54.
25. See for example, PRONI, D1071, H/H9/10, speech by Lord Dufferin to members of the Toronto Club, 2 September 1874.
26. PRONI, D1071, H/H/1/3, Dufferin to Carnarvon, 11 November 1875; Cannadine, *Ornamentalism*, pp. 27–33.
27. Where his role was to reign, not govern; something he did not always remember to distinguish, Messamore, *Canada's Governor Generals*, p. 23. He was also quick to point out to the Canadian administration that these costs (which he calculated to be £13,200 in his first six months of arriving in Canada) would be, 'what in England would be considered a modest

establishment for a Peer or an ordinary country gentleman'. As Sir John A. Macdonald, and particularly A. Mackenzie, both came from humble origins, this breezy statement may have come as something of a surprise: PRONI, D1071, H/H/4/1a, ff. 27, Dufferin to Macdonald, 26 December 1872.
28. I. R. Robertson, 'Political Realignment in Pre-confederation Prince Edward Island, 1863–1870', *Acadiensis*, 15:1 (1988), pp. 25–58.
29. J. McLaren, A. R. Buck and N. E. Wright, 'Property Rights in the Colonial Imagination and Experience', in J. McLaren, A. R. Buck and N. E. Wright (eds), *Despotic Dominion: Property Rights in British Settler Societies* (Vancouver: UBC Press, 2004), p. 3.
30. See also R. Bittermann, *Sailor's Hope: The Life and Times of William Cooper, Agrarian Radical in an Age of Revolution* (Montreal: McGill-Queen's University Press, 2010).
31. Messamore, *Canada's Governor Generals*, p. 151.
32. Bittermann, 'Upholding the Land Legislation', p. 5.
33. PRONI, D1071, H/H/1/2, Dufferin to Carnarvon, 29 May 1874; see also H/H/6/2, ff. 21, Dufferin to Herbert, C.O., 7 May 1874; Bittermann, 'Upholding the Land Legislation', pp. 3, 11–12.
34. Both the PEI government and Colonial Office recognised similar pressures ongoing in Ireland; Bittermann, 'Upholding the Land Legislation', p. 9.
35. PEI is a rare example of the use of state power to compel redistribution of resources for the benefit of ordinary citizens in Canada: Bittermann, 'Upholding the Land Legislation', p. 2.
36. Absenteeism was a critical issue in Irish politics in this period also. Robertson estimates that only 40 per cent of occupiers in PEI in 1861 were freeholders: Robertson, 'Political Realignment', p. 36; Robertson, *The Prince Edward Island Land Commission of 1860*, pp. ix–xxiii; Bitterman, 'Upholding the Land Legislation', p. 3; R. Bitterman and M. McCallum, *Lady Landlords of Prince Edward Island: Imperial Dreams and the Defence of Property* (Montreal and Kingston: McGill-Queen's University Press, 2008), p. 4.
37. Robertson, *The Prince Edward Island Land Commission of 1860*, p. x, and see p. xi.
38. Ibid. pp. xviii–xxii.
39. Ibid. p. xxii.
40. Robertson, 'Political Realignment', pp. 36–8; Lyall, *Life of Lord Dufferin*, p. 244; Drummond Black, *The Marquess of Dufferin*, p. 100; Bittermann, 'Upholding the Land Legislation', pp. 3–4, 7–8.
41. PRONI, D1071, H/H/2/1b, ff. 52, Dufferin to Kimberley, 23 July 1873.
42. Bitterman and McCallum, *Lady Landlords*, p. 5.
43. Robertson, *The Prince Edward Island Land Commission of 1860*, p. xxv.
44. PRONI, D1071, H/H/2/1a, ff. 34, Kimberley to Dufferin, 24 December 1872; Bittermann, 'Upholding the Land Legislation', pp. 8, 10.
45. Robertson, *The Prince Edward Island Land Commission of 1860*, p. xxvii.
46. M. W. Dowling, *Tenant Right and Agrarian Society in Ulster, 1600–1870* (Dublin: Irish Academic Press, 1999), pp. 290–7; P. Bull, 'Irish Land and British Politics', in M. Cragoe and P. Readman, *The Land Question in Britain, 1750–1950* (Basingstoke: Palgrave Macmillan, 2010), p. 128.
47. Bitterman and McCallum, *Lady Landlords*, pp. 10–11.
48. E. D. Steele, 'Ireland and the Empire: Imperial precedents for Gladstone's First Irish Land Act', *Historical Journal*, 11:1 (1968); W. P. Morrell, *British Colonial Policy in the Mid-Victorian Age* (Oxford: Oxford University Press, 1969); E. Delaney, 'Our Island Story? Towards a Transnational History of Late Modern Ireland', *Irish Historical Studies* 37 (2011); T. Brooking, *Land for the People: The Highland Clearances and the Colonisation of New Zealand; A Biography of John Mackenzie* (Otago: Otago University Press, 1996).
49. C. A. Bayly, 'Ireland, India and the Empire, 1780–1914', *Trans. Royal Historical Society*, 6:10 (2000), pp. 390–1.

50. Bentley, *Lord Salisbury's World*, p. 72. Dufferin oversaw a major land reform bill for Bengal while Indian viceroy, for example: B. Martin, *New India, 1885: British Official Policy and the Emergence of the Indian National Congress* (Berkley: University of California Press, 1969). Gladstone also idealised the concept of an 'aristocracy redeemed by service', itself a historicist proposition: C. Dewey, 'Celtic Agrarian Legislation and the Celtic Revival: Historicist Implications of Gladstone's Irish and Scottish Land Acts, 1870–1886', *Past and Present*, 64:1 (1974), p. 60.
51. R. Bittermann, *Rural Protest on Prince Edward Island: From British Colonisation to the Escheat Movement* (Toronto: University of Toronto Press, 2006), pp. 1–3; R. Bittermann and M. McCallum, 'When Private Rights become Public Wrongs: Property and the State in Prince Edward Island in the 1830s', in McLaren et al., *Despotic Dominion*, pp. 144–68.
52. Bittermann, 'Upholding the Land Legislation', pp. 4–5.
53. PRONI, D1071, H/H9/10, speech by Lord Dufferin to members of the Toronto Club, 2 September 1874.
54. PRONI, D1071, H/H/6/2, ff. 51, Dufferin to Holland, C.O., 9 June 1874.
55. As his initial response that he would not approve the bill demonstrates: PRONI, D1071, H/H/3/2, ff. 204, Dufferin to Mackenzie, 19 November 1874.
56. Bittermann, *Rural Protest*, p. 272.
57. Bittermann, *Rural Protest*, p. 274.
58. See PRONI, D1071, H/H/6/3, ff. 21, Dufferin to Lord Cairns, 29 May 1878; H/H/7/41, ff. 6 and ff. 6, Dufferin to Holland, C.O., 2 May 1874; 25 June 1874; Bittermann and McCallum, *Lady Landlords*, p. 14.
59. See for example his letter to Disraeli on land reform in Ireland at this time: PRONI, D1071, H/H/6/2, ff. 30, Dufferin to Disraeli, 22 May 1874.
60. Lyall, *Life of Dufferin*, p. 40.
61. A. Tindley, 'The Iron Duke: Land Reclamation and Public Relations in Sutherland, 1868–95', *Historical Research*, 82:216 (2009), pp. 303–19; E. A. Cameron, *Land for the People? The British Government and the Scottish Highlands, c.1880–1925* (East Linton: Tuckwell Press, 1996), pp. 25–6; C. O'Grada, 'The Investment Behaviour of Irish Landlords 1850–75: Some Preliminary Findings', *Agricultural History Review* 23 (1975), p. 139.
62. Dufferin often stressed the importance of landlord investments and improvements in the House of Lords; see for instance, HL Debates, 23 March 1866, vol. 182 cc. 831–7; Bentley, *Lord Salisbury's World*, pp. 95; O'Grada, 'The Investment Behaviour of Irish Landlords', pp. 146, 151, 153.
63. W. E. Vaughan, 'An Assessment of the Economic Performance of Irish Landlords, 1851–81', in F. S. L. Lyons and R. A. J. Hawkins (eds), *Ireland Under the Union: Varieties of Tension: Essays in Honour of T. W. Moody* (Oxford: Oxford University Press, 1980), p. 174.
64. J. C. Weaver, 'Concepts of Economic Improvement and the Social Construction of Property Rights: Highlights from the English-speaking World', in McLaren et al., *Despotic Dominion*, pp. 79–102.
65. McLaren, Buck and Wright, 'Property Rights', p. 7.
66. PRONI, D1071, A/F/24, 'Summarised schedule of the acreage and rental of the Clandeboye, Ards and Killyleagh estates, for the year ending 1 Nov. 1870'.
67. PRONI, D1071, A/L/41, 'Schedule showing claimants on Dufferin's estate'.
68. PRONI, D1071, A/K/1/B/24/1, Thomson to Dufferin, 27 February 1874.
69. For instance, an attempt was made to arrange a mortgage with the Royal Exchange Assurance Company in early 1874, but negotiations collapsed: PRONI, D1071, A/K/1/B/24/1, Thomson to Dufferin, 27 February 1874; L. P. Curtis, 'Incumbered Wealth: Landed Indebtedness in Post-famine Ireland', *American Historical Review* 85 (1980), p. 339.
70. Bentley, *Lord Salisbury's World*, pp. 99–100.
71. T. M. Dooley, 'Landlords and the Land Question, 1879–1909', in C. King (ed.), *Famine, Land and Culture in Ireland* (Dublin: University College Dublin Press, 2001), pp. 124–6.

72. PRONI, D1071/A/K/1/B/21/1, Dufferin to Thomson, 24 December 1874; Dowling, *Tenant Right and Agrarian Society in Ulster*, pp. 241–52, 312–14.
73. K. T. Hoppen, 'Landownership and Power in Nineteenth Century Ireland: The Decline of an Elite', in R. Gibson and M. Blinkhorn (eds), *Landownership and Power in Modern Europe* (London: Routledge, 1991), pp. 168, 176–7.
74. McLaren, Buck and Wright, 'Property Rights', pp. 10–11.
75. O. Purdue, *The Big House in the North of Ireland: Land, Power and Social Elites, 1878–1960* (Dublin: University College Dublin Press, 2009), p. 66.
76. PRONI, D1071 A/L/41 'Schedule showing the individual claimants, the amount due to each and the period at which – with due notice – the several amounts ought to be paid' (1873). Land value was calculated on annual rent multiplied by as many years as the market would bear.
77. PRONI, D1071, A/R/12, 'Lord Dufferin's descriptive Memorandum of the Clandeboye demesne and estate' (1877); F. Campbell, *The Irish Establishment 1879–1914* (Oxford: Oxford University Press, 2009), p. 38.
78. PRONI, D1071, A/K/1/B/25/1, Thomson to Dufferin, 15 January 1875.
79. PRONI, D1071, A/K/1/B/26/1, Dufferin to Thomson, 27 November 1876 and 4 December 1876; A/K/1/C/2/1, Dufferin to Howe, 17 July 1880; A/K/1/C/3/2, Dufferin to Howe, 2 August 1881.
80. Dewey, 'Celtic Agrarian Legislation and the Celtic Revival', pp. 30–1.
81. PRONI, D1071, H/B/C/95/70, Dufferin to Argyll, 7 May 1874; J. W. Mason, 'The Duke of Argyll and the Land Question in Late Nineteenth Century Britain', *Victorian Studies*, 21:2 (1978), pp. 168.
82. PRONI, D1071, H/H/7/41, ff. 6, Dufferin to Holland, 2 May 1874; British Library, Carnarvon Papers, Add. MS 60797, vol. XLI (ff.1–141, 142–246), ff. 31, Dufferin to Lord Carnarvon, 10 May 1877.
83. Robertson, 'Political Realignment', p. 38.
84. For context see R. W. Kirkpatrick, 'Origins and Development of the Land War in mid-Ulster, 1879–85', in F. S. L. Lyons and R. A. J. Hawkins (eds), *Ireland Under the Union: Varieties of Tension: Essays in Honour of T. W. Moody* (Oxford: Oxford University Press, 1980), pp. 201–35.
85. Bittermann and McCallum, *Lady Landlords*, pp. 12–13.
86. Robertson, 'Political Realignment', pp. 35, 55–8.
87. PRONI, D1071, H/H/2/1a, ff. 34, Kimberley to Dufferin, 24 December 1872.
88. PRONI, D1071, H/H/7/77, ff. 2, Robinson to Dufferin, 16 November 1872; Robertson, 'Political Realignment', pp. 57–8.
89. Bittermann, 'Upholding the Land Legislation', p. 17.
90. PRONI, D1071, H/H/6/2, ff. 51, Dufferin to Holland, C.O., 9 June 1874
91. Bittermann, 'Upholding the Land Legislation', pp. 14–15.
92. PRONI, D1071H/H/6/2, ff. 51, Dufferin to Holland, C.O., 9 June 1874. On the other hand, the PEI government was under pressure not to pay an inflated price: Bittermann, 'Upholding the Land Legislation', p. 12.
93. PRONI, D1071, H/H/3/3, ff. 75, Dufferin to Mackenzie, 1 April 1876; Robertson, 'Political Realignment', p. 38.
94. PRONI, D1071, H/H/7/14, ff. 4, Dufferin to Childers, C.O., 4 Sept. 1874; Bittermann, 'Upholding the Land Legislation', pp. 18–20.
95. PRONI, D1071, H/H/1/2, Dufferin to Carnarvon, 29 May 1874. Dufferin believed in the potential for Ireland to reap the benefits of imperial rule: F. H. A. Aalen, 'Constructive Unionism and the Shaping of Rural Ireland, *c.*1880–1921', *Rural History*, 4:2 (1993), pp. 137–8.

Part Two

Religion and Identity

SIX

Catholic Highland Scots and the Colonisation of Prince Edward Island and Cape Breton Island, 1772–1830

S. Karly Kehoe

In April 1772, Alexander Curry, his wife, Isabell Fitzgerald, and their infant son, Duncan, boarded the *Alexander* at Lochboisdale, on the island of South Uist, and abandoned Scotland forever. Bound for St John's Island, a tiny colony cradled by Nova Scotia in the Gulf of St Lawrence, this young family aspired to a life that was more secure than the one they left behind. Making the journey with them were around 210 others, including Angus Ban and Margaret Og Macdonald of Kinlochmoidart and their two children, as well as Capt. Angus Macdonald, 5th laird of Achnancoichean, Lochaber, his wife, Joanna, and their six children, counting little Donald, a toddler of two years.[1] The departure of these families and countless others was a powerful statement about the grim reality facing many people in the north-west Highlands and Islands.

St John's Island became Prince Edward Island in 1799 in honour of King George III's infant son, and these migrants came to be known as the Glenaladale settlers. What is remarkable about them is that they were the first large group of Catholic Scots to arrive in the Maritimes.[2] By this point, emigration had emerged as a symbol of many people's rejection of the new socio-economic reality. This was especially the case in the Highlands and Islands, where a rapidly transforming clan gentry were becoming increasingly preoccupied with generating cash incomes. It was a difficult adjustment for everyone, but for the Catholics, who also endured intense anti-Catholicism and debilitating penal legislation, it was doubly hard. While emigration offered the prospect of greater economic prosperity, it also promised religious toleration – an experience that would remain out of reach if they remained in Scotland. This chapter uses the arrival of the Glenaladale settlers in Prince Edward Island as a starting point for exploring the expansion of a Scottish Catholic tradition in the Maritimes. Cape Breton, an island that sat to the north-east of Nova Scotia and was independent of that colony between 1783 and 1820, will also feature in the discussion here given its popularity as a secondary destination with Highland migrants. While the first section flags the necessity of seeing these migrants, like all other Britons on the move at this time, as colonisers, the second and third sections explain how Catholicism functioned in Scotland and why the Maritime region of British North America was so important to its preservation. In becoming colonisers, Catholic Highlanders found a way to secure their faith, but it was a process that took a substantial and irreversible toll on the region's Indigenous population.

That the settler colonial enterprise in this coastal space had a major Scottish Catholic dimension merits consideration, and assessing its complexity will expand understandings of how Catholicism developed in the Empire and how it helped to extend and cement British colonisation. Exploring the Scottish Diaspora's Catholic dimension moves us beyond the prevailing explorer/exile narratives towards a deeper engagement with the interactions that these Catholic Scots had with the other Catholic groups they encountered – including Indigenous ones. In offering such preliminary insights on this theme, areas that would benefit from concentrated research are flagged.

Highland Catholics as colonisers

Prince Edward Island and Cape Breton Island were the smallest of Britain's north Atlantic colonies and were connected in ways that extended far beyond their entanglement with Scottish Highland settlement. Geographically, they were linked by the Northumberland Strait in the southern Gulf of St Lawrence, which sustained their peoples with a rich fishery. Both places had been French possessions until the 1763 Treaty of Paris turned them over to Britain and both had pre-existing Indigenous and Acadian populations. Yet their landscapes could hardly have been more different. According to one observer, John MacGregor, a merchant, writer and politician whose family immigrated first to Nova Scotia from Stornoway on the isle of Lewis in 1803 before settling in Prince Edward Island three years later, its soil, climate and surface made it ideal for agriculture, whereas Cape Breton's was largely 'unfit for profitable cultivation'.[3] In spite of these differences both islands attracted significant numbers of Scottish colonists from the last quarter of the eighteenth century, and Catholics represented a substantial proportion of them.

The Catholic settlements that grew up in this region and the Church infrastructure that emerged around them were important components of the colonial experience and were intimately tied to a British Christian missionary culture that solidified over the course of the nineteenth century. The tendency of many researchers to see Catholicism as peripheral to Britishness has meant that a much richer body of literature exists for the Protestant dimension to empire-building than for the Catholic one. Joseph Hardwick (a contributor to this volume), Rowan Strong and Stuart Wolfendale's work on the Anglican missionary experience, for example, builds upon and expands the pioneering efforts of Andrew Porter and Jeffrey Cox.[4] The Presbyterian missionary dimension of this process has benefited from the valuable research of Valerie Wallace, Philip Constable and Sarah Roddy.[5] Yet, although significant attention has been paid to Irish Catholics by scholars such as Yvonne McKenna, Deidre Rafferty, Dáire Keogh, Albert McDonnell, Colin Barr and Oliver P. Rafferty, all, with the exception of Rafferty, emphasise the Irish imperial experience as distinct from the British one.[6] While Hilary Carey's exploration of a range of missionary groups in *God's Empire* includes Catholics, her preoccupation with the Irish means that the influence of other Catholic groups, such as the Scots and the English, remains overlooked.[7] While Irish Catholics were numerically dominant in many of Britain's colonies, this was not the case in the Maritimes, because although certainly instrumental to enabling the spread of Catholicism in this region, they were not in a position to dominate Catholic culture owing to the presence of so many Catholic Highlanders.[8]

In Scottish Diaspora Studies, the coloniser element has tended to take a back seat to topics such as associational culture, education, industry and language, with the Highlanders being cast as either victims of internal colonisation or noble warriors. Notwithstanding some important exceptions, most notably Don Watson's *Caledonia Australis*, David A. Wilson and Graeme Morton's edited volume, *Irish and Scottish Encounters with Indigenous Peoples*, Ben Wilkie's *The Scots in Australia, 1788–1938* and John Reid's 'Scots, Settler Colonization, and Indigenous Displacement: Mi'kma'ki, 1770–1820 in Comparative Context', explorations of the Highland Scot as coloniser have been occasional.[9] Nevertheless, the explosion of research into Scotland's relationship with African enslavement suggests a willingness to reconfigure Scotland's imperial narrative. Research undertaken by David Alston, Stephen Mullen, Sheila Kidd, Alan Macinnes and myself is increasingly difficult to ignore and shows just how extensive and complex the Highlands' links with this global economy were.[10] While this work is slowly percolating through broader Scottish society, the need to engage audiences beyond Scotland, where emotive works such as Donald MacLeod's *Gloomy Memories in the Highlands of Scotland* and John Prebble's *The Highland Clearances* remain extremely popular, is urgent.

The post-Culloden Highlands was a dark place for many, fraught with intimidation, evictions and displacements, but what needs to be acknowledged is that in colonial settings, Highlanders became the dispossessors of Indigenous peoples. Just how much the Glenaladale settlers and those like them knew about the Indigenous people in the Maritimes is uncertain, but there was definitely some awareness, given Scottish attempts to establish a colony on Cape Breton Island and to convert its 'poore savages' as early as 1625.[11] As Ned Landsman observed, it was really during the eighteenth century, after the Treaty of Union, that the Scots established a major presence throughout the Empire and this was particularly obvious in the Maritime colonies of north-eastern British North America.[12] Some time ago, J. M. Bumsted emphasised just how disruptive Scottish settlement was to Indigenous life patterns, and that the effects were ignored by the first waves of Highlanders, who insisted on framing their experience within a clearance and exile narrative.[13] Rusty Bittermann's detailed research on one settlement at Middle River, Cape Breton, echoed this assessment and revealed how, in their haste to acquire land, resources and influence, Highlanders made little effort to accommodate the Mi'kmaq.[14] The abuse of resources was a concern from a relatively early period and Board of Trade records relating to Cape Breton, for example, include pleas from the Mi'kmaq and some settlers to stop the irresponsible exploitation of what had previously been carefully managed deer, moose, caribou and salmon stocks.[15] As John Reid rightly observes, Highland immigrants had a 'profound sense of entitlement' and cared little for the needs of their Mi'kmaq neighbours.[16]

Dispossession was as much a part of the Scottish Catholic immigrant story as that of any other Briton who settled in the Maritimes, and engaging with this fact brings into sharper focus the constituent parts of British imperialism. The survival of the communities they built depended upon their ability to create and exploit colonial opportunities and in the Maritime colonies, people moved regularly from one place to another. Many of the Highlanders who started out in Prince Edward Island – including Duncan Curry and his parents, Alexander and Isabell, who were introduced at the start of this chapter – moved to Cape Breton, where their chances of acquiring land by a petition to the Crown were high. Incidentally, the Curry family ended up at Barrachois, a community on the south-east side of the St Andrew's Channel on the Bras d'Or Lakes.[17] Settlements like these, however, had adverse effects upon the ability of the Mi'kmaq to access necessary resources.

How we understand these Scottish–Indigenous interactions is important, particularly in the context of reconciliation, as highlighted in this volume's introduction. In an insightful article on this topic, John Reid's recommendation that scholars recognise Indigenous resilience in the face of Scottish encroachment reflects the sentiments of Alan Lester and Zoë Laidlaw's assertion that settler colonialism was a series of interactions and responses.[18] Seeing the treaties between the Mi'kmaq and British as documents that were agreed upon by two parties but understood very differently is a crucial starting point because they highlight a fundamental disconnect in interpretation: whereas the Mi'kmaq saw the treaties as a formal recognition of peace and friendship, the British saw them as 'instruments of submission'.[19] As a colonial space filled with all sorts of interactions between various groups, the Maritimes were indeed 'dynamic in new ways after invasion', and this was evidenced by the accommodation of Catholicism.[20] The fact that it was a faith practised openly by both the Mi'kmaq and the Acadians meant that an important foundation had been established upon which the Highlanders and the Irish could build.[21]

Despite coming from all levels of Highland society, the majority of the

Alexander's passengers were Catholic and shared an understanding of what it felt like to belong to a proscribed faith. Ongoing persecution was a factor in many people's decision to leave, but assessing just *how* influential it was is complicated by the fact that decisions about emigration were deeply personal and informed by numerous factors. There is no question that Scotland's Catholic bishops saw Prince Edward Island as the perfect opportunity to establish a Scottish Catholic colony, but just how far this ambition was shared with the laity is unclear. Two Nova Scotian historians, Allan F. MacDonald, a Catholic priest, and D. M. Sinclair, a Presbyterian minister and Gaelic scholar, seem convinced that the preservation of Catholicism was the primary motivation for leaving.[22] In reality, there were multiple and competing factors at play. Early research on Prince Edward Island's Scottish pioneer settlers reveals that in addition to concerns about religious freedom, there was a deep frustration with the widespread agricultural change that had been sweeping through the Highlands.[23] The aggressive reorganisation of land ownership meant that tenants and sub-tenants struggled to come up with the cash rents that were being increasingly demanded. At the same time, there was a growing awareness of the opportunities available in British North America.[24] Since Highlanders tended to migrate and settle in family groups and were bound tightly by bonds of religion, kinship and language, they established themselves quickly and were intuitively self-supporting. They became fishers, farmers and traders and forged connections with an Atlantic economy that linked their region with Britain and the Caribbean.[25] Yet, in imagining new lives abroad, few anticipated the harsh reality of colonial life and the struggles they would face in re-establishing themselves abroad.

Highland Catholicism in the late eighteenth century

At the time of the settlers' departure, Catholicism in Scotland was in a precarious state. It had survived the sixteenth-century Reformation, but only just, with small and isolated pockets of adherents being confined to the north-west Highlands and Islands, Banffshire and Aberdeenshire in the north-east and Kirkcudbrightshire in the south-west. As a group, they had become instinctively quiet, incorporating little ceremony or decoration in the practice of their faith. The elites among them, such as some of the MacDonalds of Clanranald, did what they could to keep the faith alive; they provided secret places of worship, they sent their children to the Continental Scots colleges for either a secular education or seminary training, and some supported emigration schemes that took Catholic tenants away from Protestant landowners.[26] The Glenaladale settlement was one such scheme, and it was set up by the 'stolidly aristocratic' laird Captain John Macdonald of Glenaladale of the north-west Highlands.[27]

The Glenaladale Macdonalds were synonymous with Highland Jacobitism, for it was on their lands at Glenfinnan that the Jacobite standard was raised in 1745 in support of Charles Edward Stuart, the infamous Bonnie Prince Charlie. John's father, Alexander, had fought alongside the young prince at Culloden, but managed to evade capture and was subsequently pardoned.[28] After Culloden, everything changed for this family, who, like other Jacobites, faced the reality of losing their lands and their influence as the process of Highland pacification, or 'exemplary civilising', was ramped up.[29] The Catholics among them had the added pressure of belonging to an outlawed faith and the consequences were particularly devastating for the elites, some of whom lost their lands and wealth as a result of their involvement in the rising. The penal laws' exclusion of Catholics from receiving an education at home meant that those with means sent their children to the Continent for schooling – usually to France, Spain, Portugal or Italy. In John's case, he went to Germany and attended the Ratisbon seminary at Regensburg as a secular student. As the inheriting son, expectations for his future were high; and so when his father died in 1761, two years before John came into his majority, he returned to Scotland, most likely before he completed his studies.[30]

The widespread confiscation of Catholic estates following Culloden and their subsequent sale to Protestant landowners was a devastating blow to Scottish Catholicism. The growing influence of a Protestant landowning class across the Highlands made the region's Catholic population particularly vulnerable, and it became common practice for Catholic tenants to be threatened with eviction if they refused to convert to Protestantism (Presbyterianism).[31] For young men like John Macdonald, those who were not only Catholic but also tacksmen forced to watch the decline of their influence in Highland society, opportunities in the new socio-economic order were limited. It was clear that by 1770, Macdonald was deeply frustrated with his limited prospects and so, like many others of his class, he looked to the colonies for a new start. As he was contemplating his future, worrying reports began to emerge from the island of South Uist, where it was reported that Colin Macdonald of Boisedale, the major landowner in South Uist and Benbecula thanks to his father's post-Culloden land acquisitions, was pressuring his Catholic tenants to convert to Presbyterianism. When Scotland's Catholic bishops, who were extremely concerned about this sparking a broader trend, contacted John to see what might be done to arrange a major group emigration, the seeds of the Glenaladale settlement were sown.[32] George Hay, vicar apostolic of the Lowland District, saw Prince Edward Island as being able to offer a 'constant asylum for all our distressed people'.[33]

This outmigration occurred at the beginning of an intensive phase of Scottish settlement in what would later become the Canadian Maritimes, and the fact that the majority were Catholic, mostly from Moidart, Arisaig and South Uist in the north-west Highlands and Islands, is significant and suggests that Scotland's deeply entrenched culture of anti-Catholicism influenced regional demographics. When the *Alexander* left Scotland, almost half (approximately 100) of its some 210 passengers were from South Uist.[34] Despite the majority of those departing being described as 'destitute', their exodus affected the island for many years; in 1794, for example, the local minister, George Munro, lamented the loss of 'vast numbers' to 'the island of St John's, Nova Scotia, and Canada' in his report for the *Old Statistical Account*.[35]

While the Catholic Church authorities were intimately involved in the emigration scheme and provided some funds, their support was varied and sometimes indirect. Given Scotland's religious climate at the time, it is reasonable to presume that they, but specifically George Hay, had helped John Macdonald to secure land on Prince Edward Island from Sir James Montgomery, the Lord Advocate and man responsible for managing the land distribution there. While Bumsted suggests that half of the £1,500 bill was footed by the Church and that the other half came from 'emigrants themselves', archival records reveal that the actual cost was much higher and that John Macdonald's personal contribution was substantial.[36] It is unlikely that we will ever know the precise amount, but research into the state of the Church's finances at the time reveals that it was in a deeply precarious state that would worsen considerably with the almost complete loss of its French assets in the early 1790s.[37] While more research is needed to unpack Macdonald's full contribution, Jamaica money, via John's first cousin, Alexander, played a pivotal role in the settlement's survival. Known locally as 'Golden Sandy', Alexander had gone to Jamaica before the 1745 Jacobite rebellion and ended up making a fortune in (possibly) cotton. In 1773, John raised funds by selling 'the Glens' (Glenfinnan and Glenaladale) to Golden Sandy for £3,000.[38] Writing to Hay that April, John explained that 'Somewhat contrary to Mr ___[?] Macdonald's opinion I have sold the Glens to my cousins in trust for their Brother, in preference to Clanranald, to prevent as much as possible the consequences of some fresh designs he & Boisdale are said to be hatching against them in resentment to me.'[39]

Scottish Catholicism in north-eastern British North America

In the early 1770s, the population of the coastal Maritime colonies, which also included Nova Scotia and New Brunswick – the latter, like Cape Breton, becoming an independent colony in 1784 – was approximately 20,000.[40] Settlement was rapid from this point forward and census data from Statistics Canada indicates that by 1817 Nova Scotia's population had grown to 81,351. By 1827, it was 123,630 (including Cape Breton). Prince Edward Island is thought to have had just over 24,600 in 1822.[41] It is difficult to know for certain the number of Catholics, but they would have represented a significant proportion of the estimated 67,500 people who had spread across Nova Scotia, Cape Breton and Prince Edward Island by 1828.[42] The influx of so many immigrants, beginning with groups like the Glenaladale settlers, transformed the character of Catholicism in this region so significantly that its small Acadian and Mi'kmaq base was dwarfed by growing numbers of Highland Scots and Irish.[43]

Quick to petition the Crown for land, Highland colonists built settlements that served as important communication channels between friends and families and offered a sense of familiarity to the newcomers. Their settlement patterns were concentrated, defined by religious affiliation and their retention of Gaelic – a linguistic distinctiveness that set them apart from their Irish brethren, who adopted English (often French too) quickly.[44] An overall shortage of trained clergy at this time meant that religious provision was a chronic issue for the colonial missions, and this was on top of the added challenge of finding those who were Gaelic speakers. The Scottish, Irish and English colleges that had been established in Europe following the Reformation to educate the boys of elite Catholic families and to train priests for the 'home' missions could not keep up with the growing demand.[45] Records from the English College at Lisbon, like those of Scots College Rome, reveal that while they may not have been able to provide priests, they made other attempts to support their colonial colleagues. Alexander Cameron, rector of the Scots College at Valladolid, for example, worked with the president of Lisbon's English College, Edmund Winstanley, in 1821 to send missals via St John's Newfoundland to Angus MacEachern in Prince Edward Island.[46]

Moreover, the Maritime colonies were a hard sell to prospective missionaries who knew that if they went there, they faced a life that was most likely isolated, itinerant and grim in the face of an unforgiving landscape, with only paths through 'irrepressible spruce' forests at their disposal, embryonic settlements and unfamiliar wild animals such as moose and bear.[47] Donald McGillivray, who assisted the Gaelic-speaking and Scots College Paris-trained missionary Angus MacEachern on his treks through western Cape Breton, recalled 'the dreary' journeys – 'A chip out of an occasional tree served as the only landmark to guide our weary steps through the dense forests of the then rugged country.'[48] It is little wonder that it was too much to bear for many. John Macdonald, a priest who served a number of Catholic settlements on the southwest side of Cape Breton, suffered a complete health collapse in 1797 and never recovered.[49] Missionaries travelled frequently between Cape Breton, Nova Scotia and Prince Edward Island, and shared a heavy load. When Macdonald took ill, for example, it was MacEachern who covered his duties for five years because no replacement was available; only in 1802/1803 was he relieved by Alexander Macdonald, who was based at Arisaig and who was the 'first regular and permanent Catholic priest in eastern Nova Scotia'.[50] The situation was little improved by the next decade and the physical and mental strain of mission work remained palpable. An exchange between Angus (Aeneas) MacDonald, the rector of Scots College in Rome, and Prince Edward Island's bishop, Angus

(Aeneas) MacEachern, reveals some of the difficulties they faced. MacEachern wrote that in Cape Breton:

> the Barra men, with many other hundred families scattered, and thickly settled, on the shores of the Bras d'Or and I may say all over Cape Breton are depending this day on the Rev. Alexander MacDonell, which is as sulky, or more so than old ___[?], and two Irish priests, one of whom does not understand one word of Irish.[51]

In a subsequent letter he complained:

> You cannot believe the extent of the Catholic settlements in these provinces. Of 23 thousand inhabitants in this colony, nearly one half of them are Catholics. There are only, as yet, 2 priests with me on the island. One of them an Irishman is of little service among our Gaelic men. We have none in any college. The Canadian prelate will receive none from us without paying handsomely for them.[52]

Later in the nineteenth century, really from the 1840s, the colonial missions could rely upon the labour of women religious, who were drawn heavily from Irish and French congregations, but at this point, apostolic or active congregations were in their infancy and thus unable to support the growing settlements.[53] This meant that very little spiritual and/or material care was on offer to newcomers. Many of the immigrants who came in the 1820s, 1830s and 1840s had left Scotland under the extremely precarious circumstances of clearance and arrived virtually empty-handed.[54] To these later waves of colonists Cape Breton had little to offer, as scholars such as James Hunter and Daniel Samson have noted, but they required religious provision, and this was not always possible, as noted above.[55] The subtext of MacEachern's letter was a deep criticism of the Quebec clergy, who, it was felt, cared little for the plight of Catholics in the Atlantic coastal colonies. The bishops of Quebec had ecclesiastical jurisdiction for this region but they had a complicated and uneasy relationship with the Scots. Given the circumstances outlined above, the Calvinist tinge that Catholicism in Scotland had acquired was understandable, but it was by no means acceptable to the Quebec prelates, who, notwithstanding British rule, had no experience of life in a post-Reformation country and who were unable to fathom the intensity of Scotland's anti-Catholic fervour. Their disdain for the Catholic culture of the Scots was so obvious that even during his visit to Prince Edward Island in 1811–12, Quebec's 'stocky, assertive, energetic and charming' Bishop Joseph-Octave Plessis carped that 'only a priest brought up in Scotland would ever think of celebrating the Sacred Mysteries with the trash that is found therein'. 'Singing', he protested 'is as rare in their churches as ceremonies and vestments'.[56] There was little love lost between the Quebec hierarchy and the

Maritime priests and as late as 1828, MacEachern, who was made a bishop (titular) in 1819 and given responsibility for Prince Edward Island, New Brunswick and, from 1821, Cape Breton, lambasted his Quebec superiors for abandoning the Catholics of Cape Breton: 'Above 800 families, Barra men, Eigg, Knoydart, and Arisaig men are in Cape Breton, without a priest, dying without sacraments, and not one word of sending them any shoes [priests], say they have none to send.'[57] Colonial officials utilised the authority of the Quebec hierarchy to impose order upon the Catholics under their jurisdiction and while this strategy was relatively successful at official levels, and the relationship between the Quebec bishops and British officials was strong, it inflamed pre-existing tensions between the Scots and the Irish.[58]

A pivotal component of the colonisation process was territorial expansion and the control over natural resources. Catholic Highlanders, like all other Scots, were anxious to acquire land and its availability in Cape Breton was one of the main reasons it was so popular. The culture of landlordism on Prince Edward Island saw many settlers, including a number of the Glenaladale group, migrate to Cape Breton and Nova Scotia because of their fierce opposition to it.[59] These secondary migrations to other Maritime colonies expanded the reach of the Scots and their religious culture dramatically.[60] The majority were from the Western Highlands and Islands and they succeeded in introducing a strong Scottish Catholic tradition that sat alongside the pre-existing Acadian, Mi'kmaq and Irish ones.

The Nova Scotia Archives' (NSA) Cape Breton Island Petitions database includes 3,340 petitions for land between 1787 and 1843 and is an exceptional online summary resource. The actual petition documents are available for public viewing at the NSA, and they include a range of details about the specific location of the land, the number of acres requested and the name or names of the petitioner(s).[61] They offer information about who the petitioner was, how many people were in his (usually male) family, how long he had been in the colony and from where he came. Two additional pieces of information were also given if required: if the petitioner was Catholic, a statement indicating that he had sworn the oath of allegiance was included; if the plot of land requested was on or near 'Indian' lands then this was also noted.[62] While the rapid and largely uncontrolled settler growth had pushed the Church's ability to supply an adequate number of missionaries to its limit, it also had a considerable impact on the island's Indigenous population. Important work on this has been done by Andrew Parnaby and John Reid, and they provide numerous examples of Highland migrants and other European settlers coveting, requesting and even taking, without government sanction, land that was in use by the Mi'kmaq.[63] A search through the land petitions database reveals numerous examples of Scottish (Catholic and not) requests for Indigenous land or for land very near Indigenous communities. In 1822, for example, Archibald McPhaggan, a

Catholic and 'native of Scotland', petitioned for land near Whycocomagh on the western side of the Bras d'Or Lakes:

> That Your Excellency's petitioner is a Native of Scotland, thirty six years of age, married and has four children, has never received any land from the Crown nor holds any by purchase or otherwise and prays your Excellency to give him a ticket of location for the lot numbered 6 situated to the eastward of the tract reserved for the Indians on the northern side of Whycocomagh and adjoining to the western boundary of that applied for by Donald Campbell. Petitioner arrived about five weeks ago from Scotland with the rest of the families for whom these lots were reserved and he know of no claims or other improvements to the said land.[64]

There is no indication as to where, exactly, he had lived in Scotland, but he was married with four children; Archibald's mark, X, an indication that he could not write, was accompanied by a confirmation from George Leonard, a senior member of Nova Scotia's governing council that 'Archibald McPhaggan took the oath of allegiance and swore to the truth of his preceding statement 11 September 1822 at Sydney C. B. before me.'[65] A decade earlier, in 1812, Charles McNab, who had held a commission with the Rothesay and Caithness Fencibles, 'together with the whole body of Scotch settlers on the Bras d'Or Lake ask that land reserved for the ___[?] Indians be granted to McNab as a mill site, and that the Indians be induced to settle elsewhere'. The petition, which included the statement that the settlers were prepared, in the event of a war with the United States, to 'volunteer their services in defence of their beloved king and country', asked for two tracts of land, 1,000 and 800 acres respectively, at the head of the Bras d'Or Lakes. McNab complained that the 'Indians have been giving trouble to the new settlers' and had the support of almost sixty fellow Scottish settlers who gave their marks or signatures.[66] It is not known if any of the settlers who signed were Catholic – some of them probably were – but their blatant attempt to acquire Indigenous land highlights the fundamental issue of contested spaces. Both of these examples relate to land around the Bras d'Or Lakes, a space that was extremely important to Mi'kmaq survival and in continuous use by them for fishing and hunting. Scottish settlers also sought land near Chapel Island, but this seems to have been one of the few places where they were somewhat restricted and the reasons for this are spiritual. Situated on the south-eastern side of the Bras d'Or Lakes, Chapel Island was a place of immense significance to the Mi'kmaq because it was where their Catholicism and traditional beliefs intersected. Some research has been done on the junctures of Scottish and Mi'kmaq Catholic traditions, but this is an area in need of much more work.[67] There is no question that Scots of every religious persuasion engaged actively in the widespread dispossession of Indigenous land and resources – the archival records bear this out – but when it comes to the Catholics among them, we still have much to learn about how and when the Catholic cultures of these two groups crossed. We know that both practised a shared faith in distinctive ways, but what we do not yet understand is how far a common allegiance to Catholicism connected them.

This chapter has offered a preliminary sketch of the protracted process of Scottish Highland Catholic settler colonialism that gripped north-eastern British North America from the early 1770s. First-generation colonists and their descendants became active and aggressive participants and sought large tracts of land from the Crown which, when granted, turned them into instant landowners, a status that was completely out of reach to the vast majority of Highlanders back in Scotland.[68] Catholics and the numerous settlements they established were an integral component of the British colonisation process and the fact that they achieved security via landownership enabled Scottish Catholicism, and the Catholic Church as an overarching institution, to find stability, to be practised openly and to embed itself within colonial life as a mainstream faith.

Notes

1. Prince Edward Island Scottish Settlers Historical Society Alexander Committee, *Glenalladale Settlers 1772: Scotland to St John's Island* (Charlottetown: Prince Edward Island Scottish Settlers Historical Society Inc., 2016), pp. 79–80, 91–3.
2. The spelling Glenaladale was chosen over Glenalladale because the former is how the family spelled the name in Scotland.
3. John MacGregor, *Historical and Descriptive Sketches of the Maritime Colonies of British America* (London: 1828), pp. 51, 100.
4. Joseph Hardwick, *The Anglican British World: The Church of England and the Expansion of the Settler Empire, c.1790–1860* (Manchester: Manchester University Press, 2014); Rowan Strong, *Victorian Christianity and Emigrant Voyages to British Colonies, c.1840–c.1914* (Oxford: Oxford University Press, 2018); Stuart Wolfendale, *Imperial to International: A History of St John's Cathedral, Hong Kong* (Hong Kong: Hong Kong University Press, 2013); Andrew Porter, *Religion Versus Empire?: British Protestant Missionaries and Overseas Expansion, 1700–1914* (Manchester: Manchester University Press, 2004) and 'Religion, Missionary Enterprise, and Empire', in Andrew Porter (ed.), *The Oxford History of the British Empire: The Nineteenth Century* (Oxford: Oxford University Press, 1999), pp. 222–46; Jeffrey Cox, *Imperial Fault Lines: Christianity and Colonial Power in India, 1818–1940* (Stanford: Stanford University Press, 2002), p. 20.
5. Valerie Wallace, '"Preaching Disaffection" in the Presbyterian Atlantic: Jotham Blanchard and the Reform Crisis in Scotland and Nova Scotia, c.1827–37', *Journal of Imperial and Commonwealth History*, 42:3 (2014), pp. 1–23; Philip Constable, 'Scottish Missionaries, "Protestant Hinduism" and the Scottish Sense of Empire in Nineteenth- and Early Twentieth-Century India', *Scottish Historical Review*, 86:2 (2007), pp. 278–313; Sarah Roddy, '"Not a duffer among them"?: The Colonial Mission of the Irish Presbyterian Church, 1848–1900'; David Dickson, Justyna Pyz and Christopher Shepard (eds), *Irish Classrooms and the British Empire: Imperial Exchange in the Origins of Modern Education* (Dublin: Four Courts Press, 2012), pp. 144–56.
6. Yvonne McKenna, *Made Holy: Irish Women Religious at Home and Abroad* (Dublin: Irish Academic

Press, 2006). Deidre Raftery, '"Je Suis d'Aucune Nation": the Recruitment and Identity of Irish Women Religious in the International Mission Field, c.1840–1940', *Paedagogica Historica*, 49:4 (2013), pp. 513–30; Dáire Keogh and Albert McDonnell (eds), *Cardinal Paul Cullen and His World* (Dublin: Four Courts Press, 2011); Dáire Keogh, '"Bulwark of the nations": Paul Cullen, the Christian Brothers and the Evangelization of an Irish Empire', *Irish Classrooms*, pp. 80–97; Barr, Colin. '"Imperium in Imperio": Irish Episcopal Imperialism in the Nineteenth Century', *English Historical Review*, 123:502 (2008), pp. 611–50; Oliver P. Rafferty, 'The Catholic Church, Ireland and the British Empire, 1800–1921', *Historical Research*, 84:222 (2011), pp. 288–309.

7. Hilary Carey, *God's Empire: Religion and Colonialism in the British World, c.1801–1908* (Cambridge: Cambridge University Press, 2011); Keogh and McDonnell, *Cardinal Paul Cullen and his World*.

8. S. Karly Kehoe, 'Catholic Relief and the Political Awakening of Irish Catholics in Nova Scotia, 1780–1830', *Journal of Imperial and Commonwealth History*, 46:1 (2018), pp. 1–20.

9. Don Watson, *Caledonia Australis: Scottish Highlanders on the Frontier of Australia* (Sydney: William Collins, 1984); Graeme Morton and David A. Wilson (eds), *Irish and Scottish Encounters with Indigenous Peoples: Canada, the United States, New Zealand, and Australia* (Montreal and Kingston: McGill-Queen's University Press, 2019); Benjamin Wilkie, *The Scots in Australia, 1788–1938* (Woodbridge: The Boydell Press, 2017); John G. Reid, 'Scots, Settler Colonization, and Indigenous Displacement: Mi'kma'ki, 1770–1820 in Comparative Context', *Journal of Scottish Historical Studies*, 38:1 (2018). Douglas Hamilton flags this also when discussing the Caribs in the West Indies; see 'Robert Melville and the Frontiers of Empire in the British West Indies, 1763–1771'; A. Mackillop and Steve Murdoch (eds), *Military Governors and Imperial Frontiers, c.1600–1800: A Study of Scotland and Empire* (Leiden: Brill, 2003), pp. 187–9.

10. David Alston, '"Very rapid and splendid fortunes"? Highland Scots in Berbice (Guyana) in the Early Nineteenth Century', *Transactions of the Gaelic Society of Inverness*, LXIII (2002–4), pp. 208–36; Stephen Mullen, 'A Glasgow–West India Merchant House and the Imperial Dividend, 1779–1867', *Journal of Scottish Historical Studies*, 33:2 (2013), pp. 196–233; Sheila M. Kidd, 'Gaelic Books as Cultural Icons: The Maintenance of Cultural Links between the Highlands and the West Indies', in Carla Sassi and Theo van Heijnsbergen (eds), *Within and Without Empire: Scotland across the (Post)Colonial Borderline* (Newcastle: Cambridge Scholars Publishing, 2013), pp. 46–60; Allan I. Macinnes, 'Commercial Landlordism and Clearance in the Scottish Highlands: The Case of Arichonan', in J. Pan-Montojo and K. Pendersen (eds), *Communities in European History* (Pisa: Pisa University Press, 2007), pp. 47–64; S. Karly Kehoe, 'From the Caribbean to the Scottish Highlands: Charitable Enterprise in the Age of Improvement, c.1750–c.1820', *Rural History*, 27:1 (2016), pp. 37–59.

11. *Royal Letters, Charters, and Tracts Relating to the Colonization of New Scotland and the Institution of the Order of the Knight Baronets of Nova Scotia, 1621–1638* (Edinburgh, 1867), p. 297.

12. Ned Landsman, 'The Legacy of British Union for the North American Colonies: Provincial Elites and the Problem of Imperial Union', in John Robertson (ed.), *A Union for Empire: Political Thought and the British Union of 1707* (Cambridge: Cambridge University Press, 1995), p. 301.

13. J. M. Bumsted, 'Scottish Emigration to the Maritimes 1770–1815: A New Look at an Old Theme', *Acadiensis*, 10:2 (1981), p. 65; Rusty Bittermann, 'On Remembering and Forgetting: Highland Memories within the Maritime Diaspora', in Michael E. Vance and Marjory Harper (eds), *Myth, Migration and the Making of Memory: Scotia and Nova Scotia, c.1700–1990* (Edinburgh: John Donald Publishers, 1999), pp. 253–66.

14. Rusty Bittermann, 'The Hierarchy of the Soil: Land and Labour in a 19th Century Cape Breton Community', *Acadiensis*, 18:1 (1988), pp. 33–55.

15. TNA. BT6/35/f.413-6. Miscellanea, Cape Breton (1793). John G. Reid, 'Empire, the Maritime

Colonies, and the Supplanting of Mi'kma'ki/Wulstukwik, 1780–1820', *Acadiensis*, 38:2 (2009), p. 82.
16. Reid, 'Empire, the Maritime Colonies', pp. 80, 84, 99.
17. The family moved to near 'Barrasdale', probably where Barrachois is today. Many thanks to archaeologist April Mitchell-MacIntyre for her help in narrowing down this location.
18. Alan Lester and Zoë Laidlaw, 'Indigenous Sites and Mobilities: Connected Struggles in the Long Nineteenth Century', in *Indigenous Communities and Settler Colonialism: Land Holding, Loss and Survival in an Interconnected World* (Cambridge: Cambridge University Press, 2015), pp. 1–23.
19. Andrew Parnaby, 'The Cultural Economy of Survival: The Mi'kmaq of Cape Breton in the Mid-19th Century', *Labour/Le Travail*, 61 (2008), pp. 69–98; Reid, 'Scots, Settler Colonization', p. 184.
20. Lester and Laidlaw, 'Indigenous Sites and Mobilities', p. 9; S. Karly Kehoe, 'Catholic Relief'.
21. Parnaby, 'The Cultural Economy'.
22. Allan F. MacDonald, 'Captain John MacDonald, "Glenaladale"', *Canadian Catholic Historical Association Report*, 31 (1964), p. 28; D. M. Sinclair, 'Highland Emigration to Nova Scotia', *Dalhousie Review*, 23 (1943), pp. 207–20.
23. J. M. Bumsted, 'Highland Emigration to the Island of St John and the Scottish Catholic Church, 1769–1774', *Dalhousie Review*, 58:3 (1970), pp. 511–27.
24. Matthew P. Dziennik, '"Cutting heads from shoulders": The Conquest of Canada in Gaelic Thought, 1759–1791', in Phillip Bruckner and John Reid (eds), *Revisiting 1759: The Conquest of Canada in Historical Perspective* (Toronto: University of Toronto Press, 2010), pp. 241–66; Andrew Mackillop, 'Military Scotland in the Age of Proto-Globalisation, *c.*1690–1815', in David Forsyth and Wendy Ugolini (eds), *A Global Force: War, Identities and Scotland's Diaspora* (Edinburgh: Edinburgh University Press, 2016), pp. 13–31.
25. Julian Gwyn, *Excessive Expectations: Maritime Commerce and the Economic Development of Nova Scotia, 1740–1870* (Montreal and Kingston: McGill-Queen's University Press, 1998).
26. Kathleen Toomey, 'Emigration from the Scottish Catholic Bounds, 1770–1810 and the Role of the Clergy' (unpublished PhD thesis, University of Edinburgh, 1991), pp. 17–20; Alasdair B. Roberts, 'The Role of Women in Scottish Catholic Survival', *Scottish Historical Review*, 70:190 (1991), pp. 129–50.
27. F. L. Pigot, 'MacDonald of Glenaladale, John', *Dictionary of Canadian Biography*, vol. 5, <http://www.biographi.ca/en/bio/macdonald_of_glenaladale_john_5E.html> (last accessed 20 October 2019).
28. Ibid; Alastair Livingstone, Christian W. H. Aikman and Betty Stuart Hart (eds), *Muster Roll of Prince Charles Edward Stuart's Army, 1745–46* (Aberdeen,: Aberdeen University Press, 1984), p. 140.
29. Quoted in Anne MacLeod, *From an Antique Land: Visual Representations of the Highlands and Islands, 1700–1880* (Edinburgh: John Donald, 2012), p. 88.
30. MacDonald, 'Captain John MacDonald, "Glenaladale"', p. 23.
31. David Taylor flags Aberarder in Badenoch as an example. See *The Wild Black Region: Badenoch, 1750–1800* (Edinburgh, John Donald Publishers, 2016), pp. 127, 130.
32. Bumsted, 'Scottish Emigration to the Maritimes', pp. 76–7; MacDonald, 'Captain John MacDonald, "Glenaladale"', p. 24.
33. Quoted in J. M. Bumsted, *Land, Settlement and Politics on Eighteenth-Century Prince Edward Island* (Montreal and Kingston: McGill-Queen's University Press, 1987), p. 57.
34. MacDonald, 'Captain John MacDonald, "Glenaladale"', p. 25.
35. Sinclair, Sir John. *The Statistical Account of Scotland*, South Uist, Inverness, vol. 13 (Edinburgh: William Creech, 1794), p. 292, <http://stataccscot.edina.ac.uk/link/osa-vol13-p292-parish-inverness-south_uist> (last accessed 20 October 2019).
36. MacDonald, 'Captain John MacDonald, "Glenaladale"', p. 25; Bumsted, *Land, Settlement and Politics*, p. 57.

37. Darren Tierney, 'Financing the Faith: Scottish Catholicism, 1772–c.1890' (unpublished PhD thesis, University of Aberdeen, 2014), pp. 30–42; University of Durham, Ushaw College Library and Special Collections, Lisbon College Papers. LC/C732. Letter from Alexander Cameron, Edinburgh, to Jerome Allen, English College Lisbon, 9 September 1794.
38. Scottish Catholic Archives. BL/3/258/6. Letter from John MacDonald, Fort William, to Mr George Hay, in Robison's Land middle of Blackfryar's [sic] Wynd, Edinbrugh, 16 April 1773; Ian MacKay, 'Clanranald's Tacksmen of the late 18th Century', *Transactions of the Gaelic Society of Inverness*, 44 (1964–66), p. 70.
39. Scottish Catholic Archives. BL/3/258/6. Letter from MacDonald to Hay, 16 April 1773.
40. J. R. Miller, 'Anti-Catholicism in Canada: From the British Conquest to the Great War', in Terry Murphy and Gerald Stortz (eds), *Creed and Culture: The Place of English-Speaking Catholics in Canadian Society, 1750–1930* (Montreal and Kingston: McGill-Queen's University Press, 1993), p. 27.
41. Statistics Canada, Censuses of Canada 1665–1871, <https://www150.statcan.gc.ca/n1/pub/98-187-x/4064809-eng.htm#part2> (last accessed 20 October 2018).
42. SCRA. 12/111. Letters from Aeneas MacEachern, Prince Edward Island, to Aeneas McDonald, Rome, 6 May 1828. 12/112; Letter from William Fraser, Antigonish, to Aeneas MacDonald, Rome, 8 October 1828; Terrence Murphy, 'The Emergence of Maritime Catholicism, 1781–1830', *Acadiensis*, 13:2 (1984), p. 32; Heidi MacDonald, 'Developing a Strong Roman Catholic Social Order in Late Nineteenth-Century Prince Edward Island', *Canadian Catholic Historical Association Historical Studies*, 69 (2003), p. 36.
43. Murphy, 'The Emergence', p. 29; B. A. Balcom and A. J. B. Johnston, 'Missions to the Mi'kmaq: Malagawatch and Chapel Island in the 18th Century', *Journal of the Royal Nova Scotia Historical Society*, 9 (2006), pp. 115–41; Ruma Chopra, 'Maroons and Mi'kmaw in Nova Scotia, 1796–1800', *Acadiensis*, 46:1 (2017), p. 14.
44. John G. Reid, *Six Crucial Decades: Times of Change in the History of the Maritimes* (Halifax, NS: Nimbus Publishing, 1987), p. 76.
45. University of Durham, Ushaw College Library and Special Collections, Lisbon College Papers. LC/C871. Letter from William Poynter, London, to Edmund Winstanley, English College Lisbon, 18 May 1819. Regarding the need for missionaries in England, 'it is to them [Continental colleges] that we look for a supply of the wants of the mission in our present distress'.
46. University of Durham, Ushaw College Library and Special Collections, Lisbon College Papers. LC/C902. Letter from Alexander Cameron, Scots College Valladolid, to Edmund Winstanley, English College Lisbon, 11 November 1821. LC/C908. Letter from Alexander Cameron, Scots College Valladolid, to Edmund Winstanley, English College Lisbon, 9 January 1822.
47. Charles Dunn, *Highland Settler: A Portrait of the Scottish Gael in Cape Breton and Eastern Nova Scotia* [1953] (Wreck Cove: Cape Breton Books, 1991), p. 28.
48. Quoted in A. A. Johnston, *A History of the Catholic Church in Eastern Nova Scotia: Volume I* (Antigonish: St Francis Xavier University, 1960), pp. 133–5, 162.
49. Ibid. p. 157.
50. J. L. MacDougall, *History of Inverness County Nova Scotia* (Strathlorne, Nova Scotia, 1922), p. 37. Quoted in Johnston, *A History of the Catholic Church in Eastern Nova Scotia*, p. 197.
51. Scots College Rome Archives (SCRA). 12/110. Letter from Aeneas MacEachern, Prince Edward Island, to Bishop Aeneas MacDonald, Rome, 1827 (no day or month given).
52. Scots College Rome Archives. 12/111. Letter from Aeneas MacEachern, Prince Edward Island, to Bishop Aeneas MacDonald, Rome, 6 May 1828.
53. See chapters 2 and 3 in S. Karly Kehoe, *Creating a Scottish Church: Catholicism, Gender and Ethnicity in Nineteenth-Century Scotland* (Manchester: Manchester University Press, 2010).
54. Eric Richards, *The Highland Clearances* (Edinburgh: Birlinn, 2002), pp. 189–91; Stephen J.

Hornsby, *Nineteenth-Century Cape Breton: A Historical Geography* (Montreal and Kingston: McGill-Queen's University Press, 1992), pp. 49, 57, 71–4.

55. Daniel Samson, *The Spirit of Industry and Improvement: Liberal Government and Rural-Industrial Society, Nova Scotia, 1790–1862* (Montreal and Kingston: McGill-Queen's University Press, 2008), pp. 226–33; James Hunter, *Scottish Exodus: Travels among a Worldwide Clan* (Edinburgh: Mainstream, 2007), p. 156.
56. Beaton Institute, Cape Breton University, Sydney, Canada (hereafter BICBU). MG 13/43. The English translation of 'The Plessis Diary of 1811 and 1812', pp. 77–8; Terence J. Fay, *A History of Canadian Catholics* (Montreal and Kingston: McGill-Queen's University Press, 2002), p. 45.
57. Scots College Rome Archives. 12/110. Letter from Aeneas MacEachern, Prince Edward Island, to Bishop Aeneas MacDonald, Rome, 6 May 1828.
58. Heidi MacDonald, 'Developing a Strong Roman Catholic Social Order in Late Nineteenth-Century Prince Edward Island', *Acadiensis*, 69 (2003), pp. 34–51; Kehoe, *Creating a Scottish Church*.
59. Allan I. Macinnes, Marjory-Ann D. Harper and Linda G. Fryer, *Scotland and the Americas, c.1650–c.1939: A Documentary Source Book*, 'Doc. A5, Letter from Rev. James MacDonald, Tracadie, to Rev. Dr. Sir', 4 November 1776, pp. 174–5; MacDonald, 'Captain John MacDonald, "Glenaladale"', p. 35; Lucille H. Campey, *'A Very Fine Class of Immigrants': Prince Edward Island's Scottish Pioneers, 1770–1850* (Toronto: Natural Heritage Books, 2001), pp. 29–30; Annie Tindley, 'New World, Old Problems', this volume; R. Bittermann, *Rural Protest on Prince Edward Island: From British Colonisation to the Escheat Movement* (Toronto: University of Toronto Press, 2006); R. Bitterman and M. McCallum, *Lady Landlords of Prince Edward Island: Imperial Dreams and the Defence of Property* (Montreal and Kingston: McGill-Queen's University Press, 2008).
60. Stephen J. Hornsby, 'Patterns of Scottish Emigration to Canada, 1750–1870', *Journal of Historical Geography*, 18:4 (1994), pp. 400–4.
61. Cape Breton Island Petitions, 1787–1843, <https://novascotia.ca/archives/land/> (last accessed 20 October 2019).
62. Ibid.
63. Parnaby, 'The Cultural Economy of Survival'; Reid, 'Scots, Settler Colonization', p. 184; Reid, 'Empire, the Maritime Colonies'.
64. NSA. Cape Breton Island Petitions, 1787–1843. 1822 Archibald McPhagan, Cape Breton no. 2874, mf. 15798.
65. Ibid.
66. NSA. Cape Breton Island Petitions, 1787–1843. 1812 Charles McNab, Cape Breton no. 854, mf. 15791. The vast majority signing the document were illiterate and used an X to mark their names.
67. Parnaby, 'The Cultural Economy of Survival', p. 91; Balcom and Johnston, 'Missions to the Mi'kmaq', p. 129.
68. A simple search through the petitions will show the size of tracts being requested.

SEVEN

The Church of England, Print Networks and the Book of Common Prayer in the North-Eastern Atlantic Colonies, *c.*1750–*c.*1830

Joseph Hardwick

The Church of England has featured only intermittently in histories of Atlantic Canada. Scholars focus on Roman Catholics and those Protestant evangelical groups – Baptists, Presbyterians and Methodists – that supposedly injected a democratic and dynamic element to the region's religious scene.[1] When it is discussed, the Church of England appears as a conservative and cumbersome institution, one that had struggled with financial and recruitment problems from its foundation in the early eighteenth century. In the mid-1830s, for example, two-thirds of New Brunswick's eighty Anglican parishes lacked resident clergy.[2] Mission work to indigenous communities was rarely prioritised, and the determination of churchmen to replicate old world traditions in new world environments, 'everything from the parish church to the Book of Common Prayer's set services', meant Anglicanism extended itself unsurely in frontier environments.[3]

Yet historians who focus on the Church's financial difficulties and recruitment troubles paint too bleak a picture of Anglican fortunes in the Atlantic Canadian region. It was the Church of England that made an early and vital contribution to the development of higher education in Nova Scotia with the establishment of King's College, Windsor, in 1789.[4] The Church was also a more popular, adaptable and rooted institution than historians have appreciated. The Church's historic relationship to the British Crown (prayers for the monarch were offered in Anglican churches every Sunday), coupled with its accessible forms of worship, made attendance at Anglican places of worship undemanding and a strategic choice for many.[5] The Anglican bishopric established at Nova Scotia in 1787 was a new kind of non-political or 'limited' episcopate specially adapted to colonial conditions.[6] Michael Gauvreau's research also shows that the region was home to a uniquely lay-orientated and cosmopolitan Church.[7] Both the clergy and the congregations they served were ethnically diverse, and as in colonial America, Canadian congregations wielded considerable power over church property and the appointment of clergy. Calvin

Hollett, writing on Newfoundland fishing communities, has highlighted the strength of a 'popular', 'vernacular' or 'evangelical Anglicanism': this was a religion that emphasised 'the word' and that was not dependent on bishops, clergy or institutional churches.[8]

Recent research has also uncovered the networks which grew up within and outside the Church of England and which enabled Anglicans to maintain an overseas presence. Historians have described the range of metropolitan-based voluntary societies that supplied colonial churchgoers with Bibles, Prayer Books, cheap tracts and printed sermons.[9] Jeremy Gregory's research on pre-revolutionary America shows that texts maintained a viable Church of England in places with few resident churches and purpose-built churches. The provision of the Book of Common Prayer, the Church of England's manual, was particularly important, as without it, communities would not understand and could not participate in Anglicanism's distinctive forms and services. Indeed, through its provision of a standard set of forms of prayer and Bible readings for every week in the year, the book had the potential to connect colonial churchgoers to far-reaching communities of worshippers.[10] Historians have also appreciated the importance of religious literature in sustaining 'imagined communities' of worshippers in Atlantic Canada. Calvin Hollett has traced the distinctive evangelical spirituality that characterised nineteenth-century Newfoundland fishing communities to influential texts, namely the King James Bible and the Prayer Book.[11]

This chapter uses work by Gregory and Hollett as a starting point to examine the organisation of Anglican print networks in Atlantic Canada. A study of the circulation and use of religious literature opens new questions and fresh perspectives about imperial networks, the expansion of institutional churches and the development and maintenance of common denominational identities across large territories and among cosmopolitan communities. More specifically, this chapter suggests that Anglicanism in the Atlantic Canada region was not as fragmented, lay-led or unpopular as much of the existing literature implies. It was the case that the Church of England appeared in a variety of forms as it took root in communities of differing ethnic origins. There was a long tradition of laypersons leading prayers, delivering sermons and providing unofficial baptism, marriages and burial services from the Prayer Book. Yet the Prayer Book was a flexible text that could meet local needs and preferences as well as provide a point of unity. There was considerable conformity to the Prayer Book's forms of worship and lay communities looked to ordained clergy to validate the Church of England's services. Anglicanism in Atlantic Canada may have been distinct because it was so cosmopolitan and diverse, but it still retained strong connections with both Church of England tradition and the wider 'Anglican Communion'.

The study begins with the foundation of congregations in the middle of the eighteenth century and ends in the 1830s. This was the moment when the authority of bishops pressed more heavily on congregations, and also when the provision of religious literature changed, as new forms of print and local sources of supply emerged. The first section surveys the patchy Anglican presence in Atlantic Canada up to the 1830s and shows that Anglicanism was much shaped by local circumstances and the decisions and preferences of lay communities.

The Church of England and north Atlantic region to c.1830

It was not until the American War of Independence – a conflict that transformed the Church of England's colonial ministry – that north-eastern British North America became a primary focus of Anglican concern.[12] Since the early eighteenth century the British Crown had relied on the Society for the Propagation of the Gospel (SPG), an Anglican outreach organisation formed in 1701, to maintain clergymen and schoolteachers in Newfoundland and Nova Scotia, territories taken from the French in 1713 and 1749. Importantly, the initiative for Church expansion in Newfoundland came from the colony's fishing communities. In 1729 the inhabitants of Trinity petitioned the SPG for a clergyman and committed themselves to erecting a place of worship and paying part of the minister's salary.[13] This example of lay initiative was replicated across Atlantic Canada in the decades to come, with women joining men in signing petitions to the SPG, bishops and the Crown. Late in the eighteenth century, black people who had come to Nova Scotia as part of the loyalist relocations of the American Revolution petitioned the Anglican authorities for bibles, Prayer Books and funds for schools.[14] Colonial Anglicanism was not imposed on reluctant colonial populations but grew in response to local demand.[15]

In Nova Scotia after 1750, non-Anglicans enjoyed religious toleration, but the Church of England possessed privileges as the official state religion. British authorities used religion and the settlement of Protestant migrants to serve imperial goals, with the Church forming part of an effort to 'anglicise' the French-speaking Acadians. In the 1760s, Thomas Wood, vicar at Halifax, ministered among the indigenous Mi'kmaq, who, during French rule, had come under the influence of Roman Catholic priests.[16] Charles Lawrence, governor of Nova Scotia from 1756, also thought the Church of England could be the agent through which the colony's plural mix of English, Scottish, New England and German Protestant settlers could be brought into 'union & Harmony with the rest of His Majesty's subjects'.[17] Initially, the SPG appointed bilingual missionaries to serve Nova Scotia's communities of French Protestants and German-speaking Lutherans, though a more aggressively anglicising strategy was adopted when Robert Vincent (appointed 1762), who spoke only English, was sent to Lunenburg's German community. Though the project was not entirely successful – later ministers were bilingual, and the German community broke off and formed a Lutheran congregation in 1771 when a minister became available – nothing like this was tried elsewhere in colonial America. Here is another reminder that the interventionism and authoritarianism of the eighteenth-century British state in Atlantic Canada marks the region off from much of British North America.[18]

Yet in the 1770s the Church of England had only established a marginal presence in the region. Newfoundland was a backwater: religion there was largely led by the laity, as at any time before the second decade of the nineteenth century the island had only three Anglican clergymen (at St John's, Harbour Grace and Trinity). After the American Revolution the imperial government made more concerted efforts to strengthen the established Church in Nova Scotia, St John's Island (formed 1769 and renamed Prince Edward's Island in 1798) and New Brunswick and Cape Breton (both formed in 1784). The extension of Anglicanism was partly a response to the migration of thousands of loyalist refugees – not all of whom identified with the Church of England – from the revolted colonies. It also reflected new imperial policies: for the architects of Britain's 'second empire', a privileged Church of England establishment, complete with bishop, would project British authority and tie the colonies to the imperial centre.[19] In 1787 Charles Inglis, a New York loyalist, became bishop of Nova Scotia, with episcopal jurisdiction over the whole of British North America, and the SPG provided funds for more missionaries. In Nova Scotia, the Church monopolised higher education until the 1820s, and from 1808 the bishop sat on the legislative council. In New Brunswick, only Anglican clergymen had the legal right to solemnise marriages after 1791. Newfoundland's 1817 marriage act prohibited (in all but exceptional circumstances) the celebration of marriages by anyone other than Anglican ministers and Roman Catholic priests.[20] In the 1810s the British parliament granted money for the support of additional SPG missionaries in Nova Scotia (from 1813), Newfoundland (1814) and New Brunswick (1816).[21]

For all this metropolitan backing, the 'Anglican design' was given limited support by the colonial authorities and was wound up in the 1830s.[22] Anglicans remained a minority denomination in most regions (though concentrations of Church of England members grew up in provincial urban centres and at Shelburne, Windsor and Annapolis in Nova Scotia).[23] In Newfoundland, Roman Catholicism was so dominant that one Anglican missionary called the island an 'Irish plantation'.[24] Yet even in the era of financial support Anglican bishops and clergy could not maintain an independent status or impose the required moral and spiritual authority. Charles Inglis had little control over the expansion of the Church: his clergy were paid by and answered to the SPG and he had to negotiate with governments and congregations before he could make appointments to vacant posts. Many clergy lived in poverty and most lacked the glebe lands that would have provided a source of remuneration and given the Church a foundation in the soil.[25] Michael Gauvreau points out that Anglican ministers had to negotiate with congregations about everything, from the building of parsonages to the appointment of churchwardens and modifications to church services.[26] With clergy in short supply, missionaries undertook demanding visitations of their huge 'parishes', with rough services offered to small congregations in private homes, the open air, or, worse still, places of worship belonging to other denominations. Ministry in Newfoundland was particularly difficult, as the seasonal nature of the fishing industry meant clergymen might have no congregation in the winter months.

Yet despite these troubles, there is evidence that the Church drew into its fold Irish Calvinists, Scottish Episcopalians, American Loyalists, 'foreign Protestants' and the expected English 'church people'. The French- and German-speaking immigrants who settled in Halifax and Lunenburg in the 1750s – the so-called 'foreign Protestants' – initially attended Anglican services because no others were available.[27] Roger Aitken, missionary at Lunenburg, said in 1822 that the people of Nova Scotia made 'no distinction between one communion and another' and considered 'the best communion' the Church of England, because its services were cheap and provided by government and the SPG.[28] The SPG wanted to encourage local initiative, but in many cases the poverty of colonial congregations meant British donors covered the missionary's entire income. Missionaries reported that colonists came to the Church to hear sermons and to have important rites of passage – baptism, marriage and burial – validated by the Church of England through the services in the Book of Common Prayer. Missionaries often reminded inhabitants of the Church's special relationship with the British monarchy, and for many – particularly those of non-British descent – attendance at church was a way to claim respectability, loyalty and British subject status.[29] Though clergymen often worried about what they called 'occasional conformity', it seems the Church of England community divided into a core of active laypersons who regularly attended church and frequently took Holy Communion, and a larger constituency that maintained dual or multiple denominational identities, and who accessed the Church for special services and occasions.[30]

Atlantic Canada in the age of revolution was, then, a region where the authority of bishops tended to press lightly, and where congregations and churches had freedom to develop peculiar characters and features.[31] One nineteenth-century missionary called Newfoundland an island of 'peculiar contrasts' where the character of neighbouring settlements differed so markedly that the people seemed to be 'of quite difference races'.[32] A similar diversity emerged in the Church of England. The composition of congregations varied considerably. In some places, people who had grown up in other faith communities attended Church of England services if the missionary was personally liked and if non-Anglicans had no ministers and places of worship. Ministers who reached out to other faiths tried to be examples of 'moderation' who, on their own authority, might adapt Anglican forms of worship to meet local tastes and prejudices. Gauvreau cites examples of Nova Scotian clergymen giving up the sign of the cross at baptism to satisfy New England dissenters.[33] Wealthy patrons of both sexes had the freedom to shape local church services. In 1830, Edward Wix, archdeacon of Newfoundland, found an influential American-born woman at Saint George's who included hymns and psalms from the American Episcopal Church in services.[34]

A multiplicity of forms of local church government emerged in Nova Scotia, with congregations developing different rulings on the composition, responsibilities and voting qualifications of vestries.[35] Some vestries, such as that at St Paul's Halifax, exercised the same kind of 'lay trusteeship' found in Roman Catholic churches (the St Paul's vestry took its right to appoint new ministers so seriously that for a time in the mid-1820s it resisted Crown authority).[36] Until 1811, St George's church, Halifax – a congregation composed of Lutheran Germans – ran a system by which only people of German descent could stand as churchwardens, attend church meetings and vote on new appointments. Though the process of anglicisation continued in the church through the appointment of an English clergyman in 1799 and the use of English-language prayers and sermons, the congregation insisted on retaining 'the Psalmody of our native Church in our native language' as a 'relic of our native worship'.[37]

Within this context the circulation of religious literature took on tremendous significance. In their letters to the SPG, Anglican clergymen recognised that by distributing Prayer Books they could, at little expense, create a sense of unity, commonality and identity across huge territories, scattered populations and diverse congregations. Other kinds of religious literature, such as tracts, pamphlets and printed sermons, educated inhabitants on the meaning the Church of England's distinctive rituals and services. The next two sections consider how religious texts were distributed in Atlantic Canada before 1830, and how the use of this literature might work to strengthen lay authority and both fragment and unify the Church of England in Atlantic Canada.

Religious literature and Church of England print networks

In the late eighteenth and early nineteenth centuries colonial Anglicans looked to the home country to provide clergymen, church bells and, on occasion, gravestones.[38] Atlantic Canada's primitive printing industry meant that Anglicans also relied on Britain – and sometimes colonial America and the United States – for Bibles, Prayer Books, tracts, sermons and other religious literature. These materials came to the colonies through various channels: some were formal, regular and institutional, others were personal and more ephemeral.

What might be termed Anglican 'associational activism' was an important element in the spread of religious literature at home and abroad.[39] The SPG and the Society for the Promotion of Christian Knowledge (SPCK), another Anglican outreach society formed in 1699, made huge efforts to connect metropolitan and colonial churchgoers through the spread of Church propaganda.[40] Like its SPG partner, the SPCK aimed to galvanise local action:[41] a district committee was set up in Halifax in 1814, and other committees appeared in New Brunswick, Prince Edward Island and Newfoundland. A third of the money gathered by these committees was sent to the SPCK in England, with the remainder returned as books to the parishes that contributed.[42] Books would then be sold, lent out or distributed gratis in each parish. Texts commonly distributed by the SPCK included Bibles, Prayer Books, devotional aids, tracts that explained aspects of Anglican worship, religious literature for groups such as children and the military, and religious biographies and histories.[43]

Religious literature also passed between individuals through personal and familial networks. Charles Inglis, Nova Scotia's first Anglican bishop, particularly valued the episcopal 'charges' that he received from English bishop friends, especially those that came from George Pretyman-Tomline, the bishop of Lincoln and metropolitan lobbyist and networker for the Canadian churches.[44] Inglis said that because he was 'shut out from personal intercourse' with fellow bishops, such texts served to connect his diocese to the episcopate in England. It is noteworthy that Pretyman-Tomline sent Inglis a copy of one 1794 charge, as the circulation of such a ferociously counter-revolutionary text reveals that the conservative reaction to 'French principles' was transatlantic in scope.[45] The Newfoundland historian Calvin Hollett notes that religious literature also travelled across the Atlantic through family and personal links established by laypersons. For example, archdeacon Edward Wix discovered isolated settlers who possessed Prayer Books that had been sent to them after family members had represented their needs to English clergymen.[46]

Throughout the eighteenth and early nineteenth centuries it was the missionary that served as the primary vector through which religious literature was distributed in the colonial world. Regardless of where they were stationed, the SPG provided each missionary in the Atlantic region with the same standard library that had been sent to missionaries in the pre-revolutionary American colonies. SPG libraries were intended to help missionaries define, advance and defend the Church of England's teachings.[47] Many of the printed materials that came through clergymen were, however, cheap tracts and pamphlets that the SPG sent out in great quantities, and which missionaries distributed to inhabitants free of charge. The distribution of Anglican religious literature partly relied on official connections. In the 1790s, for instance, books for Newfoundland passed through Poole, Devon and the collector of customs, Richard Routh, who spent much of his year in England. The SPG recorded the books it sent to its missionaries in the field, and one surviving volume, that covering the period 1791–1821,[48] reveals that Anglican missionaries across Atlantic Canada received a standard set of titles. It also shows that only occasionally were missionaries provided with specialist literature for their region. The literature sent out was of different types, and some explanation is therefore necessary.

First, missionaries received works that had been authored back during the moral reform campaigns (the 'reformation of manners' movement) of the early eighteenth century.[49] Why elderly works on swearing, lying, drunkenness and the 'profanation of the Sabbath' should have been sent out, or why missionaries continued to request them, can only be conjectured at. It is probable that such literature, with its emphasis on duties and obligations, was considered particularly suited to new societies, such as those in Atlantic Canada, where the loyalty of inhabitants could not be assumed. The second class of religious literature consisted of private devotional manuals, the type designed to encourage spiritual self-examination and repentance and to prompt people to pray in their homes.[50] Key examples, such as James Merrick's *Short Manual of Prayers for Common Occasions* (1774), Henry Crossman's *An Introduction to Knowledge of the Christian Religion* (1742), William Burkitt's *Help and Guide to Christian Families* (1787) and Thomas Wilson's *A Form of Family Prayer* (1790), provided colonists with forms of prayer for the morning and evening, for worship outside church and during services, for personal needs (such as during sickness and bereavement) and for old people and children. This literature was distinctively Anglican, as it stressed that private prayer would follow set forms, and not be improvised or extemporary. That missionaries requested such works is another example of how Anglican missionaries quickly adapted to 'personal religious rituals' and the culture of 'informal family worship' that blossomed throughout Canada.[51] Encouraging family and private worship might seem to have boosted lay authority and furthered the fragmentation of the Church of England. What the transatlantic spread of such prescriptive literature really shows is that clergymen wished to standardise worship in the Anglican Communion, and ensure that even in private homes colonial inhabitants offered similar prayers as their co-religionists in other parts of the 'British world'.

Third, missionaries received works that defined and explained the Church of England's distinctive teachings and forms of worship. Paulus Bryzelius, a Swedish-born minister who served Lutherans in Lunenburg, had requested German translations of such works as early as the 1760s.[52] This literature was premised on the notion that religious adherence was hereditary but also a matter of choice, and that non-Anglicans could through discussion only be weaned from 'that religion wherein they were bred'.[53] Sermons and private visits were useful for educating the illiterate, but books could help reach harder-to-access communities. A popular tract titled *The Englishman Directed in his Choice of Religion* (1729), one which continued to be sent to Newfoundland as late as the mid-1810s, analysed the truths of the Anglican religion, disparaged the claims of Protestant dissenters and said that Anglican membership was the duty of all British subjects, as it alone promoted 'Order and Decency'.

Missionaries also asked for works that explained rituals, notably confirmation and Holy Communion. It was a long-running complaint of missionaries in North America, and not just those in Atlantic Canada, that worshippers were reluctant to participate in the sacrament because they felt unworthy and unprepared.[54] Well into the 1820s Atlantic Canada missionaries continued to ask for[55] and receive works on the sacrament by Thomas Wilson, Edmund Gibson, William Assheton, Edward Synge and William Fleetwood, all of which had been sent to missionaries in colonial America before the Revolution.[56] So much emphasis was placed on regular participation in Holy Communion because taking the sacrament was considered a sign of true faith and a marker of Church membership.

The important point is that in sending this literature the SPG and SPCK did not, for the most part, take much notice of regional peculiarities and differences. As the historian Jeremy Gregory points out, Anglicans assumed that the threats to colonial churches took the same form everywhere.[57] Clergy who had served in one part of Atlantic Canada were moved on to parishes elsewhere in the region, and, as was noted earlier, Charles Inglis saw no difficulty with introducing in his part of the world the practices he read about in English episcopal charges. Nevertheless, the books sent to Atlantic Canada reveal that Anglican administrators had some appreciation of regional particularisms. Missionaries requested tracts – again, some very elderly – that challenged the claims of competitor denominations. The SPG sent Newfoundland missionaries tracts against 'popery', though some missionaries thought that such 'controversial Pamphlets' could not be distributed safely and might damage Anglican fortunes and strengthen attachment to Roman Catholicism.[58] In Nova Scotia, where the Baptists had always been strong, missionaries asked for tracts that explained the necessity of infant baptism, justified Anglican baptismal ritual and defended Anglican teaching on baptismal regeneration.[59] Abridged versions of William Wall's *History of Infant Baptism* (1705) were a standard issue in Nova Scotia up to the 1820s, and in 1815 the missionary at Fredericton received two bundles of 100 copies of a recent work by Lewis Bagot, bishop of St Asaph.[60] Other deliveries of books give tantalising glimpses of the social issues confronting missionaries in particular places. In 1800, for instance, both Roger Viets and John Harries, missionaries at Digby, Nova Scotia and St John's, Newfoundland, respectively, received copies of a tract on suicide by Zachary Pearce.[61]

Interestingly, towards the end of the period some missionaries developed a sharper sense of regional peculiarity and doubted whether tracts written for eighteenth-century England were appropriate for the colonies. Abel Gore, a schoolmaster in Halifax, told bishop John Inglis in 1829 that all books sent out by the SPG should be selected by missionaries, as they were 'best acquainted with the wants of the people' and most of the texts on the SPG catalogue (he mentioned *The Englishman Directed in his Choice of Religion*) had little use in Atlantic Canada, presumably because such works assumed that the Church of England was the majority, 'national' church, when in Atlantic Canada it was not.[62] Indeed, around this time the SPG was winding down its provision of literature, and new forms of print, notably locally produced Church periodical literature, would become important vehicles by which Anglicans advanced the claims of their denomination. Those who advocated a Church of England press in the 1820s reckoned that Nova Scotians should follow the example of the productions of the Episcopal Church of the United States, as that institution also faced the task of 'explaining and vindicating' forms of worship 'not generally understood or duly valued'.[63] Colonial Anglicans had begun to diversify their networks and to look beyond metropolitan Britain for inspiration.[64]

If literature was to have an impact, missionaries had to rely on laypeople to circulate copies and read texts aloud to the illiterate. The available sources reveal little about how inhabitants used this printed material. What is known is that some clergymen granted laypersons a considerable degree of authority in the use of religious literature. Lay preaching was a radical step; indeed, in parts of the empire this was policed, as while reading prayers could be allowed, since prayers were addressed to God, preaching was an exhortation to a community on how individuals should act and think.[65] Yet lay sermonising was encouraged to a surprising extent, especially in Newfoundland, even though this practice threatened to collapse the distinctions between the Church of England and its 'dissenting' rivals. What was preached was regulated. Ministers approached the SPG for 'plain' and 'practical' printed sermons which laymen could read aloud, and David Rowland, minister at St John's, Newfoundland, wanted only sermon books authored by the 'most orthodox divines', citing such eighteenth-century orthodox high churchmen as Thomas Secker, archbishop of Canterbury, and Thomas Wilson, bishop of Sodor and Man.[66] But the SPG and SPCK never had a monopoly on importing religious literature into Atlantic Canada and senior Anglicans, among them Edward Wix in Newfoundland, worried that sermon books distributed by non-Anglican societies, such as the interdenominational Religious Tract Society (formed 1799), spread damaging evangelical principles.[67] Senior clergymen who identified with the high church tradition, such as Wix, particularly resented the influence of the Newfoundland School Society (NSS), an evangelical voluntary organisation that had been set up in 1823 to teach Newfoundlanders 'the knowledge of the Holy Scriptures and the way of salvation'.[68] Wix suspected that the NSS fraternised too closely with Methodists and taught the Bible without the Prayer Book.

Senior clergymen assumed that for all Atlantic Canada's variety, a sense of simultaneity, unity and common identity could be promoted if worship was standardised around set forms – this meant providing inhabitants with copies of the Book of Common Prayer and educating them on its use. The Prayer Book was the most requested and most circulated Anglican religious text in the eighteenth and nineteenth centuries. The final section considers how the book was adapted to local conditions, as well as used to create an imperial and global community of settlers, converts and missionaries.

The Book of Common Prayer in the north Atlantic region

Ever since 1662 and the Act of Uniformity, the Prayer Book had been, alongside the thirty-nine articles, the foundational text of Anglican belief and identity. Every ordained clergyman was required to follow the forms of prayer and worship as laid down in the 1662 book: its rules for when and how the Bible and psalms should be read; the collects and epistles to be used throughout the week; its services of morning and evening prayer; and the forms for baptism, marriage, confirmation and ordination. Dissenters argued that Prayer Book liturgy made services in the Anglican Church repetitive, rigid and, as one Nova Scotian missionary put it, 'forms without spirit'.[69] Anglicans, by contrast, emphasised the value of set forms of prayer. Thomas Taylor's *Why Are You a Churchman?* (1811), a tract widely distributed in Atlantic Canada, noted that 'the purposes of prayer are most effectively answered, when all the congregation unite in a known and accustomed formulary'.[70] Set forms of prayer made worship understandable and collective: they were shared by the community, and strengthened the bonds between worshippers and between congregations and ministers. Forms also reminded worshippers that other people, elsewhere in the world, participated in the same services with 'identical words and formulations'.[71] Interestingly, one Nova Scotian missionary thought set forms allowed the Church to appeal to deaf people who could read; such individuals would have been lost in evangelical churches where improvised prayer was prioritised.[72]

To assess the significance of the Prayer Book in Atlantic Canada it must be known how regularly it was read, heard and used. Anglican missionaries usually wanted a book distributed gratis to every person, as unless the book was frequently read, inhabitants might retain their old biases against liturgical worship and would not understand or join in the service (missionaries tended to assume that hostility to Anglican worship would wither away as worshippers became more familiar with Prayer Book worship). William Twining, SPG missionary at Liverpool, Nova Scotia, said people stayed away from his church services because there were too few free books and it was widely believed 'that whoever goes to Church should have a book to follow the minister in his devotions'.[73] Though there were grumbles throughout the eighteenth and nineteenth centuries about insufficient copies, the SPCK's distribution networks bore fruit from the second quarter of the nineteenth century. Ministers gave

Prayer Books as prizes to schoolchildren, and in the 1850s some parishioners could buy their own copies.[74] Yet limitations in distribution networks meant books were cherished by families of worshippers. Stories of prized books that had been handed down from generation to generation often made it into missionary publicity, and give some indication of the value that was attached to the book by both clergy and laity.[75]

Provision was made for non-English speakers. Jean-Baptiste Moreau, the first missionary to Halifax's French-speaking 'foreign Protestants', secured French-language Prayer Books from the SPG in the early 1750s, and Paulus Bryzelius applied to Philadelphia for German-language books and then received German Prayer Books with the Anglican communion rite from the SPG in 1771. The society sent Gaelic books to Scottish Highlanders in Prince Edward Island in the 1820s.[76] The Prayer Book was forced on some communities. Attendance at Anglican worship was part of a short-lived plan to transform the Maroons – a community of fugitive slaves who had been resettled from Jamaica to Preston, Nova Scotia in 1796 – into a 'godly community' and a 'black peasantry'.[77] Thomas Wood worked on a Mi'kmaq translation Prayer Book in the mid-1760s, but generally the civil and ecclesiastical authorities left the task of educating and 'civilising' the Mi'kmaq to French and Irish Catholic priests.[78] Only for a brief time in New Brunswick in the early 1800s did another voluntary society, the New England Company, attempt to wean the Mi'kmaq from Roman Catholic influence through the establishment of Anglican schools and apprenticeships for Mi'kmaq children. Overall, it is questionable whether the arrival of Anglicanism in Atlantic Canada represented a significant moment in Mi'kmaq history.

Jeremy Gregory points out in a recent study that in Georgian England the Prayer Book was popular and deeply embedded in community life. Parishioners heard the same words and forms of prayer again and again and could memorise large parts of it. The book also connected the individual to a larger community. Family, friends and congregations witnessed the key rites of passage – baptisms, marriages and burials. Prayer Book forms were highly regarded, even among dissenters.[79] In the colonial world too, there are examples of illiterate colonists repeating prayers and services on their death beds.[80] Missionaries remarked that non-Anglicans knew 'where to apply for the Ordinances in time of needs', and in Newfoundland people asked for baptisms in homes rather than churches, either because they had no suitable clothing, or because they drew a distinction between services and the institutional Church.[81] The text could be an element in an English diasporic identity. The aptly named Horatio Nelson Arnold ministered to an English settlement in New Brunswick in 1834 where the inhabitants 'seemed delighted to respond to those prayers which in former days they had been accustomed to offer up in the Church of their native land'.[82]

But rather than being an ethnic text, Anglican ministers considered their

Prayer Book to be the foundational text of a 'common Protestantism'.[83] Moreau, missionary to French-speaking Protestants in Halifax, had 'some difficulty' in bringing his congregation at Lunenburg to 'answer to the Common Prayers', but in 1760 he said his congregation 'now answer to the Common Prayers as well as any English church'. Peter Delaroche, missionary at Lunenburg, said in 1771 that French-language Prayer Books were in great demand, and when the German Lutheran congregation of St George's, Halifax, applied to the SPG and bishop of Nova Scotia for money for building work on the church in 1807, they confirmed that theirs was a 'Church of the Established Religion wherein Divine Service has been and is to be at all times hereafter Solemnized according to the Order prescribed in the Book of Common Prayer'.[84] The popularity and ethnic appeal of the Prayer Book should not be overstated, however. In the 1790s, it was reported that Maroons continued to bury their dead according to 'Coromantie ceremonies' rather than the Anglican burial service.[85] Robert Vincent, Anglican vicar in Halifax in the 1760s, said the Mi'kmaq population were 'very averse to the Ceremonies of the Church of England, as they have not that Show which is used in the Romish Church'.[86] Black people attended Anglican church services, and after 1800 Anglican bishops commissioned prayer leaders from such communities to set up independent churches and schools for free and enslaved black people. How far worship in these self-governing churches followed Prayer Book forms is unclear since a distinctively experiential and personal religion grew up in these congregations, one that nurtured a wider sense of separation, community and special election.[87]

The prayer book symbolised uniformity, authority and unchanging tradition; its common forms of prayer connected worshippers across space as well as time. By law, the smallest departure from its forms could see a clergyman deprived of his position in New Brunswick.[88] Only in the twentieth century would Canadians adopt a revised version. Yet colonial clergy understood that services might be altered or added to meet circumstances, needs and tastes. In times of war, pestilence and royal celebration, colonial bishops composed special forms of prayer so that communities could implore God's intervention or give thanks for blessings received.[89] Lower clergy were prepared to make unauthorised changes to Prayer Book forms in the interests of retaining a congregation. William Ellis of Windsor, Nova Scotia denied that clergymen had a 'discretionary power' to alter forms, but in the 1770s even he had to leave the Athanasian Creed out of worship (the book instructed the Creed to be read for festivals and some other holy days) because his people – mostly New Englanders from dissenting backgrounds – considered it harsh and dogmatic.[90] Roger Aitken, the Lunenburg missionary, complained that his congregation, which included many of German descent, forced him to leave out the offertory collection for the poor from Holy Communion. Aitken's parishioners also asked him to drop the Litany, the general supplication used throughout the week, presumably because it was so long, though possibly also because it was a political text that contained prayers for the royal family, the nobility, bishops and other guardians of the English status quo.[91]

To survive, the Church had to hand over use of the Prayer Book to laypersons. In Newfoundland especially, Anglican ministers recognised that the Church could only maintain a presence if 'well-disposed' laypersons – usually male – read services and prayers whenever clergymen were absent.[92] Clergymen who came later in the nineteenth century complained that the freedom enjoyed by lay leaders damaged the standing of the ministry. The missionary at Harbour Briton said in the 1850s that his community had an 'utter ignorance of the office and benefit of the ministry', as there was a 'rooted idea that any one who could read was equally competent'.[93]

Yet lay usage of the Prayer Book did not necessarily separate laity from clergy, nor did it mean the Church in these Atlantic colonies fragmented to the extent that it had no point of unity.[94] Communities prized resident clergy for various reasons. Ministers enjoyed 'gentlemanly' status and gave new settlements kudos. Clergymen read and wrote letters for illiterate colonists and led freemason lodges. Missionaries provided spiritual and medical care to the sick.[95] Significantly, children who had been baptised at lay-led services were subsequently presented at authorised ceremonies when travelling missionaries arrived. Gauvreau may also have overestimated the extent to which clergymen negotiated with congregations about appropriate forms of worship. Most clergymen in this region refused to dispense with prayers for the monarchy (Gauvreau finds instances of this elsewhere in Canada), and some ministers continued to give the sign of the cross at baptism, against the wishes of their dissenting congregations.[96] Indeed, what emerges from the sources is that what congregations demanded from their clergy was strict adherence to the Prayer Book's forms and instructions. Congregations might look to remove ministers if church services did not take place, if Holy Communion was celebrated infrequently and if festivals were ignored.[97]

Conclusion

The Anglican world described in this chapter was challenged after the 1830s, as Church of England bishops became more visible and authoritative figures. Additional Church of England bishoprics appeared at Newfoundland in 1839 and Fredericton in 1845, and the first incumbents – Edward Feild and John Medley – were high churchmen who had been influenced by a revival of ritualistic high churchmanship known as the 'Oxford Movement' (or 'Tractarianism' to its detractors). This revival of Anglican high churchmanship brought along new conceptions of priestly authority and a harder attitude towards the culture of lay-led worship.[98] Hibbert Binney, the Oxford-influenced bishop of Nova

Scotia from 1850, faced accusations of 'Popery' when he required baptisms and marriages to be 'performed with the proper service in Church instead of in the midst of a festive party in the Drawing-room'.[99] New bishops needed cathedrals, and this meant converting parish churches and wrestling control of ecclesiastical property from lay trustees.[100] Developing a sense of unity and 'diocesan consciousness'[101] between congregations was another chief preoccupation of these bishops. Each set up the diocesan 'church societies' and synods that would organise church finances and government and draw the attention of clergy and churchgoers away from purely local concerns. The kind of mixed denominational congregations often found in the early colonial period also died away as non-Anglican ministers and permanent places of worship became more numerous. The flow of religious literature across the Atlantic decreased as religious publishing developed in the colonies and as new types of church party – low church, orthodox high church, Tractarian and broad church – used religious periodicals to broadcast their versions of Anglicanism.

Yet it took time for such Tractarian forms as Gothic architecture, surpliced choirs, sung services, kneeling at prayer, altar lights, incense and the elevation of the elements at Holy Communion to take root in what would become eastern and north-eastern Canada. Though Tractarians insisted that their changes were in conformity with the Prayer Book rubric, many churchgoers, those who would be identified as 'evangelical' or 'low church', regarded such signs of advanced ritualism as innovations and unjustifiable alterations to an ancient tradition of Prayer Book worship.[102] Other aspects of the pioneer Anglicanism sketched in this chapter continued to shape the Church of England experience in Atlantic Canada after 1850. Anglican missionaries still baptised dissenting children in private homes and continued to bend Anglican teachings (for instance, fully immersing children as opposed to sprinkling them with font water) to maintain an appeal. The diocese remained a distant and insignificant entity for many churchgoers. Some congregations, among them St Paul's, Halifax, wanted nothing to do with episcopal authority and refused to send lay representatives to synods. Binney in Nova Scotia noted as late as 1880 that the two wealthiest congregations in his bishopric, St Paul's, Halifax, and St Paul's, Charlottetown, were controlled by Irish evangelical rectors and were 'not even nominally connected' to the diocese.[103] John Medley complained to the SPG in the 1850s that in the Church of England in New Brunswick there was 'no centre of unity other than the bishop'.[104] While such a statement says a good deal about the new emphasis on the figure and authority of the bishop in Anglican expansion in the second half of the nineteenth century, it overlooks the fundamental role that prayer books and laypersons continued to play in maintaining what had always been a dispersed and cosmopolitan Anglican communion.

Notes

1. Phillip A. Buckner and John G. Reid (eds), *The Atlantic Region to Confederation: A History* (Toronto: University of Toronto Press, 1994); Valerie Wallace, *Scottish Presbyterianism and Settler Colonial Politics: Empire Of Dissent* (Basingstoke: Palgrave Macmillan, 2018); S. Karly Kehoe, 'Catholic Relief and the Political Awakening of Irish Catholics in Nova Scotia, 1780-1830', *Journal of Imperial and Commonwealth History*, 46:1 (2018), pp. 1-20; Terrence Murphy and Cyril J. Byrne (eds), *Religion and Identity: The Experience of Irish and Scottish Catholics in Atlantic Canada* (St John's: Jesperson Press, 1987); G. A. Rawlyk, *Ravished by the Spirit: Religious Revivals, Baptists, and Henry Alline* (Montreal and Kingston: McGill-Queen's University Press, 1984). The standard survey of Anglicanism in Atlantic and Maritime Canada is Thomas R. Millman, *Atlantic Canada to 1900: A History of the Anglican Church* (Toronto: Anglican Book Centre, 1983).
2. Barry L. Craig, *Apostle to the Wilderness: Bishop John Medley and the Evolution of the Anglican Church* (Madison-Teaneck: Fairleigh Dickinson University Press, 2005), p. 54.
3. Judith Fingard, *The Anglican Design in Loyalist Nova Scotia, 1783-1816* (London: SPCK, 1972).
4. Henry Roper, 'Aspects of the History of a Loyalist College: King's College, Windsor and Nova Scotia Higher Education in the Nineteenth Century', *Anglican and Episcopal History*, 60:4 (1991), pp. 443, 447.
5. D. G. Bell, 'Charles Inglis and the Anglican Clergy of Loyalist New Brunswick', *Nova Scotia Historical Review*, 7:1 (1987), pp. 46-7.
6. Ross Hebb, *Samuel Seabury and Charles Inglis: Two Bishops, Two Churches* (Madison: Fairleigh Dickinson University Press, 2010), pp. 13, 42.
7. Michael Gauvreau, 'The Dividends of Empire: Church Establishments and Contested British Identities in the Canadas and the Maritimes, 1780-1850', in Nancy Christie (ed.), *Transatlantic Subjects: Ideas, Institutions, and Social Experience in Post-Revolutionary British North America* (Montreal and Kingston: McGill-Queen's University Press, 2008), pp. 199-250.
8. Calvin Hollett, *Beating Against the Wind: Popular Opposition to Bishop Feild and Tractarianism in Newfoundland and Labrador, 1844-1876* (Montreal and Kingston: McGill-Queen's University Press, 2016), pp. 77, 109, 291.
9. Scott Mandelbrote, 'The Publishing and Distribution of Religious Books by Voluntary Associations: From the Society for Promoting Christian Knowledge to the British and Foreign Bible Society', in Michael F. Suarez and Michael L. Turner (eds), *The Cambridge History of the Book in Britain. Volume V: 1695-1830* (Cambridge: Cambridge University Press, 2009), pp. 613-30.
10. Jeremy Gregory, 'Introduction', in Jeremy Gregory (ed.), *The Oxford History of Anglicanism. Volume II: Establishment and Empire* (Oxford: Oxford University Press, 2017), pp. 15-16; Gregory, 'Transatlantic Anglican Networks, c.1680-c.1770: Transplanting, Translating and Transforming the Church of England', in Gregory and Hugh McLeod (eds), *International Religious Networks* (Woodbridge, 2012), pp. 127-43; Michael Gladwin, 'The Book of Common Prayer in Australia', *St Mark's Review*, 222 (2012), pp. 75-88; Brian Cummings, *The Book of Common Prayer: A Very Short Introduction* (Oxford: Oxford University Press, 2018), ch. 5.
11. Hollett, '"I'd rather have a Prayer Book than a shirt": The Printed Word among Methodists and Anglicans in Nineteenth-Century Outport Newfoundland and Labrador', *Newfoundland and Labrador Studies*, 12:2 (2017), pp. 315-43.
12. James B. Bell, 'North America', in Gregory, *Oxford History of Anglicanism*, II, pp. 177-87.
13. Ernest Hawkins, *Historical Notices of the Missions of the Church of England in the North American Colonies* (London: B. Fellowes, 1845), p. 348.
14. James W. St G. Walker, *The Black Loyalists: The Search for a Promised Land in Nova Scotia and Sierra Leone, 1783-1870* (Toronto: University of Toronto Press, 1976), p. 82.

15. Gregory, 'Refashioning Puritan New England: The Church of England in British North America, c.1680–1770', *Transactions of the Royal Historical Society*, 6.20 (2010), p. 101.
16. C. E. Thomas, 'Wood, Thomas', *Dictionary of Canadian Biography*, vol. 4, <http://www.biographi.ca/en/bio/wood_thomas_1711_78_4E.html> (last accessed 20 October 2019).
17. Charles Lawrence to the Board of Trade, 12 January 1760, Heritage Canadiana. Available at <http://heritage.canadiana.ca/> (hereafter HC), United Society for the Propagation of the Gospel fonds, microfilm H-1994, B25, f. 19.
18. Jerry Bannister, 'Atlantic Canada in an Atlantic World? Northeastern North America in the Long 18th Century', *Acadiensis*, 43:2 (2014), pp. 16, 24–5.
19. Fingard, *Anglican Design*.
20. Trudi Johnson, '"A matter of custom and conscience": Marriage Law in Nineteenth-Century Newfoundland', *Newfoundland and Labrador Studies*, 19:2 (2003), <https://journals.lib.unb.ca/index.php/nflds/article/view/159/270> (last accessed 20 October 2019).
21. James B. Bell, 'North America', pp. 185–6; Fingard, *Anglican Design*, pp. 111–12.
22. D. G. Bell, 'Charles Inglis and the Anglican Clergy', pp. 33, 36.
23. Fingard, *Anglican Design*, p. 42.
24. John Harries to SPG, 28 October 1788, USPG Archives (hereafter USPG), Bodleian Libraries Special Collections, Oxford, C/CAN/NFL/1/219/62.
25. Fingard, *Anglican Design*, p. 26; Bell, 'Charles Inglis and the Anglican Clergy', pp. 39–41.
26. Gauvreau, 'The Dividends of Empire', pp. 199–213.
27. Winthrop P. Bell, *The 'Foreign Protestants' and the Settlement of Nova Scotia* (Toronto: University of Toronto Press, 1961), pp. 586–98.
28. Roger Aitken to Bishop John Inglis of Nova Scotia, 20 September 1822, HC, H-1995, C/1/1/19, f. 649.
29. Ranna Cossit, missionary in Cape Breton, told his congregation in the 1790s that only Anglicans could be 'true subjects' of the King: Cossit to SPG, 30 September 1795, HC, H-1995, C/1/1/15, f. 199.
30. Fingard, *Anglican Design*, p. 117.
31. Ibid., pp. 169–70.
32. Jacob G. Mountain, *Some Account of the Sowing Time on the Rugged Shores of Newfoundland* (London: SPG, 1857), p. 33.
33. Gauvreau, 'The Dividends of Empire', p. 213.
34. Edward Wix to SPG, 12 October 1830, USPG, C/CAN/NS/16/6.
35. Fingard, *Anglican Design*, pp. 164–70.
36. Terrence Murphy, 'Trusteeship in Atlantic Canada: The Struggle for Leadership among the Irish Catholics of Halifax, St John's, and Saint John, 1780–1850', in Terrence Murphy and Gerald Stortz (eds), *Creed and Culture: The Place of English-speaking Catholics in Canadian Society, 1750–1930* (Montreal and Kingston: McGill-Queen's University Press, 1993), pp. 126–50; George W. Hill, 'History of St Paul's Church', *Collections of the Nova Scotia Historical Society*, vol. II, (Halifax, NS: Morning Herald, 1883), pp. 14–69.
37. Fingard, *Anglican Design*, 166; congregation of Saint George's to lieutenant governor Sir George Prevost, 7 May 1811, Public Archives of Nova Scotia (PANS), Saint George's Church, Parish Records, 1799–1814, Microfilm 11,475.
38. Imported English gravestones are noted in *Church in the Colonies. No. XXI. Journal of the bishop of Newfoundland's voyage of visitation and discovery, of the south and west coasts of Newfound and on the Labrador, in the church ship 'Hawk', in the year 1849* (London: SPG, 1849), p. 51.
39. David Manning, 'Anglican Religious Societies, Organizations, and Missions', in Gregory, *The Oxford History of Anglicanism*. II, p. 430.
40. Mandelbrote, 'The Publishing and Distribution of Religious Books', pp. 616–22, 629.
41. Manning, 'Anglican Religious Societies', p. 439.

42. W. O. B. Allen and Edward McClure, *Two Hundred Years: The History of the Society for Promoting Christian Knowledge, 1698–1898* (London: SPCK, 1898), pp. 312–13.
43. Janet B. Friskney, 'Christian Faith in Print', in Patricia L. Fleming, Gilles Gallichan and Yvan Lamonde (eds), *History of the Book in Canada. Volume One: Beginnings to 1840* (Toronto: University of Toronto Press, 2004), pp. 140, 143.
44. Richard Vaudry, *Anglicans and the Atlantic World: High Churchmen, Evangelicals and the Quebec Connection* (Montreal and Kingston: McGill-Queen's University Press, 2003), pp. 10–11, 73–87.
45. Charles Inglis to George Pretyman-Tomline, 23 June 1795, PANS, MG1-480, Letters of Charles Inglis, ff. 80–1; Pretyman-Tomline, *A Charge Delivered to the Clergy of the Diocese of Lincoln, at the Triennial Visitation of that Diocese. In May and June 1794* (London: T. C. Adell, 1794), p. 20.
46. Edward Wix, *Six Months of a Newfoundland Missionary's Journal, from February to August, 1835*, 2nd edn (London: Smith, Elder and Co., 1836), pp. 27, 39–40; Hollett, 'The Printed Word', p. 328.
47. Gregory, 'Transatlantic Anglican Networks', p. 133.
48. USPG, X-755, 'Catalogue of books delivered and sent to the Society's missionaries, 1791–1821'.
49. Common titles included Josiah Woodward's *A Disswasive from the sin of Drunkenness* (first published 1701), *An Earnest Perswasive to the Serious Observance of the Lord's Day* (1704) and his *The baseness and perniciousness of the sin of slandering and back-biting* (1706).
50. Andrew Braddock, 'Domestic Devotion and the Georgian Church', *Journal of Anglican Studies*, 16:2 (2018), pp. 188–206.
51. Nancy Christie and Michael Gauvreau, *Christian Churches and Their Peoples, 1840–1965: A Social History of Religion in Canada* (Toronto: University of Toronto Press, 2010), pp. 18–19.
52. Paulus Bryzelius to SPG, 9 January 1769, HC, H-1994, B25, f. 344.
53. Peter Delaroche (Lunenburg, NS) to SPG, 2 August 1779, HC, H-1994, B25, f. 677.
54. Gregory, 'Transatlantic Anglican Networks', pp. 136–7. For similar objections among English worshippers, see Gregory, '"For all sorts and conditions of men": The Social Life of the Book of Common Prayer during the Long Eighteenth Century: Or, Bringing the History of Religion and Social History Together', *Social History*, 34:1 (2009), pp. 41–4.
55. William Walker (missionary at St Eleanor's, PEI) to SPG, 2 July 1829, USPG, C/CAN/NS/5/63/258; Horatio Nelson Arnold (Granville, NS) to SPG, C/CAN/NS/4/50/194; James Somerville (Fredericton, NB) to SPG, 2 December 1823, C/CAN/NB/1/157/124.
56. Gregory, 'Transatlantic Anglican Networks', pp. 136–7.
57. Ibid. p. 138.
58. Examples include Beilby Porteus, *Archbishop Secker's Five Sermons against Popery* (1781) and Edmund Gibson, *Preservative against Popery* (1738). Harries to SPG, 20 November 1809, USPG, C/CAN/NFL/1/219/84. Peter Delaroche in Nova Scotia made the point about unintended consequences as early as 1771: Delaroche to SPG, 28 November 1771, HC, H-1994, B25, f. 514.
59. Horatio Nelson Arnold (Granville), 12 July 1824, USPG, C/CAN/NS/4/50/194.
60. Lewis Bagot, *A Serious Caution against the Dangerous Errors of the Anabaptists* (London, F. and C. Rivington, 1807).
61. Zachary Pearce, *A Sermon on Self-Murder* 3rd edn. (London, 1736).
62. Abel S. Gore to John Inglis, 10 April 1829, USPG, C/CAN/NS/4/39/15.
63. James Cochran to John Inglis, 10 June 1829, USPG, C/CAN/NS/8/68/368.
64. Joseph Hardwick, *An Anglican British World: The Church of England and the Expansion of the Settler Empire, c.1790–1860* (Manchester: Manchester University Press, 2014), ch. 5.
65. Miles Ogborn, *The Freedom of Speech: Talk and Slavery in the Anglo-Caribbean World* (Chicago: Chicago University Press, 2019), ch. 4.

66. John Clinch to SPG, 2 December 1803 and 8 August 1817, USPG, C/CAN/NFL/1/218/41 and /61; John Burnyeat to Bishop John Inglis, 22 August 1820, C/CAN/NS/3/32/339; David Rowland to SPG, 22 December 1812, USPG, C/CAN/NFL/2/232/217.
67. Wix to SPG, 15 October 1831, USPG, C/CAN/NS/16/20.
68. Carey, *God's Empire*, pp. 154–8.
69. Joseph Wright (Horton) to SPG, 9 November 1824, USPG, C/CAN/NS/3/19/243.
70. Thomas G. Taylor, *An Answer to the Question: Why Are You a Churchman?*, 5th edn (London: F. C. and J. Rivington, 1811), p. 48.
71. Gregory, 'Introduction', p. 16; Cummings, *The Book of Common Prayer*, p. 45.
72. James Cochran (Lunenburg) to bishop of Nova Scotia, 10 February 1843, USPG, C/CAN/NS/8/68/389.
73. William Twining to SPG, 3 January 1824, HC, C1/1/12, f. 113–15.
74. William Cochran to SPG, 24 January 1831, HC, C1/1/16, f. 265; G. Schofield to SPG, 12 December 1859, HC, microfilm H-1997, ff. 443–5.
75. Hollett, 'The Printed Word', pp. 326–7.
76. Paulus Bryzelius to SPG, 18 December 1767 and August 1771, HC, H-1994, B25, f. 299, 434; L. C. Jenkins to SPG, 30 November 1823, UPSG, C/CAN/NS/4/41/23.
77. Ruma Chopra, 'Maroons and Mi'kmaq in Nova Scotia, 1796–1800', *Acadiensis*, 46:1 (2017), pp. 20–1.
78. Helen Ralston, 'Religion, Public Policy, and the Education of Micmac Indians of Nova Scotia, 1605–1872', *Canadian Review of Sociology*, 18:4 (1981), pp. 478–82, 485–6.
79. Gregory, 'The Social Life of the Book of Common Prayer', pp. 29–54.
80. Joshua W. Weeks (New Dublin, NS) to SPG, 1 January 1842, USPG, C/CAN/NS/564/271.
81. Charles Inglis (Sydney, CB) to bishop of Nova Scotia, 1 January 1839, HC, H-1995, C.1/1/18, f. 409; Wix, *Six months*, 44. For private baptisms where church services were available, see Henry Starmer to SPG, 26 September 1850, HC, microfilm H-1995, D10, ff. 110–14.
82. Horatio Nelson Arnold to SPG, July entry from 1834 journal, C/CAN/NB/4/191/522; Edward Langman (St John's) to SPG, 15 November 1773, HC, H-1994, B6, f. 237.
83. Gauvreau, 'The Dividends of Empire', p. 218.
84. Moreau to SPG, 15 October 1760, and Delaroche to SPG, 28 November 1771, HC, H-1994, B25, f. 25–6, 513; Winthrop P. Bell, *The 'Foreign Protestants'*, pp. 628–9; Congregation of St George's to Charles Inglis, 31 March 1808, PANS, Microfilm 11,475.
85. R. C. Dallas, *The History of the Maroons, from their Origin to the Establishment of their Chief Tribe at Sierra Leone*, vol. II (London: A. Strahan, 1803), pp. 221–9; 251–2.
86. Robert Vincent to SPG, 29 April 1765, HC, H-1994, B25, f. 160.
87. St G. Walker, *The Black Loyalists*, pp. 67–71, 80–7.
88. Hebb, *Samuel Seabury and Charles Inglis*, pp. 91–2.
89. Hardwick, 'Fasts, Thanksgivings and Senses of Community in Nineteenth-Century Canada and the British Empire', *Canadian Historical Review*, 98:4 (2017), pp. 675–703.
90. William Ellis to SPG, 14 September 1776, HC, H-1994, B25, f. 617.
91. Roger Aitken to John Inglis, 20 September 1822, HC, H-1995, C/1/1/19, f. 592; Cummings, *The Book of Common Prayer*, p. 56.
92. James Balfour to SPG, 18 June 1770, HC, microfilm H-1994, B6, f. 166.
93. Mountain, *Some Account*, p. 13.
94. Gregory, 'The Social Life of the Book of Common Prayer', p. 30.
95. Diary of Henry Lind, OMF.002, Memorial University of Newfoundland's Department of Archives and Special Collections, St John's.
96. William Ellis to SPG, 14 September 1776, HC, microfilm H-1994, B25, f. 617.
97. Petition of inhabitants of St John's, Newfoundland, to SPG, complaining about Edward Langman: 9 November 1765, HC, H-1994, B6, f. 105.

98. Hollett, *Beating Against the Wind*; Craig; *Apostle to the Wilderness*.
99. Hibbert Binney to SPG, 17 February 1853, HC, H-1996, D10, f. 598.
100. Craig, *Apostle to the Wilderness*, pp. 56-8.
101. The term is from Arthur Burns, *The Diocesan Revival in the Church of England, c.1800–1870* (Oxford: Oxford University Press, 1999).
102. Christopher F. Headon, 'Developments in Canadian Anglican worship in Eastern and Central Canada, 1840–1868', *Journal of the Canadian Church Historical Society*, 17 (1975), pp. 26-36.
103. Binney to SPG, 17 January 1880, HC, H-2004, D54, f. 313.
104. Medley to SPG, 10 July 1856, HC, H-1997, D11, f. 240.

EIGHT

'For Christ and Covenant': Scottish Presbyterian Dissent and Early Political Reform in Nova Scotia, 1803–1832

Holly Ritchie

In 1928, an American delegate stood before the Church of Scotland General Assembly and asserted that 'wherever a great piece of work is being done a Scot is at the back of it, and whenever there is an ecclesiastical dispute a Scot is at the bottom of it'.[1] A century prior to this speech, a missionary described as a man of 'inflexible firmness not inferior to John Knox himself', made his way across the Atlantic.[2] Reverend Dr Thomas McCulloch, who had been sent to Nova Scotia on behalf of the Anti-burgher Secession Synod, was convinced by Reverend James MacGregor, of the General Associate Presbytery, along with the town's influential merchant, Edward Mortimer, to join them in Pictou, Nova Scotia.[3] While much is known about McCulloch's educational work, less attention has been paid to the ways in which his political activism and Scottish Presbyterian background informed his relationships within the colony. Events in Pictou County, located in eastern Nova Scotia, offer an important insight into the strains of sectarianism transported by Scottish migrants and reflect the way in which Scottish religious identity was exhibited in a British colonial context.[4] This chapter explores how McCulloch applied a politico-religious approach to his struggle to secure permanent pecuniary aid for Pictou Academy on the same basis as the colony's first institution of higher learning, King's College. While McCulloch's institution was intended to be the colony's first non-sectarian institute of higher education, the Pictou Academy was an institution closely aligned with dissenting Presbyterianism, and King's College was the design of established Anglicanism. As a consequence, both were deliberate attempts to impose religious ideology upon Nova Scotia's emerging educational landscape. The Academy debate, however, extended far beyond this, and represented the beginning of party politics in Nova Scotia.

The formation of a Scottish Diasporic identity has attracted significant interest from academic researchers and from the wider public, but a less well understood aspect of Scottish settlement is just how influential Presbyterian dissenters were to the development of colonial politics. Nova Scotia presents an important opportunity to explore this theme, particularly in relation to how far Scottish dissenting politics shaped strategies for securing equal consideration for non-conforming Protestants: the Church of England was established by law in Nova Scotia and enjoyed privileges that McCulloch believed to be undue. By focusing on the dissenting tradition that connected Scotland and Nova Scotia, this chapter's exploration of McCulloch's influence over colonial reform expands our understanding of how far the colonial environment could accommodate Scottish religious identity within the context of Britain's imperial world. There is no doubt that McCulloch saw his campaign – a movement designed to end Anglican privilege and replace it with a system which afforded dissenting communities equal consideration in government decisions – as one that was couched within the context of Scottish Covenanting ideology. Valerie Wallace has demonstrated the importance of Covenanting ideology to McCulloch's political strategy and at the same time has emphasised the tendency in Canada's politico-religious historiography to ignore the importance of the Atlantic colonies.[5] All the same, Michael Gauvreau's examination of the Covenanting influence on politics in Upper Canada has emphasised the importance of understanding the environment in which dissidence was reared. He has observed that early political disaffection was often fought across religious lines and so frustration was regularly expressed within a shared language.[6]

In Nova Scotia, McCulloch viewed the contest with the Anglican establishment as analogous to the Covenanting struggle in Scotland, and he drew upon that memory to authenticate and advance his campaign for equal consideration. Scotland's Covenanting tradition stemmed from a radical movement which sought to preserve Presbyterianism as the 'true religion' by preventing state intrusion into spiritual affairs following the ascension of King James VI and I in 1603 and, later, Charles II. The Covenanters possessed a form of radical constitutionalism that challenged the notion of the divine right of kings.[7] The intransigence of Charles II on this point led to a series of armed revolts, and culminated in the 1679 battles at Bothwell Brig and Drumclog. In 1685 the Privy Council sanctioned the execution of the Covenanters, who bore arms in protest against prerogative power. This became known as 'The Killing Time', even though few people were actually executed. This episode became pivotal to the emergence of a 'Covenanting martyrology', and enshrined a culture of religious dissent that would shape Scottish society for generations and follow many of its people abroad.[8]

Covenanting itself had grown out of the widespread adoption of a particular strain of Protestantism in Scotland. Following the sixteenth-century Reformation, Scotland's reformers looked to Geneva and to John Calvin's doctrinal model, which emphasised Predestination and the sovereignty of God, for theological inspiration.[9] Calvin's spiritual doctrine was implemented aggressively across much of Scotland, and Catholicism was all but wiped out save a few pockets in the Western Highlands and Islands, Aberdeenshire and Kirkcudbrightshire.[10] Calvinism was expressed through the Westminster Confession of Faith; unlike the Reformed English Church, the Kirk (as the Presbyterian Church came to be known) had no prayer-book and instead called for a strict adherence to the liturgy of a community church and informal prayer, family worship and the Holy Fair.[11]

The primacy of Presbyterianism in Scotland, with its myriad of internal divisions, meant that significant tensions between Presbyterianism and Anglicanism informed local religious practice, culture, state development and colonial interactions. Significantly, the structural differences between the reformed churches shaped how the British settler population engaged within the political sphere in a place like Nova Scotia. The Church of England was essential to the formation of the British state, for it provided protection against religious and political dissidence. Moreover, its top-down structure, headed by the Sovereign, shaped the early governance of the colonies. Scottish Presbyterians, however, rejected the 'unholy' partnership between the church and state and opted instead to promote 'twa kingdoms': the spiritual realm guided by Christ, and the temporal kingdom supervised by a 'worldly monarch'.[12] Additionally, the Kirk was governed by a system of four Church Courts, which, with the exception of Kirk sessions, were open to every class of people for observation. This style of participatory decision-making certainly informed McCulloch's political strategy and colonial vision, and led to assertions of the Kirk's democratic character.[13] The Stuart dynasty disrupted this dualism, and the events that culminated in 'The Killing Time' were invoked centuries later to justify resistance to state interference with spiritual affairs in Scotland and Nova Scotia.

The religious divisions which beset Scotland were transported across the Atlantic by the settlers. McCulloch, for example, was an ardent critic of Anglican privilege, and an examination of his ineffectual campaign to challenge this in Nova Scotia reveals how the Scots asserted Presbyterian values in this colonial environment and how they interacted with each other and other settler communities. Pictou Academy thus became a 'magnet for old resentments' between those who supported the established Church of England, the Kirk, and dissenting Presbyterians who did not.[14] In Nova Scotia, these factions clashed, and by targeting the Academy and supporting the campaign of the colony's governing council to undermine efforts to 'increase the levelling spirit', adherents of the Kirk revealed a preference for a closer connection with the established Church in the colony.[15] The Kirk in Nova Scotia sought to establish a foothold within the British Empire; it was not really challenging the Church of England's hegemony. The Scots could be, as Richard J. Finlay noted, loyal to both their Scottish and British identities without contradiction.[16] This essential dichotomy is perhaps why McCulloch felt that, as a loyal citizen, he was perfectly entitled to criticise the colonial government and why the Kirk's support of the colonial establishment in Nova Scotia failed to generate genuine criticism at a civic level. As T. C. Smout pointed out, it was perfectly reasonable for the Scots to think of themselves as Scottish when connecting with a particular region and culture, and British when discussing Empire, foreign policy and the Crown.[17] Such concentric loyalties complemented the Scots' colonial ambitions and allowed them to manage their identities at both the civic and governmental levels; to challenge or to adapt to the colonial environment of Nova Scotia.

While Nova Scotia's demographic landscape was characterised by a diverse settler population, Anglicanism was prioritised by the governing elite. Although the liturgy of the Church of England was established by law as the national religion of the colony, toleration was afforded to non-conforming Protestants when 'The Act of the Establishment of Religious Publick [sic] Worship in this Province and for Suppressing Popery' was sanctioned in 1758.[18] This Act was significant because it enshrined free liberty of conscience, the right to establish meeting houses and an exemption from the payment of rates and taxes levied in support of the Church of England on non-conforming Protestants. Although this culture of toleration was initially intended to keep dissenting groups on side following the American War of Independence, it was seen as unsustainable because it demonstrated to the metropole the danger of creating political establishments without the security of an ecclesiastical body.[19]

At the end of the Revolutionary War, Loyalist Anglican clergymen had assembled in New York to devise a strategy to protect the established status of the Church of England in Britain's remaining colonies. In 1783, they, with Sir Guy Carleton, the governor general of British North America, submitted a plan to the British government that would protect the primacy of Anglicanism in this region. Their strategy called for a stronger bond between the church and state in Nova Scotia to avoid future rebellion. Specifically, they advised on the establishment of a colonial episcopate, endowed with ecclesiastical authority, alongside the creation of a liberal 'College or Seminary of learning' where 'youth may receive a virtuous education'.[20] This course of action would be, they argued, 'conducive to the permanent loyalty and future tranquillity of that colony'.[21] In both Presbyterian and Anglican circles, education was recognised as the surest means to remedy the ills of society, though dissenting Presbyterians saw it more as a solution to immorality, whereas their Anglican counterparts perceived it more in terms of combating radicalism and securing loyalty to the Crown.

In 1787, Charles Inglis, one of the Loyalist clergymen present at the New York negotiations, was appointed the first colonial bishop. It was a demanding position, and Inglis complained of it being 'difficult and laborious'.[22] He did not see eye to eye with Lieutenant Governor John Parr, who described Inglis as a 'high Churchman . . . who [had] never drank the Glorious memory of King

William'.²³ Yet Inglis proved to be a man strong in the 'old faith', with a hard-line conservativism, and in a sermon preached at St Paul's Church in Halifax in 1793, he emphasised the two pillars of society – government and religion:

> There is a close connection between the duty which we owe to God, and the duty we owe to the King, and to others in authority under him. So intimate is this connection that they can scarcely be separated. Whoever is sincerely religious towards God, from principle and conscience, will also, from principle and conscious, be loyal to his earthly sovereign, obedient to the laws and faithful to the government which God hath placed over him.²⁴

In viewing the Church of England as an apparatus for upholding the loyalty of the inhabitants and as a means of preventing another insurrection in British North America, Inglis spread the doctrine of divine right in Nova Scotia.

The loss of the thirteen colonies marked a 'decisive watershed in shaping colonial Anglicanism' and confirmed for colonial officials, who believed in the interdependency of the church and state, the risk of affording toleration to dissenting groups.²⁵ This thinking shaped decision-making in Nova Scotia. Inglis was acutely aware of the shortage of missionaries and urged the legislative council to assist in developing education in the colony as a means of preventing student departures to the United States, where young people would likely absorb republican principles unfriendly to the British Constitution.²⁶ When King's College was established at Windsor in 1788, the colonial government awarded it a permanent grant of £400 for maintenance: this money was to come from the duties imposed on brown loaf and refined sugars.²⁷ Indeed, King's promised a progressive future for the White Protestant settler population until 1802, when a Royal Charter awarded a further £1,000 in perpetuity on the condition that a committee of governors be appointed to draft statutes based on the model of Oxford University.²⁸ Once drafted and adopted, two points in the statutes meant that 80 per cent of the population was excluded from being able to attend. Firstly, no student was permitted to attend any place of worship where Divine Service was not performed according to the liturgy of the Church of England.²⁹ Secondly, students were required to subscribe to the thirty-nine articles of the Church of England, and the three Articles contained in the 36th Canon of the Synod of London at matriculation and again at convocation.³⁰ Given that the articles of the Church of England made it a 'distinctively English national Church', King's College was moulded as an English institution.³¹

A monopoly over the higher branches of education was just one of the privileges enjoyed by the Church of England. Although King's College emphasised, to the dissenting population, that toleration, as opposed to equality, was the ruling doctrine, McCulloch's campaign for equal consideration centred around the inequitable composition of the legislative council and the authority of the Anglican Bishop. Established in 1719, the council was designed to be an advisory body to the lieutenant governor. While this post was central to the management of colonial affairs, the lieutenant governors assigned to Nova Scotia usually had little experience of colonial administration and no prior knowledge of local conditions; the council had significant authority as a result.[32] Following Inglis's appointment, the church–state relationship was cemented in Nova Scotia because this position came with a seat on the council, a position that was permanent and guaranteed. As a political solution, McCulloch advocated popular sovereignty and retained, with Covenanting vigour, an uncompromising stance against a government founded upon divine right, holy alliances and family compacts.[33] Though an elected legislative assembly had existed since 1758, it lacked autonomy and was regularly challenged by the governing council. What began as a nominal dispute over the distribution of public revenue, as highlighted by McCulloch's failure to secure permanent aid for Pictou Academy, became a larger issue involving the council's right to interfere with legislation after it had secured the approbation of the assembly. McCulloch's campaign to secure permanent pecuniary aid for Pictou Academy, though fought across religious lines, became politicised by default.

The granting of the Royal Charter to King's College and the implementation of the corresponding statutes coincided with the third wave of Scottish immigration to Nova Scotia.[34] McCulloch, who had intended to settle in Prince Edward Island, was among the migrants. In his writing, McCulloch frequently noted his distaste for Anglican privilege and his suspicion of Catholicism, and in 1804, he was engaged in a pamphlet war with Bishop Inglis against Edmund Burke, the Roman Catholic priest who was serving as vicar general in Halifax.[35] Notwithstanding their fleeting allegiance and the fact that the relationship between Inglis and McCulloch was initially polite, their conflicting views on the church–state relationship proved too significant to facilitate any further collaboration. Inglis was not the only Anglican to attempt to connect with McCulloch; in 1809, William Cochran, the Loyalist president of King's College, asked him to transfer his allegiance to the Church of England from the associate presbytery of Pictou. Cochran believed that church government was a 'thing of inferior importance'; McCulloch rejected that position, and the invitation.[36]

Pictou Academy was born out of similar anxieties to those that were expressed by the clergymen in New York and by Bishop Inglis. Reverend James MacGregor, McCulloch's ally, wrote a letter to the *Christian Magazine* wherein he reflected upon the 'mournful state' of the country settlements and opined that the lack of missionaries had hindered the progress of Presbyterianism in the colony.[37] Despite their doctrinal differences, the dissenting Presbyterian ministers agreed with Inglis that an institution for the instruction of home-grown missionaries was the only resolution to the 'destitute situation'.[38] They concurred that education was the surest way to maintain peace, increase piety and secure economic prosperity for the 'benefit of mankind'.[39] In 1818, McCulloch made a final bid to solicit the support of the legislative assembly and invoked the memory of the American War, reminding officials of the consequences of allowing young minds to be charmed by the 'specious appearance' of republicanism.[40]

A lack of funds did not deter McCulloch, who initially gave lessons in his home until the reputation of his school necessitated a larger space. On his property, he constructed a log building which became a grammar school and the foundation for Pictou Academy. As young men travelled from 'almost every county, Cape Breton Island, Prince Edward Island and the West Indies', McCulloch recognised the urgent need for expansion.[41] The colonial legislature's 'Act to Establish Grammar Schools in Several Counties and Districts', which had been passed in 1811, enabled him to apply for support, and later that year he was awarded an annual grant of £150 from the provincial treasury.[42] His teachings, though influential, were not universally supported, and in 1815 the log college was burned down in a reputed act of arson.[43] The hinterland communities operated beyond colonial surveillance and were often governed and controlled by the 'paternalistic rule' of mercantile leaders.[44] Pictou County was overseen by the Legislative Assembly representative Edward Mortimer, who believed that the advancement of the county settlements was impeded by the governing elite in Halifax. The loss of the log college stirred community spirit in Pictou and many of its residents pushed for its reconstruction to 'counteract the influence of the evil element in their midst'.[45] Mortimer approved the construction of a sizeable building on his land, which 'promise[d] with a little cooking and care to become a thriving seminary'.[46] As King's College became a symbol of religious privilege, the rebuilding of McCulloch's school as Pictou Academy was seen as an attempt to promote higher education unimpeded by sectarianism.[47]

McCulloch founded an elected body to devise a plan for Pictou Academy with the approval of the lieutenant governor, George Ramsay, the Earl of Dalhousie.[48] According to their final proposal, the Academy was to be a non-sectarian degree-granting institute that would serve as a seminary for local Presbyterian missionaries. Since Pictou was viewed as a 'den of radicalism', owing to the number of Scottish dissenting settlers, the elected group had to be strategic in their request, and so separated their proposal into parts to expedite approval.[49] Their design could never be adopted in full, since the creation of a non-sectarian but denominational institution of higher learning would challenge the status of the Church of England and create a space wherein dissenting Protestants could unite against Anglicans.[50] The literary historian Gwendolyn Davies notes that Pictou Academy was indeed perceived as a threat to the authority of King's College, and was deeply unsettling to Halifax's governing elite.[51]

The elected body submitted their proposal to the legislative assembly, highlighting only that no religious tests would be administered and that students would not be obliged to attend divine worship within the Academy. The only restriction specified was a prohibition on professing or propagating any 'atheistical or deistical opinions, or any opinions repugnant to loyalty'.[52] Although the legislative assembly approved the bill to establish Pictou Academy, the governing council and acting bishop, John Inglis, Charles Inglis's son, raised concerns over the Academy's open policy. In soliciting the assistance of secessionist lawyer S. G. W. Archibald, who was a member of the legislative assembly and a trustee of Pictou Academy, the elected body secured the Act of Incorporation for the Academy, but with one condition: all Protestant students could attend the institute, but professorships and trusteeships were restricted to Anglicans and Presbyterians. McCulloch agreed to the condition, but the impact of this stipulation was damaging. It was the first time the council successfully hindered the development of Pictou Academy.

As the Anglican-dominated council continued its assault on the Academy, opposition from the Kirk also surfaced. Prior to 1823, Presbyterian spheres of influence did not overlap much in Nova Scotia because Kirk missionaries were concentrated in Halifax and the dissenters were more focused on the remote country settlements. As the Kirk began to evolve, however, its authority spread into dissenting dominated regions such as Pictou County, and in 1823 the first provincial presbytery of the Church of Scotland was established in the county; the bitter sectarianism that plagued Presbyterianism in Scotland and would bring about the 1843 Disruption had been transported to Nova Scotia. McCulloch had recognised the necessity of presenting a united front in support of the Academy and had pushed for a union between the Presbyterian dissenting factions and succeeded in forming the Presbyterian Church of Nova Scotia (PCNS).

On his mission through Nova Scotia, John Inglis remarked that Pictou was a 'fine and rapidly improving country'.[53] He observed that although the majority of the Scottish settlers were originally of the Kirk, the lack of missionary support prior to 1823 had meant that they sought the guidance of the dissenting factions. He noted the growing influence of the Kirk and wrote that 'several ministers ha[d] settled among them, which ha[d] naturally caused some division'.[54] The following year, Kirk minister Kenneth McKenzie, a native of Stornoway, arrived in Pictou. The encroachment of the Kirk into a region considered to be 'the seat of Secessionism', and its attempt to form a partnership with the established Church of England, adds a layer of complexity to the politico-religious environment of Nova Scotia.[55] Although McCulloch believed that he was fighting against the authority of the Church of England, the expansion of the Kirk moved the debate more into the realm of a wider critique of established hierarchies that cut across denominational lines.

In an effort to secure transatlantic support for the Academy, McCulloch returned to Scotland in 1825 and managed to raise £583.16.6.[56] In 1826, the Glasgow Society for Promoting Interests of Religion and Liberal Education among Settlers in British North America was established to consolidate the Scottish connection. The Glasgow Society circulated a pamphlet that outlined the necessity of supporting the development of education in Nova Scotia because of the Anglican threat. It argued that King's College in Windsor was so closely connected with Anglicanism that the 'great body of the inhabitants must either violate their conscientious convictions or exclude themselves from its advantage'.[57] The Oxford model of education was declared too exclusive and unaccommodating to facilitate the development of the colonial environment. This matter was addressed by the Glasgow Society, which argued that:

> It is enough that such evil should exist in England, where it is met by many very effectual antidotes; but it is intolerable that in Nova Scotia, without any antidote, this *virus* should be injected into that infant community, and made to rankle in all its veins.[58]

The Glasgow Society argued that Pictou Academy provided the necessary protection for Protestantism in the colony, and it was clear that McCulloch needed to secure financial support from Scotland if the Academy was to survive the weight of 'insecure and temporary Episcopal ascendency'.[59] In linking Scotland's early religious struggles against unwanted prerogative power with the difficulties unfolding in Nova Scotia, the Glasgow Society sought to inspire a collective responsibility among the Lowland Scots.

In the spring of 1827, the Academy failed to secure the endorsement of the legislative assembly and was publicly criticised by the governing council, which released a report outlining its reasons for refusing its support. The report narrated the council's relationship with Pictou Academy, noting that it had taken an 'active part' in the procurement of their incorporation and that some of its 'most zealous advocates' were of the Church of England.[60] In outlining their reasons for its initial support, the council highlighted that the majority of the inhabitants of the county were 'descendants from natives of Scotland, or emigrants from that country'.[61] Accordingly, the Academy was not born out of hostility towards the Church of England, but rather a natural preference for the Kirk and a longing that many immigrants had to educate their children in the 'religious principles of their forefathers'.[62] In their original design, the trustees had tried to assure members of the legislative assembly that the institution would neither undermine the Church of England nor provoke opposition towards King's College. This fell upon deaf ears. The governing council's report stated that the trustees of 'that Academy' had approved measures to 'excite a spirit of hostility towards the established church among all classes of dissenters' and explained that the council could only support the Academy if the board of trustees were appointed by the lieutenant governor.[63] As an instrument of the state, it is unsurprising that the council nominated the lieutenant governor to replace the disaffected trustees with 'safer' candidates, in an effort to protect their established position, to control information and to supervise more carefully religious dissent in the country settlements. Following the publication of the report, the legislative assembly eventually approved the Academy's £400 grant application, but the governing council remained inflexible on their condition for permanent financial aid.

In the absence of regular colonial support, and dependent on subscriptions which were rarely if ever paid, the Academy's debt mounted. The launch of a Pictou-based newspaper, however, helped reinvigorate support for the school. The *Colonial Patriot* was the first newspaper to be issued outside of Halifax, and according to one commentator it gave a 'voice to the Scottish radicalism of the province and played no small part in the initiation of reform'.[64] The paper was edited by Jotham Blanchard, one of the first graduates of Pictou Academy and the secretary of its board of trustees, who had been influenced by the positive results of the 'unshackled press in Britain'.[65] Although Blanchard is credited with having been the sole editor of the *Patriot*, the strong Covenanting spirit of the periodical suggests that McCulloch influenced a number of its editorials. Although he denied writing for the newspaper, in private correspondence with his friend, Reverend James Mitchell of Glasgow, McCulloch admitted to occasionally writing editorials.[66]

The alliance between the church and the state was regularly commented upon by the *Colonial Patriot*. In 1828, for example, it reported that a 'church support by legal sanctions, had admitted into its constitution an authority which religion declaims: and wherever it uses this authority either to enforce its principles or to ensure its support, it acts in direct opposition to the injunction of Christ'.[67] The article concluded that 'no Scotsman acquainted with the sufferings of the noble army of martyrs, who resisted unto death the tyrannical attempts of Charles II to establish Episcopacy in Scotland, [would] dare to hold up his voice against a constitutional opposition'.[68] In consideration of the growing resistance to passive obedience in the colony, a later editorial declared that the 'community [would] not be put down: it has passed the days in which loyalty claiming its rights quailed in the presence of prelacy and arbitrary power'.[69] By linking the politico-religious struggle unfolding in Nova Scotia to the struggles of the Scottish Covenanters, the paper reinforced the connection between the two campaigns as imagined by McCulloch and became an important tool in his campaign for equal consideration. The Covenanting wars were used in Nova Scotia as a symbol of justified resistance against the authority of the Church of England and the colony's Anglican-dominated governing council.

In the meantime, the *Pictou Observer and Eastern Advertiser*, edited by the Church of Scotland's Kenneth McKenzie, was established to counteract the strength of the dissenters. McKenzie adopted the same view as the Anglicans and used his newspaper to denounce Pictou Academy as an 'Antiburgher nursery', which 'smelt rank of disloyalty and republicanism'.[70] In echoing Bishop Charles Inglis's fears of the 'levelling spirit' claimed by the dissenting population, McKenzie criticised the growth of the 'dangerous spirit of democracy' and condemned those who espoused radical ideologies.[71] The 'levelling spirit', he continued, be it under the guise of an 'assumed liberality of sentiment or the more specious appearance of an anxious desire for the reformation of all abuses', threatened established institutions.[72] In attacking McCulloch's campaign as unjustified, undesired and in danger of 'polluting the stream of good British feeling', McKenzie confirmed his position as an enemy of dissenters.[73] He maintained that national religion was inseparable from the state, and that when 'Britain cease[d] to have an established Church she would cease to have an established kingdom'.[74]

The politico-religious issues that divided Nova Scotia had solidified into a two-sided debate by the 1830s. At a grassroots level, McCulloch viewed his campaign for permanent funding as a religiously charged matter and continued to criticise the unconstitutional privilege of the Church of England, with its oligarchical structures and the Anglican-dominated governing council. While McCulloch failed to recognise the strength of opposition emanating from the Kirk, he did emphasise that Bishops Inglis, junior and senior, were a central obstacle to the progress of Pictou Academy. Like McCulloch, Bishop Inglis's motives, though veiled in religious language, were politically driven. Concerned with retaining the privilege of the Anglican Church, they advised settlers that attachment to the sovereign was strengthened only with the advancement of the established Church and that supporting the church in the colony meant suppressing Pictou Academy.[75] In an effort to avoid the deadlock, George Smith, a trustee and member of the legislative assembly, appointed a committee to examine the journals of the governing council in 1828 and 1830.[76] They found that on two occasions, it was the bishop who had cast the deciding vote against the Academy, and within the council there existed an extreme faction who consistently objected to supporting public schools that did not have established religion as a foundation. Although the group was primarily composed of Anglicans, councillor Michael Wallace of the Church of Scotland, expressed a 'chronic grudge against . . . the secessionist Presbyterians of the Pictou area'.[77] Conversely, in the governing council moderate Anglicans sought to reward the steady loyalty of dissenting Protestants and drafted a report in favour of equal consideration. They cautioned that to continue support for King's would mean exciting further hostility, surmising that every attempt to 'give or retain exclusive privileges to the Church of England had invariably operated to its disadvantage'.[78] The councillors concluded that ruling Anglicans must wield their privilege with caution, and in lending their support to the Academy they would be able to prove to Protestant dissenters that they had 'nothing to fear from the diffusion of knowledge'.[79]

While the reports failed to win government support for the Pictou Academy, they did anticipate a general swing toward political reform in the colony. The 1830 session of the legislative assembly was dissolved following the death of King George IV (1762–1830), necessitating a general election. It was fortuitous that this event coincided with a dispute over the tax collected on imported spirits, which was very much a concern of the privileged. Dubbed the Brandy Election, it gave McCulloch's campaign the opportunity to reach a wider group of Protestant dissenters and led to a rise of political reporting in printed media. The *Colonial Patriot* reported that the brandy dispute had presented Nova Scotians with a 'golden opportunity to agitate for greater representation'; a failure to do so would leave them 'pin[ing] under unconstitutional and oppressive power for another half century'.[80] By contrast, the Halifax-based *Free Press* vindicated the position of the governing council and maintained that pro-reformers sought the removal of the council's privilege to reject decisions made by the legislative assembly only to dispose of 'all the money at [their] own pleasure'.[81] In the lead-up to the election, the *Novascotian*, edited by Joseph Howe, who secured Responsible Government for the province in 1848, continued to write favourably of their position but acknowledged that the council possessed no hereditary rights and held their position only at the 'pleasure of the crown'.[82] Howe's political vision changed dramatically in the post-election period and he conceded that the 'first county of Nova Scotia [had] spoken out with decisions that cannot be misunderstood'.[83] He condemned the governing council as a 'vindictive and irresponsible body'.[84] In response to the victory of the pro-reform candidates, Howe shared in their celebration alongside the *Acadian Recorder* and the *Colonial Patriot*. Although a minor victory, the success of the pro-reform candidates marked an important turning point – it secured greater representation within the colony, and consolidated the partisan role of the press and the development of party-based politics in Nova Scotia. Despite the outcome of the Brandy Election, by the end of the decade McCulloch had failed in his objectives for the Pictou Academy because the governing elite remained intact.

The Pictou Academy controversy had alerted many to the absence of equal consideration in Nova Scotia, and this realisation marked the first step towards dissident communities agitating for greater representation. Using the Academy and King's College as a case study, this chapter has illustrated how religious struggles divided early Nova Scotian politics. Although McCulloch's campaign continued to be fought across religious lines, the debate became politicised because of interdenominational networking on both sides. Indeed, the emergence of early party politics in the province was facilitated by the rise of the print media that had emerged during the controversy. Despite the collapse of McCulloch's campaign, the discussions it prompted, at both civic and governmental levels, surrounding the establishment of a non-sectarian institute of higher learning, provide insight into how dissenting Scottish Presbyterians navigated the demands of the colony while mediating their ambitions as agents of the British Empire. Giving consideration to their concentric loyalties, and to the theological and societal predilections embedded in the Covenanting tradition transplanted from Scotland, helps to explain why McCulloch felt he could criticise the colonial government without surrendering his role as a loyal subject, and why Kirkmen in Nova Scotia opted to support the Church of England and the idea of established hierarchies more broadly rather than consolidating the position of dissenting Presbyterians in the colony.

Notes

1. Lord Sands, 'Historical Origins of the Religious Divisions in Scotland', *Records of the Scottish Church History Society*, 3 (1929), p. 94.
2. Thomas McCulloch, *The Prosperity of the Church in Troublous Times, A Sermon Preached at Pictou Friday February 25 1814 with Introductory Remarks by Rev. Robert Grant* (New Glasgow: S. M. MacKenzie, 1882), pp. 3–4.
3. The Secession Church in Scotland divided in 1747 over the Burgess Oath. The burghs [burgesses] of Edinburgh, Glasgow and Perth were obliged to take the Oath agreeing to adhere to the true religion of Scotland. The ambiguity of the phrase 'true religion' caused many to reject the Oath as unlawful, for they believed that it alluded to the Church of Scotland, which they had rejected. Others argued that it referenced recognised Protestant faith and was intended to protect the burghs against the resurgence of popery. This created a schism within the dissenting church between those who accepted the Oath – the Burghers – and those who denounced it, the Anti-burghers. For more information see: Joel Hiatt and William Owen, *Diary of William Owen from November 10, 1824 to April 20, 1825* (Indianapolis: The Bobbs-Merrill Company, 1906), p. 466; Finlay Macdonald, *From Reform to Renewal: Scotland's Kirk Century by Century* (Edinburgh: Saint Andrew Press, 2017), pp. 103–5; George Patterson, *Memoir of the Reverend James MacGregor, D. D.* (Philadelphia: J. M. Wilson, 1859), pp. 27–8; Alan Wilson, *Highland Shepard: James MacGregor, Father of the Scottish Enlightenment in Nova Scotia* (Toronto: University of Toronto Press, 2015), p. 12; Susan Buggy, 'Mortimer, Edward', *Dictionary of Canadian Biography*, <http://www.biographi.ca/en/bio/mortimer_edward_5E.html> (last accessed 20 October 2019); Holly Ritchie, *For Christ and Covenant: A Movement for Equal Consideration in Early Nineteenth Century Nova Scotia* (MA thesis, Saint Mary's University, 2017), pp. 10–26.
4. Throughout this chapter, sectarianism is used to denote the tensions between various Protestant sects of the Church of Scotland, which formed when the church began to fracture, and the interactions between dissenting Protestants and the established Church of England.
5. Valerie Wallace, *Exporting Radicalism within the Empire: Scots Presbyterian Political Values in Scotland and British North America, c.1815–c.1850* (PhD thesis, Glasgow University, 2010).
6. Michael Gauvreau, 'Covenanter Democracy: Scottish Popular Religion, Ethnicity, and the Varieties of Politico-religious Dissent in Upper Canada, 1815–1841', *Histoire Sociale/Social History*, 36:71 (2003), pp. 55–83.
7. Gauvreau, 'Covenanter Democracy', p. 61.
8. Nicholas Terpstra, *Religious Refugees in the Early Modern World: An Alternative History of the Reformation* (Cambridge: Cambridge University Press, 2015), p. 125.

9. Stewart J. Brown, 'Religion in Scotland', in H. T. Dickinson (ed.), *A Companion to Eighteenth Century Britain* (Oxford: Blackwell, 2002), p. 260.
10. S. Karly Kehoe, *Creating a Scottish Church: Catholicism, Gender and Ethnicity in Nineteenth-Century Scotland* (Manchester: Manchester University Press, 2010), pp. 22–48.
11. Throughout this chapter, the colloquial term 'Kirk' is used to reference the established Church of Scotland as guided by primary documents and to differentiate it from the established Church of England when discussing the politico-religious environment of Nova Scotia. Holy Fair, though there are varied definitions, can be understood as communion/a communal event. For further discussion of Holy Fairs see: Michael P. Carroll, *American Catholics in the Protestant Imagination: Rethinking the Academic Study of Religion* (Baltimore: Johns Hopkins University Press, 2007), pp. 19–20; Leigh Eric Schmidt, *Holy Fairs: Scottish Communions and American Revivals in the Early Modern Period* (Princeton: Princeton University Press, 1989); Gauvreau, 'Covenanter Democracy', p. 59.
12. Mark Goldie, *Locke: Political Essays* (Cambridge: Cambridge University Press, 2004), p. 231; Alasdair I. C. Heron, *Table and Tradition: Towards an Ecumenical Understanding of the Eucharist* (Philadelphia: Westminster Press, 1983), p. 84.
13. H. Moncreiff Wellwood, *Account of the Life and Writings of John Erskine* (Edinburgh: Archibald Constable & Company, 1818), p. 414; Callum G. Brown, 'The People in the Pews: Religion and Society in Scotland since 1790', *Studies in Scottish Economic and Social History*, 3 (1993), p. 10.
14. Wilson, *Highland Shepherd*, p. 159.
15. *Pictou Observer*, 'Sign of the Times', 22 February 1832; 'Political Review', *Pictou Observer*, 7 March 1832. This was in contrast to Upper Canada, where William Morris, a Scottish immigrant and member of the Legislative Council, championed the idea of a dual establishment – Church of Scotland and Church of England. While this failed, Queen's University in Kingston, Ontario was founded as the Presbyterian college in Upper Canada largely due to Morris's efforts. Harry Bridgeman, 'Morris, William', *Dictionary of Canadian Biography*, <http://www.biographi.ca/en/bio/morris_william_8E.html> (last accessed 20 October 2019).
16. Richard J. Finlay, 'Keeping the Covenant: Scottish National Identity', in T. M. Devine and J. R. Young (eds), *Eighteenth Century Scotland: New Perspectives* (East Linton: Tuckwell Press, 1999), p. 122.
17. T. C. Smout, 'Problems of Nationalism, Identity and Improvement in Late Eighteenth Century Scotland', in T. M. Devine, *Improvement and Enlightenment: Proceedings of the Scottish Historical Studies Seminar University of Strathclyde 1987–88* (Edinburgh: John Donald Publishers, 1989), pp. 1–22; Finlay, 'Keeping the Covenant: Scottish National Identity', p. 122.
18. J. M. Bumsted, 'Church and State in Maritime Canada, 1749–1807', *Historical Papers*, 21 (1967), p. 41; Alan L. Hayes, *Anglicans in Canada: Controversies and Identity in Historical Perspective* (Chicago: University of Illinois Press, 2004), p. 226; James Robertson, *History of the Mission of the Secession Church to Nova Scotia and Prince Edward Island from its Commencement in 1765* (Edinburgh: John Johnstone, 1847), p. 278.
19. V. T. Harlow, *The Founding of the Second British Empire, 1763–1793*, vol. 2 (London: Longman, Green and Co., 1964), p. 735.
20. Guy Carleton, 'King's College and Episcopate in Nova Scotia: Plans Submitted to the British Government in the Year 1783', in *Nova Scotia Historical Society*, vol. 4 (W. M. MacNab Printer, 1884), p. 123.
21. NSA: 'Inglis Papers: Copy of a Letter from General Sir G. Carleton to the Honourable Lord North', New York, 26 August 1783 MG 100, vol. 121 #23; *Acadian Recorder*, 'Sir Alexander Croke to Walter Bromley', 14 August 1813.
22. NSA: 'Inglis Papers: Memoirs of Bishop Inglis, Nova Scotia, Letter to Lord Dorchester', Halifax, 27 December 1787 MG 1 vol. 479 (a) #1.
23. NSA: 'Inglis Papers: Memoirs of Bishop Inglis, Nova Scotia, Letter to Lord Dorchester',

Halifax, December 1787 MG 1 vol. 479 (a) #1; John S. Moir, *Church and State in Canada, 1627–1867: Basic Documents* (Toronto: McClelland and Stewart Limited, 1967), pp. 39–40; Judith Fingard, 'Inglis, Charles', *Dictionary of Canadian Biography*, <http://www.biographi.ca/en/bio/inglis_charles_5E.html> (last accessed 20 October 2019).

24. Bishop Charles Inglis, *Steadfastness in Religion and Loyalty Recommended, in a sermon preached before the legislature of His Majesty's province of Nova* (Halifax, 1793), p. 28.
25. Judith Fingard, *The Anglican Design, in Loyalist Nova Scotia, 1783–1816* (London: S.P.C.K., 1972), pp. 1–4; Nancy Christie, *Transatlantic Subjects: Ideas, Institutions, and Social Experience in Post-Revolutionary British North America* (Toronto: McGill-Queen's University Press, 2014), pp. 223–4.
26. NSA: 'Memoirs of Bishop Inglis: A Letter from Charles Inglis to Lord Hawkesbury', Halifax, 4 December 1789; NSA: 'Memoirs of Bishop Inglis: A Letter from Charles Inglis to Archbishop of Canterbury', Halifax, 26 December 1787; NSA: 'Memoirs of Bishop Inglis: A Letter from Charles Inglis to Archbishop of Canterbury', Halifax, 20 April 1789.
27. NSA: 'Memoirs of Bishop Inglis: A Letter from Charles Inglis to Mr. Cumberland', Halifax, 20 April 1789.
28. John Inglis, 'Memoranda Respective King's College at Windsor in Nova Scotia Collected and Prepared for the Purpose of making Evident the Leading Object in Suggesting and Establishing that Institution' (Halifax, NS: Gossip & Coade Printers, 1836), p. ii.
29. The Statutes, Rules and Ordinances of the University of King's College at Windsor in the Province of Nova Scotia (Halifax, NS: John Howe, 1803), pp. 27–8.
30. Ibid. p. 27–8.
31. Stewart J. Brown, *The National Churches of England, Ireland, and Scotland, 1801–46* (Oxford: Oxford University Press, 2001), p. 5.
32. Helen Taft Manning, *British Colonial Government after the American Revolution* (New Haven: Yale University Press, 1933), p. 101.
33. *Colonial Patriot*, 'State of the Province', 21 May 1831.
34. J. M. Bumsted, 'Scottish Emigration to the Maritimes 1770–1815: A New Look at an Old Theme', *Acadiensis*, 10:2 (1981), p. 66.
35. B. Anne Wood, 'Thomas McCulloch's Use of Science in Promoting a Liberal Education', *Acadiensis*, 17:1 (1987), p. 56.
36. NSA: 'McCulloch Papers: William Cochran to Thomas McCulloch', Windsor, 15 May 1809, MG 1 No. 550 vol. IV.
37. *Christian Magazine*, 31 October 1805, found in George Patterson, *Memoir of Rev. James MacGregor* (Pictou, 1859), pp. 350–1.
38. NSA: 'McCulloch Papers: Thomas McCulloch, Draft Essay Putting Forth Reasons for the Establishment of Pictou College', 1806, MG 1 vol. 544 #4.
39. Ibid.
40. *Acadian Recorder*, 'Investigator', 24 January 1818.
41. William McCulloch, *Life of Thomas McCulloch D.D.* (n.p., 1920), p. 42.
42. Statues of Nova Scotia, 1811, Cap. 9; NSA: 'Pictou Academy Papers, An Article from the Nova Scotia Royal Gazette Office following the act passed in the last session of the General Assembly', RG 14 vol. 50–1.
43. William McCulloch, *Life of Thomas McCulloch D.D.*, pp. 43–4.
44. B. Anne Wood, 'Pictou Academy: Promoting "Schooled Subjectivities" in 19th-Century Nova Scotia', *Acadiensis*, 28:2 (1999), section 5.
45. William McCulloch, *Life of Thomas McCulloch D.D*, p. 44.
46. NSA: 'McCulloch Papers: 'A Letter from Rev. Dr. Thomas McCulloch to Rev. James Mitchell', Pictou, 9 December 1815, MG 1 vol. 553 #1.
47. William McCulloch, *Life of Thomas McCulloch D.D.*, p. 44.
48. Dalhousie, born in Scotland, was a Church of Scotland adherent who would propose another

non-denominational college, opened in Halifax in 1820, that now bears his name. Peter Burroughs, 'Ramsay, George', *Dictionary of Canadian Biography*, <http://www.biographi.ca/en/bio/ramsay_george_7E.html> (last accessed 20 October 2019).
49. Joseph Howe, *Western and Eastern Rambles: Travel Sketches of Nova Scotia* (Toronto: University of Toronto Press, 1973), p. 146; W. Hamilton, *Education, Politics and Reform in Nova Scotia 1800–1848* (MA thesis, University of Western Ontario, 1970), p. 210; *The Novascotian*, 31 October 1833.
50. NSA: 'Pictou Academy Papers 1806–1846, Laws and Ordinances for the Regulation and Management of the Academy', Reel 1; NSA: 'Plans for Providing the means of instruction in the branches of liberal education and rules', June 1807, MG 1 vol. 554 #2.
51. Gwendolyn Davies, *Thomas McCulloch: The Mephibosheth Stepsure Letters* (Ottawa: Carleton University Press, 1990), p. xix.
52. NSA: 'Pictou Academy Papers 1806–1846, Laws and Ordinances for the Regulation and Management of the Academy', Reel 1.
53. 'Report from the Society for the Propagation of the Gospel in Foreign Parts, 1823', in Thomas McCulloch, *A Memorial from the Committee of Missions of the Presbyterian Church of Nova Scotia to the Glasgow Society for the Promoting the Religious Interests of the Scottish Settlers in British North America with Observations on the Constitution of that Society, and upon the Proceedings and First Annual Report of the Committee of Directions* (Edinburgh: Oliver and Boyd, 1826), p. 37.
54. Ibid. p. 37.
55. B. Anne Wood, 'The Significance of Evangelical Presbyterian. Politics in the Construction of State Schooling: A Case Study of the Pictou District, 1817–1866', *Acadiensis*, 20:2 (1991), p. 67.
56. William McCulloch, *Life of Thomas McCulloch D.D.*, p. 83; NSA: 'Subscriptions for the Pictou Academy 1825/26', MG1 vol. 554 #24.
57. *Report of the Glasgow Society for Promoting Interests of Religion and Liberal Education Among the Settlers in the North American Provinces* by the Glasgow Society for Promoting the Religious Interests of Scottish Setters in British North America (Glasgow, 1828), pp. 21–2. The Glasgow Society was allied to the established Church of Scotland and its reports reflect this perspective. See also Elizabeth Ann Kerr MacDougall and John Moir (eds), *Selected Correspondence of the Glasgow Colonial Society* (Toronto: Champlain Society, 1994).
58. Ibid. pp. 21–2.
59. Ibid. p. 30.
60. JHA: Thursday 5 April 1827.
61. Ibid.
62. Ibid.
63. Ibid.
64. D. C. Harvey, 'The Intellectual Awakening of Nova Scotia', in G. A. Rawlyk, *Historical Essays on the Atlantic Provinces* (Toronto: McClelland and Stewart, 1967), p. 117.
65. *Colonial Patriot*, 'Editorial', 7 December 1827.
66. NSA: 'McCulloch Papers: A Letter from Rev. Dr. Thomas McCulloch to Rev. James Mitchell', 21 November 1829, MG 1 vol. 553 #145.
67. *Colonial Patriot*, 'Editorial', 14 December 1828.
68. Ibid.
69. *Colonial Patriot*, 'State of the Province', 21 May 1831.
70. Valerie Wallace, 'Exporting Radicalism within the Empire: The Scots Presbyterian Political Values in Scotland and British North America', pp. 133, 216.
71. *Pictou Observer*, 'Sign of the Times', 22 February 1832; 'Political Review', *Pictou Observer*, 7 March 1832.
72. Ibid.
73. *Pictou Observer*, 'Sign of the Times'.

74. *Pictou Observer*, 'Grand Conservative Dinner Glasgow', 12 August 1834.
75. *Colonial Patriot*, 'Pictou Academy', 19 June 1830.
76. JHA: Wednesday 5 March 1828; JHA: Wednesday 31 March 1830.
77. Wallace had lost a bitter election contest to Edward Mortimer in 1799, when Pictou was part of the Halifax County riding, and the Lanarkshire-born Virginia Loyalist was also a slaveholder, which put him at odds with another McCulloch ally, Rev. James MacGregor – who had aggressively denounced the continuing practice of bondage in the colony. As fitting a beneficiary of a long-term government council appointment as treasurer and a twice president of the North British Society, Wallace's own sons attended King's College. See H. Amani Whitfield, *North to Bondage: Loyalist Slavery in the Maritimes* (Vancouver: University of British Columbia Press, 2016) and D. A. Sutherland, 'Wallace, Michael', *Dictionary of Canadian Biography*, <http://www.biographi.ca/en/bio/wallace_michael_6E.html> (last accessed 20 October 2019).
78. NSA: 'Pictou Academy Papers: Document No. 2, Judge Brenton Halliburton enters protest against the dismissal of the Pictou Academy Bill with Judge Stewart, S. B. Robie and Charles Morris', RG 14 vols 50–1.
79. Ibid.
80. *Colonial Patriot*, 'To all the Representatives of the Province, now at Halifax, except messrs Uniacke, Hartshorne and Barry', 17 April 1830.
81. *Free Press*, Signed 'A Constitutionalist', 4 May 1830.
82. *The Novascotian*, 'Council's Vindication', 15 April 1830.
83. *The Novascotian*, 'The County Election', 7 October 1830.
84. Ibid.

Part Three

Reappraising Memory

NINE

Fenian Ghosts:
The Spectre of Irish Republicanism in Ethnic Relations in Newfoundland

Willeen G. Keough

In the thriving town of Port de Grave, Newfoundland, a small, desolate graveyard marks the spot where a chapel once stood to serve the spiritual needs of local Irish Catholics. In the 1860s, they comprised one-third of the town's population; but by the turn of the century, their numbers had dwindled to one single resident, earning Port de Grave the reputation of 'the town that drove out the Catholics'. They and their English Protestant neighbours had been caught up in ethno-religious tensions that often cut across class solidarity within the fishing population of the ethnically mixed Conception Bay area, north-west of the capital of St John's.[1] The Port de Grave incident was a local manifestation of the 'Fenian scare' experienced by various British North American colonies in the mid-1860s. Because no archival evidence has surfaced of a formal Fenian presence in Newfoundland, there is a tendency in the historiography to dismiss such moments of tension as mere sectarianism on the part of fishers, tradespeople and the working poor, who were supposedly gulled into struggle by local religious and political leaders. Yet ordinary Irish Catholics, particularly in Conception Bay and St John's, were attuned to broader trends in Irish republican nationalism and drew from them understandings of how to fight for greater equity in the Newfoundland context. Further, their efforts to assert their claims were cause for concern among English Protestants of all classes.

In post-colonial discourse in Canada, 'white settler society' is represented as if it were homogeneous and universally privileged. Yet there was considerable diversity among white settlers, and unequal access to power even among those who came from the 'British Isles' – itself, a loaded term that requires intersectional analysis on the bases of gender, class, religion, ethnicity and region. In Newfoundland, there were ethnic tensions between English Protestants and Irish Catholics throughout the nineteenth century and into the twentieth, especially in mixed areas such as St John's and Conception Bay. In both areas, Irish Catholics positioned themselves as marginalised by English Protestant privilege, while English Protestants of all classes reasserted the Protestant nature of the colony/dominion. In St John's, an ambitious Irish middle class increasingly made inroads into political, economic and social power, while the Irish working class and poor asserted their ethnicity through their own associations and occasional street violence. While much of the middle-class rhetoric drew from Irish constitutional nationalism and became increasingly pro-imperial in nature, there were tracings of oppositional, more militant voices that suggest a more complex tone in the capital than we currently acknowledge. In Conception Bay, ethnic tensions between Irish Catholics and English Protestants manifested clearly in individual assaults and communal violence, as well as in an increasing segregation of these ethnic groups within the bay, not just in terms of separate ethnic neighbourhoods but also separate communities within the region.[2] These tensions were certainly informed by local conditions, particularly the island's gradually declining economy throughout most of the nineteenth century and the resulting struggle over entitlement to employment and resources. But in articulating their frustrations, groups also tapped into older understandings of ethnic difference that were sometimes challenged, but also sometimes reinforced, in this new context. Particularly intriguing is how often physical conflicts coincided with republican and proto-republican activities in Ireland in the same period. This chapter will explore Newfoundland moments such as a United Irish mutiny, a Fenian Scare, the 'Harbour Grace Affray' and the development of a local branch of the Friends of Irish Freedom to argue that Irish Catholic assertions of ethnic identity were often filled with the thrum of subversiveness and resistance common to republican discourse, and that English Protestant responses were tied, at least in part, to a fear that Irish militant nationalism had reached Newfoundland.

Shades of early republicanism

A historical collective memory of grievance among the Newfoundland Irish was rooted not only in the history of Irish and British relations but also in the discrimination that they encountered from British naval authorities during the early migratory fishery and settlement period on the island. Early authorities recognised that Irish fishing 'servants' (boat and shore crews in the fishery) were essential to the industry, but they issued numerous orders to ensure that this undesirable group did not remain on the island – requiring that fishing masters return their servants to Ireland after the fishing season was over and, on one occasion, banning the recruitment of Irish women servants altogether.[3] Nonetheless, an increasing number settled, particularly in St John's, Conception Bay and the southern Avalon Peninsula.

Colonial authorities in Newfoundland were clearly wary of the presence of relatively large numbers of transient fishing servants moving back and forth between Ireland and Newfoundland annually. They had already taken stringent actions against Irish fishers in Conception Bay for flying the Irish colours, hiding priests and maintaining mass houses in 1755.⁴ In the wake of the 1798 United Irishmen Rebellion, their fears seemed to be realised when, on the night of 24 April 1800, Irish troops of the Newfoundland Regiment stationed at St John's mutinied, purportedly with the intention of murdering colonial authorities and principal inhabitants of the town. While some escaped capture, seventeen were arrested; four informed on their co-conspirators, and the remaining thirteen were charged and found guilty of treason.⁵ Local authorities feared broad disaffection of the Newfoundland Irish. Deputy Naval Officer Thomas Tremlett, Jr, reported that a directory of five United Irishmen had been administering the oath to the local Irish population since 1798. '[T]hey are sworn to sacrifice their dearest friends if necessary,' he observed. 'Their signs and words are nearly as in Ireland and the Parole on the 24th inst. was Death or Liberty.'⁶

Authorities were particularly concerned about the concentration of Irish fishers in the southern Avalon area. Surrogate and Deputy Naval Officer John Ogden reported to Governor Waldegrave that 'the Inhabitants of this and all the Out Harbours, particularly to the Southward almost to a Man have taken the United Oaths . . .'⁷ The ethnic composition along the southern Avalon, however, was quickly becoming Irish Catholic through intermarriage, so there were few ethnic quarrels at the local level. Furthermore, the inshore fishery in the area was increasingly carried out by household production units in small, isolated communities, providing little opportunity for the type of networking necessary for organised protest and secret societies.⁸

But circumstances were different in Conception Bay, where ethnic tensions resonated both on the ground and in formal politics well into the twentieth century. In this area, the negotiation of ethnic identity and otherness was much more clearly articulated; and there was a heightened sense of ethno-religious political identity and purpose in a number of collective actions. Additionally, this region developed a migratory Labrador fishery and a sealing industry, both of which brought harvesters together on vessels for lengthy periods. These conditions encouraged the formation of popular class consciousness, but when resources were particularly scarce, ethnicity sometimes trumped class in confrontations in the nineteenth century.

Two episodes of ear-lopping in Conception Bay in the 1830s strongly suggest that there was a Ribbon society at work in the area. Ribbonism had emerged in Ireland in the early nineteenth century. Given that this period witnessed peak immigration of Irish people to Newfoundland, it is very likely that at least some of these newcomers had participated in Ribbon activities and brought the ethos of that movement to the island (just as earlier migrants had engaged in Whiteboy activities in the colony). Ribbon societies, like the Whiteboys, responded to agrarian injustices with threatening and violent activities, but the movement also involved a heightened sense of ethno-religious identity vis-à-vis an ethnic other, politicisation around shared oppression by the Anglo-Protestant ascendancy, a sense of Irish Catholic nationalism and often a broader political agenda to achieve Irish independence from the United Kingdom.[9] Most of these elements were present in the ear-lopping incidents in Conception Bay. The two episodes must also be situated within the context of a highly charged political environment in the colony itself. When Newfoundland obtained representative government in 1832, ethno-religious tensions surfaced in formal politics, as predominantly Anglican conservatives filled the ranks of the legislative council, exercising considerable control over power and patronage, while predominantly Catholic and Dissenter liberals dominated the assembly. Complicating the tensions was the active political participation of the Roman Catholic bishop Michael Fleming, with his very Irish nationalist agenda, and Chief Justice Henry Boulton, whose recommendations to reform the legal system were seen by the liberals as an attempt to maintain the Anglo-Protestant oligarchy. Additionally, Boulton had become very unpopular among many Irish Catholics because of his efforts to tamper with the customary credit arrangements of the fishery. Two local newspaper editors aggressively championed opposing sides. Robert Parsons, of the liberal *Newfoundland Patriot*, sympathised with Irish Catholics and branded the conservatives as 'bumptious despots'.[10] Henry Winton, of the conservative *Public Ledger*, supported Boulton and accused the liberals of being strangers to the 'rational principles of civil and religious liberty'.[11] Winton was anonymously placarded and warned that 'the people' would 'set a mark upon him and have his life'[12] – signalling the possible presence of a coherent, politicised group of Irish Catholics who were operating outside the formal legal system. This group delivered on its threat after Boulton imprisoned Parsons on 18 May 1835 for publishing a particularly unflattering article on the chief justice.[13]

Late in the afternoon of the very next day, Winton was travelling with Capt. William Churchward from Carbonear to Harbour Grace – the two largest towns in Conception Bay. A group of assailants attacked them on Saddle Hill, an isolated stretch of road that had recently been dubbed 'Liberty Hill', a symbolic place to a population that had recently mounted a successful sealers' strike there in 1832.[14] The attackers were carrying large stones and had painted their faces with red and yellow ochre – an element of disguise suggestive of Ribbonism, which commonly used the colour red to symbolise revenge. Two of the assailants dragged Churchward into the woods and held him there under threat of death, while their colleagues brutally beat Winton with stones, and severed his left ear and parts of his right ear.[15] A reward of £1,300 was raised by Governor Henry Prescott and public subscription for information leading to the arrest of the perpetrators. But the notices were defaced, with abusive language and drawings of an Irish harp ascendant over a falling crown.[16] Ultimately, no one was ever charged with the crime.[17] Such was the level of solidarity, or the ability to impose sanctions to ensure secrecy, or both, that no one in these two towns would identify the attackers.

Traces of Ribbon discourse lingered after the main event. In early June, a placard was erected in Harbour Grace, threatening to cut off the ears of Peter Rogerson, a local merchant. It was signed 'Croppy'[18] – an epithet that harked back to the United Irish rebels of 1798. That same month, the unpopular Boulton received an anonymous warning in the capital that he should stop his suit against Parsons or suffer the consequences, 'for I am here as well as I was at SADLEHILL But Better provided Whit a leaden Nife'.[19] Ethno-political tensions continued to simmer on the north-east Avalon, and resurfaced in 1840 when by-elections were called for St John's (in May) and Conception Bay (in December).

Late in the night of 13–14 February 1840, Herman Lott, Winton's overseer at the *Public Ledger* office, was accosted, blindfolded and forcibly escorted to a house just outside St John's, where he was interrogated about his own religious persuasion (Protestant) and various affairs of his employer, including the number of firearms at the *Ledger*'s office. Before his release, he was told to warn Winton that 'there was a RIBBON Society in this contry equally as terrible as ever it was in Ireland, and that he [Mr Winton] would soon find his house too hot for him'.[20] Although Lott had been warned not to divulge any details about the interrogation, Winton convinced him to report the incident to authorities. Three months later, Lott was attending to business in Conception Bay. At midday on 15 May, he left Carbonear for Harbour Grace and was attacked on Saddle Hill by four men, disguised with black crepe over their faces. One of them cried out, 'Long looked for, come at last.'[21] Lott's assailants easily overcame him, dragged him into the woods, beat him, cut off his ears and filled his ear canals with dirt. When Lott was revived, he tried to obtain assistance from passers-by. One man reluctantly helped him along for a few steps, Lott later deposed, but then abandoned him; another observed, 'Oh, you're nipped,' and passed on.[22] They likely recognised that Lott had been purposefully marked and chose to avoid potential sanctions for rendering assistance.[23]

As in the case of the attack on Winton, the incident was shrouded in mystery – even though a man had been violently assaulted in daylight on a public road. Two women who had passed Lott on the hill just before the attack never came forward. A couple of witnesses said that they had seen four men running over Saddle Hill from Carbonear – two of them wearing hats painted green under the brim (another symbolic colour). Lawrence Dulhanty or Delahunty, late of Saddle Hill, was arrested and brought before the magistrates, but there was insufficient evidence to charge him. Governor Prescott offered a reward of £300 for information leading to the arrest of the perpetrators, and even a pardon for any accomplices who had not actually committed the mutilation, but without results.[24]

Several people were specifically examined by the police but were unable to help authorities with their inquiries.[25] David Connor, who had been measuring out a new potato garden on Saddle Hill when Lott was attacked, deposed that he had heard and seen nothing. Patrick Keefe, who lived nearby, attested that neither he nor his wife had heard any cries of distress or calls for assistance during the day. Matilda McGrath, who had initially told her aunt that several Harbour Grace men had suspiciously left a funeral in Carbonear early, just before the assault on Lott had taken place, later swore to local magistrates that she had not seen any unsavoury people or dubious activities.[26] Also quite intriguing was the presence of some Irish-Newfoundland individuals who seemed to fit the occupational profile of Ribbon leaders: a disaffected schoolmaster from St John's, a publican from the Mosquito Road and a local bookkeeper (recently fired for drunkenness) who had been seen walking back and forth over Saddle Hill on the afternoon of the incident. All denied their involvement. Throughout various depositions, there was clearly a refusal to cooperate – a tight ring of influence that suggested the existence of a secret society.

Indeed, there were many indications in these incidents that Ribbonism was operating in a nexus between St John's and major towns in Conception Bay: the choice of mutilation; the use of disguise, symbolic colours and a symbolic place; the presence of likely personnel; the enforcement of silence; and the defence of the ethno-religious group. Both ear-lopping moments speak of an awareness and commitment to this form of proto-nationalism that was steeped in Irish Catholic grievance. And their discontent was seen as threatening, not just by authorities, but by the broader English Protestant population in Newfoundland.[27] These Irish Newfoundlanders may not have been fighting for their own republic on the island, but they were claiming political, economic and cultural ground, and they were engaging in a physical-force tradition that emanated from, and was reinforced by, proto-republican nationalism in Ireland.

Fenian scare in Port de Grave

A further moment of transatlantic connection occurred in the 1860s, just after the formation of the Irish Republican Brotherhood (IRB) in Ireland and the Fenian Brotherhood in the United States. These organisations were strongly linked (the umbrella term for both was 'Fenianism') and advocated the use of revolutionary means to remove the British presence from Ireland. By 1865, the American Fenians had hatched a strategy to invade key centres of British North America and hold them ransom for Irish independence. Colonial authorities were placed on high alert, and the Newfoundland government opened an investigation on the Fenian threat, while local newspapers speculated about whether the movement had reached the island.[28] Central authorities soon dismissed rumours of Fenian activity. Nonetheless, fears percolated on the ground among English Protestants that Fenianism, 'having for its object the massacre of their protestant fellow subjects', had already arrived in the colony.[29] While the liberal press with Catholic sympathies ridiculed local Protestant '*gobemouches*' for believing that they were under siege by troops of imaginary 'Fenian ghosts',[30] conservative newspapers accused their liberal colleagues of being suspiciously strenuous in their denials of local sympathy for the brotherhood.[31] Certainly, ethnic tensions were heightened in ethnically mixed Conception Bay, and there was a full-blown Fenian scare in Port de Grave.

In late January and February 1865, an intriguing exchange of letters appeared in the local press about worrisome activities by local Catholics. 'Gamma' claimed that large bands of armed men had recently paraded through the town 'on direful acts intent' in a demonstration of Fenian strength. 'Port-de-Grave' dismissed these allegations as 'second-hand slanders', but Gamma countered that the riots had indeed been Fenian in nature, with the specific purpose of intimidating Protestant neighbours. 'J.C.F.' declared that Gamma's accusations against the 'peace-loving Catholics of Port de Grave' were a 'monstrous falsehood', the product of Protestant/Orange duplicity. However, 'Philo-Gamma' of Conception Bay 'unequivocally corroborate[d]' reports that a large number of 'infatuated and misguided people' had been involved in Fenian demonstrations and warned 'that pikes, *a la mode* of those of Vinegar Hill [the Wexford site where Irish Catholic rebels had finally been defeated in the 1798 United Irishman rebellion] with many modern improvements', were being manufactured in nearby Bay Roberts to fend off Fenian invaders.[32]

Meanwhile, local police constable Matthew Rielly had reported to his superiors that Protestants had begun retaliation against Catholics in Port de Grave. A local man had been reading a Harbour Grace newspaper to members of the Protestant community, 'telling them to Get there Guns to rites that the ware all going to be ki'd by the Catholicks'. That Saturday evening, they had begun firing guns in the hills around the town. The following day, when Father O'Keefe arrived to hear confessions, about fifty 'rowdies' surrounded and fired upon the Catholic chapel. Upon hearing that Rielly had stored powder and shot in a Mrs Shea's house, the rioters surrounded her premises and threatened to tear it down. Rielly concluded that the Protestant population were 'Going about in Gangs' and that if there was 'not a stop put to the leaders bad will be the end of it'.[33] Authorities took depositions from about forty local people and finally determined that the matter had been overblown[34] – a finding that some locals claimed was a complete whitewashing.[35]

But while the episode was downplayed by local authorities, there is a strong collective memory in the area of the deteriorating relations between Irish Catholics and English Protestants and a heightened state of mistrust in 1865 within the broader context of Fenian activities in British North America.

According to oral tradition, Protestants were warned that Catholics from 'up the bay' were arming a vessel to attack Port de Grave, intending to pick up reinforcements at communities along the way. Protestants prepared for the invasion by mustering their sealing guns and confiscating any arms found in Catholic households. They then set up camp on the shoreline between their community and nearby Bareneed to await the coming 'Fenians'. Meanwhile, the local Catholic merchant, Peter Butler, sent his clerk to Harbour Main to warn potential Protestant reinforcements: 'If ye come to Port de Grave, ye had better bring the boards to build your caskets!' As in St John's, the 'Fenian ghosts' did not materialise, but a number of Protestants remained in hiding for several days, firing off their guns to stake their claim to the shore.[36]

Ultimately, organised Fenianism had not come to Conception Bay. But there is much to suggest that local Catholics were keeping abreast of the movement's development, that a number supported its aims in spirit, and that, at the very least, the local Irish Catholic community was using the building fear of Fenianism within the broader context to shore up their interests locally. And its imagined presence in the mental landscape of local English Protestants was as important as the reality in terms of ethnic relations in the area, for the spectre of Fenianism arose in moments of tension throughout the rest of the century and into the next.

Territorial claims and physical-force responses

In the wake of a failed IRB–Fenian rebellion in Ireland and unsuccessful Fenian raids in Canada, the American brotherhood underwent reorganisation and expansion under the name of Clan na Gael. Yet 'Fenianism' continued as an umbrella term for republican sympathies and activities on both sides of the Atlantic. Constitutional nationalism rallied under the Home Rule Association (HRA), which became increasingly assertive under the firebrand Charles Stewart Parnell. By 1877, the IRB, Clan na Gael and the HRA were in conversations about cooperation to attain Ireland's freedom. In 1878, Clan na Gael proposed a 'new departure', by which the Home Rulers would harden their stance on Ireland's self-government and the land question, while the republican groups would generate support for suitable Home Rule candidates in Ireland. By 1879, the three were coordinating the Land War, harnessing the agrarian discontent of Irish farmers and agricultural workers, who had been enjoying a reasonable standard of living since the Great Famine but found their circumstances much changed in the poor harvests and shifting market demands of the late 1870s.[37] Newfoundland newspapers regularly carried news of these developments and disturbing accounts of agrarian violence.[38]

Meanwhile, Newfoundland's two major fisheries – the cod fishery and the seal harvest – continued to decline in the latter nineteenth century, and efforts to diversify the economy by utilising landward resources met with limited success. In this context, ethnic claims were rearticulated in Conception Bay in the form of Orangeism and militant Irish Catholic responses to Orange marching – an echoing of Ribbon societies' reactions to the Orange Order in Ireland itself.[39] These assertions of ethnic identity and difference at the local level were very much affected by the scarcity of work and resources and therefore the contested entitlement to the means of earning a livelihood. But they also involved the reinterpretation of cultural 'traditions' from the old world, a reshaping of historical consciousness to address contemporary concerns. That rearticulation included awareness of recent assertions of Irish republican nationalism in Ireland as well as a perception by Irish Newfoundlanders that the local Orange Order, having rallied behind pro-Confederate candidates in the 1869 elections, was itself an agent of Confederation – a federal union with Canada that was as undesirable to most Irish Newfoundlanders as the original union of Ireland with Great Britain.[40]

The Orange Order had arrived late in Newfoundland; the first lodge, in St John's, appeared in 1863, but the movement spread quickly and extensively in areas with significant Protestant populations.[41] In Newfoundland, Orangemen were almost completely English Protestant, as there were very few Irish Protestants in the colony. They soon began articulating their ethnic identity and interests in the face of an increasingly assertive Irish Catholic population. And there were various incidents in which Orange marching met with resistance from Irish Catholic communities, especially in ethnically mixed areas like Conception Bay.

On 18 January 1878, for example, there was a major flare-up between Orangemen and Irish Catholics from the communities of Portugal Cove, Kelligrews and Long Pond in Conception Bay.[42] Having threatened that 'no Catholic would be spared' along the shore, the Orangemen attempted to march to their lodge in full regalia. But some 50 to 60 local Catholics, massed behind two green flags with harp insignias, tore the sashes from the Orangemen's bodies and forced them to retreat. On their way home, the Orangemen took shelter in the house of the widow Maria Moyse, but the Catholic crowd paraded around the house, wielding fence pickets and making verbal threats, until the Orangemen were finally removed under police escort.[43]

The conflict sprouted from seeds of dissension that had already been sown between groups who were making rival claims to space in which it was becoming increasingly more difficult to eke out a living. The legitimacy of one claim over the other was underscored by government authorities, who stated that the Orange parade had been peaceful in intent and that neither the police nor the government had any authority to prohibit it or interfere with it in any way; the Catholic response, by contrast, they deemed illegal.[44] Irish Catholics interpreted this response as a defence of English Protestant privilege, and resentments continued to simmer in the bay.

Throughout the late 1870s and into the 1880s, news of intensive Land League activities, the 1882 Phoenix Park murders by the IRB splinter group the Invincibles, and Clan na Gael bombing campaigns in Britain appeared regularly in Newfoundland newspapers. The press also reported Clan na Gael activities in America and the formation of an American Land League as well as rumours that Invincible leaders who had fled the UK were in hiding in the United States.[45] In May 1883, the threat of Irish republican militancy again moved closer to home when the Canadian prime minister, Sir John A. MacDonald, warned the lieutenant governor of Nova Scotia, Sir Adam George Archibald, that two Clan na Gael vessels armed with torpedoes were sailing from Boston to attack Halifax because of its strategic military position.[46] And in December of that year, the Newfoundland press reported that a large meeting of Fenians in New York had sworn to avenge the death of Patrick O'Donnell, who had been executed for the assassination of James Carey, an Invincible who had turned Queen's evidence in the Phoenix Park murder trials.[47]

In the midst of this highly charged discourse, and in the height of Ireland's Land War, another confrontation between Irish Catholics and English Protestants took place in Newfoundland – this time with tragic consequences.[48] On St Stephen's Day, 1883, Orangemen parading in full regalia in Harbour Grace attempted to march into the Irish Catholic area of Riverhead – a neighbourhood that had been flagged as a hotbed of Irish nationalist activity by authorities as early as the mid-1700s.[49] They were confronted by a Catholic crowd determined to stop any encroachment into their territory, and in the ensuring fracas, at least twenty-three men were wounded – five of them fatally. The Orangemen had marched through the main part of town several times previously, and the Riverhead community had responded with counter-marching of their own. But the stopping point for both groups had always been at the Pipe Track – the boundary line between two neighbourhoods, Irish Catholic Riverhead and English Protestant Courage's Beach. There, a serious fault line had developed in relations between the two ethnic groups in Harbour Grace, with tensions building proportionately to the slide in the local fishing economy and successive poor growing seasons that had wreaked havoc with subsistence crops. And in 1883, when a rumour surfaced that the Orangemen intended to march beyond that boundary into Riverhead, the people of Riverhead (men, women and children) likewise marched toward the Pipe Track, planted their green flag with harp insignia at Brennan's corner and awaited the society's approach. The people of Courage's Beach felt that their territory was under attack and began 'running to and fro, singing out that the Riverhead Fenians were coming down'. They warned the approaching Orange procession to turn back, but neither side would retreat, and the fighting began.[50]

Again, the immediate official response to the incident demonstrated a predisposition to see Orange marching as innocuous and to portray the Irish Catholic response as dangerous and illegal.[51] Indeed, the procession had actually been protected by extra police reinforcements, brought in to prevent 'interference' by the Catholic Riverhead party.[52] All the initial arrests, and most of the arrests overall (twenty-seven out of thirty-four), targeted the Irish Catholic community, although ultimately several members of the Protestant community, most of them from the working-class Courage's Beach area, were also charged.[53] Two trials were held between May 1884 and January 1885. There was an impressive array of Protestant power on the prosecution and the bench,[54] and a bill of indictment was readily handed down against nineteen Riverhead men. But the petty juries in both cases were Catholic, and this, combined with the maze of contradictory evidence from both sides, made it virtually impossible to obtain a conviction.

The Riverhead people maintained a conspiracy of silence in the aftermath of the affray – a refusal to cooperate with authorities that reflected both strong solidarity within the group and a prevailing attitude that it was impossible for Irish Catholics to obtain justice at the hands of a legal system that was still dominated by English Protestants. According to most Catholic testimonies, no one had left Riverhead that day with any intent to confront the Orange march. 'Someone' had hoisted a green flag and started to walk with it; others had just followed along. They had not been rowdy; no one had armed themselves with guns, pickets or stones. Somehow, they had ended up at the site of confrontation just as the Orangemen tried to march down Pippy's Lane into Riverhead. This cover-up speaks eloquently to both the extent of solidarity and the fear of sanctions operating in the area. And the lack of cooperation on the part of Irish Catholics resonates with a Ribbon oath not to reveal the group's secrets or to give evidence against a brother if prosecuted by an 'Orangeman or heretic', as well as Fenian and IRB oaths to protect the secrecy of those organisations.

Ultimately, no one was found guilty of the Harbour Grace Affray, but there was a surge of reaction from Protestants in Conception Bay, evidencing a strong sense of British Protestant identity and entitlement. At 'Indignation Meetings' held in Carbonear and Harbour Grace, Protestants expressed their 'horror' at the 'outrageous miscarriages of justice' at the trials and called for an amendment of jury laws to ensure 'unbiased juries, untrammelled by outside influence'.[55] Several discursive themes emerged at these meetings: a construction of Catholicism as anathema to reason and justice; the sense of a separate Protestant world; the perception that Protestantism should be properly protected under the British constitution; and an increasing identification of Protestantism with a pan-British imperial identity.

The concern about 'outside influence' is particularly interesting. This may have been a reference to the Catholic Church, but it may also have reflected anxieties about the influence of Irish Catholic nationalism, and even physical force nationalism. For running in counterpoint to discourse around British entitlement was the rhetoric of Fenianism or sometimes *about* Fenianism, reflecting concerns that had first arisen specifically in the mid-1860s but were rooted in earlier tensions manifested in the 1800 mutiny and incidents of proto-republican Ribbonism. Throughout the trials, Protestant witnesses deployed the term when referring to the Catholic Riverhead party. Three women deposed that they were warned not to 'go around the river' because 'the Fenians were providing for the Orangemen' and were 'blowing off their guns and had their flag hoisted'. Another was told that 'there would be terrible work ... between the Fenians and the Orangemen, and a good deal of blood spilt' that day. In the midst of the fighting, police constable Andrew Fahey was heard by several Protestant witnesses declaring himself to be 'as good a Fenian as them that's behind me'. Later, Margaret and Roseanne Wiseman were confronted on Harvey Street by several Orangemen, who were swearing, brandishing pickets and threatening to muster enough guns to 'blow up the whole of Riverhead'. Two of them called Roseanne 'a Fenian b—d of a b—h' and swore that if the girls were men, they would 'go no further'.[56] The term 'Fenian' may have been employed by Protestants as a term of abuse or a means of coding illegitimacy – casting aspersions on the Irish Catholic action by linking it to an illegal secret society. But it also revealed a fear of the assertiveness of the Irish Catholic community and its potential for undermining the English Protestant interest – a concern that popular-class Catholics appeared content to let fester in the Protestant psyche. So the spectre of Fenianism lingered, despite official efforts to exorcise it. Further, the willingness of Irish Catholics to fight physically for their group interests and the coincidence of these events with significant moments in Ireland's struggle for independence are highly suggestive of a transatlantic sharing of republican ideals, tailored to local circumstances.

Republican discourse in the aftermath of the Easter Rising

A final case study, located early in the twentieth century, is worth mentioning here, not only because of its clear ties to Irish republican nationalism but because of the involvement of middle-class and upper-middle-class Irish Catholics, a number of whom were wavering in their support of empire when confronted with a large-scale nationalist struggle in Ireland. Within the context of World War I and its aftermath, there was a growing sympathy for protecting the rights of small nations. When Irish nationalists of various (often overlapping) stripes brought rebellion to the streets of Dublin in April 1916, Newfoundland newspapers provided constant coverage of the 'Sinn Fein Revolt' and its aftermath.[57] Among Irish Newfoundlanders, there was both sympathy and disdain for the rebels, but soon most were calling for understanding and mercy, as news reached the dominion of the summary executions of key leaders and imprisonment of Irish Volunteers and supporters in British jails. And when

Irish republican forces fought against Britain in the Irish War of Independence (1919–21), and news reached Irish populations everywhere of retributive activities of British forces and the notorious Black and Tans on Irish soil, a groundswell of support within diasporic populations gave rise to movements such as the Friends of Irish Freedom (FOIF) and the Self-Determination for Ireland League (SDIL). The FOIF was established in the United States in March 1916 to provide moral and financial support for the Easter Rising. It remained a radical republican group into the 1930s, but it fell out with the IRB and Sinn Fein in October 1920 over the management of funds raised in America. Eamonn de Valera convinced Canadian organiser Katherine Hughes – formerly a strong imperialist, now turned republican – to establish a support group for Irish independence among Irish diasporic populations in the empire. Thus, the SDIL was born in 1920. It maintained a more neutral, constitutional façade than the FOIF's to attract those who did not want to sever imperial ties, but it still had a significant tolerance level for those with republican sympathies. Both had a substantial presence, and sometimes overlapping memberships, in Newfoundland.[58]

News of the more radical FOIF had reached Newfoundland as early as 1917, with accounts that the group had been waging a successful petition campaign in the United States for Irish independence and had been branded as 'treasonous and seditious' for their 'hyphenated' nationalism by the American Defence Society.[59] While no official records of a local branch of the FOIF have yet surfaced, Patrick Mannion indicates that the group was established in St John's by late 1919.[60] In the following year, traces of the monthly meetings and growing membership of the 'Padraic Pearse' branch (named for one of the leaders of the 1916 Rising and a signatory to the Proclamation of the Irish Republic) appeared in the pages of local newspapers such as the *St John's Daily Star* and the *Evening Telegram*. April was a busier month than usual, with meetings on the 8th and 15th as the fourth anniversary of the Easter Rising approached. They planned to celebrate the 'the birth of the Irish republic' on 23 April with a programme that included nationalist orators and Irish musical programming; cables would be sent to friends in Ireland to mark the day and maintain transatlantic connections to republican nationalism.[61] Upon hearing concerns about these events, Governor Charles Harris opened a file on the FOIF but remained phlegmatic. He noted that the presence of an American political society in a British colony was unusual, but that it would be unwise to pay too much attention to these 'well intentioned faddists'. Nonetheless, he asked the Inspector General of the Constabulary to monitor the group and report 'any tendency to disloyalty'; he also wrote to Viscount Milner, Secretary of State at the Dominions Office, to advise him of the matter.[62]

That July, there was another flurry of FOIF meetings, with further reports of an increasing membership. The *Daily Star* praised the movement for its non-sectarian ethos, its purpose to provide 'intimate knowledge of Irish history both current and past', and its goal to 'stimulate a just pride of Irish ideals and achievements' in Newfoundland. The Padraic Pearse branch had been quite successful in generating 'much sympathetic appreciation of the Irish race in their struggle for freedom', the paper declared.[63] It is intriguing to note the coming together of cultural and republican nationalism in this moment, just as had happened in Ireland in the decades leading up to the Easter Rising. In its endorsement of the FOIF in its editorial comments, in contrast to other papers that merely reported the basic facts about FOIF meetings, the *Daily Star* may well have been positioning itself as a vehicle for republican sympathies in the colony.

Some writers suggest that enthusiasm for the FOIF had fallen off in Newfoundland by the fall of 1920 because their activities were no longer reported in the press. However, the reality is slightly more complex. The first meeting of a branch of the SDIL in Newfoundland (SDILN) was held on 6 October 1920, the day after a tempered lecture by Katherine Hughes on the issue of the right of all small nations to self-determination. During that month, the FOIF actually amalgamated with the SDILN, and the joint membership moved forward under the banner of self-determination for Ireland.[64] Yet we should not read this consolidation to mean that the spirit of Irish republicanism was no longer alive in the country. Rather, it suggests that more radical supporters were making the same pragmatic choice that de Valera and Hughes had made: to maximise impact and maintain momentum with larger numbers. More radical voices can still be heard in press coverage. A correspondent named 'Democrat', for example, wrote to the editor of the *Daily Star* to congratulate the SDILN on choosing John Devine and John Meaney as representatives of the forthcoming national convention in Ottawa because of their open support of Irish freedom (as opposed to the diluted concept of 'self-determination'). The writer singled out Meaney for particular praise, describing him as 'a type of Irishman that Friends of Irish Freedom can point to with pride. Self-made, courageous, fearless and able'.[65] Meaney had certainly become a republican sympathiser. His speech at the SDIL's national convention in Ottawa (16–17 October) was quite anti-imperial in tone; he revealed that his own son had died in the British war effort in World War I, but that given recent British reprisals against Irish forces and civilians during the War of Independence, he 'would not have permitted my son to fight for the British flag, because of what had been perpetrated under its aegis. Ireland never could and never should trust the word of a British stateman.'[66] It was hardly surprising to see that, during the ensuing treaty negotiations with Britain that led to civil war in Ireland, Meaney declared his support for de Valera and his anti-treaty side.

How did such anti-imperial commentary and demonstrations of sympathy for Irish independence play out in terms of ethnic relations in Newfoundland?

Although various reports of FOIF and SDILN meetings had already been stirring some anti-republican reactions,[67] an incident in late October seemed to push the tolerance level of local Protestant imperialists too far. A well-attended meeting of the SDILN (now amalgamated with the FOIF) on 28 October passed several resolutions that many Protestants deemed to be subversive. Terence MacSwiney, a Sinn Fein playwright and mayor of Cork, had been imprisoned by the British for being in possession of seditious documents and a code key; he and eleven other republican prisoners had embarked upon a hunger strike in Brixton Prison to protest their internment. On 25 October, after seventy-three days, MacSwiney died, as did two fellow protestors shortly thereafter, and reverberations were felt around the Irish world. The SDILN resolutions expressed admiration for their 'heroism' and 'martyrdom'. The meeting condemned the 'tyranny' of the British court that had 'tried these men on trumped-up charges' and denounced the 'blind perversity that exacted their lives rather than accede to their just protest'. Members congratulated the Irish nation 'on the dauntless heroism of its sons ... the latest of Ireland's martyrs' and demanded, 'in the name of sanity and decency', that the remaining prisoners in Cork be released. The league finally pledged 'to spare no effort to ensure that [the hunger-strikers] have not died in vain'.[68] These were not the words of a group that was pro-imperial and neutral on the issue of Irish independence.

The 28 October resolutions provoked a strong sense of outrage in the Orange Order and a concern that the Protestant nation they had vowed to protect was in imminent danger. In a special two-day session held by the Grand Orange Lodge in St John's and attended by large numbers from the capital and outports, the Orange Order responded with their own resolutions. They accused the SDILN of disseminating anti-British propaganda and charged that the whole purpose of the league, despite its innocuous name, was to have Ireland secede from the United Kingdom and form a separate republic. They condemned the SDILN's allegations of 'tyranny', 'dishonesty' and 'infamy' against British justice, and argued that these 'crimes' were more typical of the Sinn Fein movement. They charged the league of sedition in its pledge to ensure that the hunger-strikers had not died in vain. And they called upon the Government to remove from office any politicians and public servants who were involved in this 'strike against the integrity of the British Empire'.[69] Fenian ghosts were again haunting ethnic relations in the colony.

But authorities continued their policy of watchful waiting, while debates continued in local papers into the following year. Strong anti-imperial sentiments and the merging of cultural and republican nationalisms were exemplified in a lengthy letter to the editor of the *Daily Star* written by G. Roude of St John's and published on 13 January 1921. Roude's opening remarks were ironic:

Verily we Irish are a turbulent people, a race of extremists, a nation afflicted with a double dose of Original Sin. British statesmen have said all those things of us – yea, and much more . . . And if they say such things who can doubt their words; are they not all honourable men.

He then identified himself as 'one of those impossible Irishmen, and perhaps . . . even a Sinn Feiner'. He argued that, despite England's ambitions to seize control of all the land and seas across the globe, 'God made Ireland for the Irish' and therefore 'set the four seas as her irremovable frontier forever'. He accused England of trying to drown Ireland's voice in blood and spoke of the 'people's agony' and Ireland's 'willing martyrs' to the 'holy cause of freedom'. As evidence, he pointed to the horrors of the Anglo-Irish War: 'No day or night passes now without its own tale of men butchered and homesteads burned,' he declared. 'The story of England's love of liberty is lit up by the blaze of Irish towns and in their glare we see that the page is writ red with Irish blood.' The Irish people were victims of English tyranny, and any outsiders who 'knowingly and willingly aided and abetted the criminal conspiracy of a foreign tyranny against the freedom and welfare' of the Irish Republic should be warned of potential consequences. 'The sanction of English rule in Ireland is measured in terms of armoured cars, machine guns, bayonets and bombs,' he posited; 'her moral sanction is an exploded myth'. The way forward for Ireland would be difficult, Roude observed, but 'Ireland cannot die. If sword and gun could break her; if rope could strangle her, then her epitaph had long since been written.'[70] Like Cromwell, who had tried to conquer Ireland, these 'petty imitators' would fail. God would hear the prayer of the Irish people, in their 'agony', and would value it more than English gold. 'And because of the faith and the hope that is in us,' he concluded, 'and because of the noble ones that have gone before, we tread undismayed through sorrow's night the path to the dawning day.' Here was the stuff of the writings and speeches of Padraic Pearse, the namesake of the St John's branch of the FOIF; here was a lament for centuries of oppression by the English tyrant, the Irish people's agony in the garden of Gethsemane, the blood sacrifice required of the people to obtain freedom, and the martyrs who had already given their lives for the just cause of Irish freedom.

Conclusion

I am not arguing that most Irish Newfoundlanders in this moment, or in the earlier incidents discussed here, held republican sentiments, but it is important to recognise that not all Irish Newfoundlanders were supporters of the British Empire. There has been a tendency in the historiography to interpret the views of Irish Newfoundlanders through the lens of the middle class and elites – in no small part because they have left behind written records in the archives, so their perspectives are more readily accessed. The records of the Benevolent Irish Society, for example, resound with toasts to sitting monarchs and empire from many of the well-heeled Irish-Newfoundland population.[71] But even among the more affluent Irish population, attitudes were not uniformly or consistently pro-empire. Furthermore, reading against the grain of archival sources and engaging with oral history, we can uncover greater complexity in the ways that Irish Newfoundlanders positioned themselves in the new world. Some were clearly republican in outlook; others were tapping into physical force traditions to ensure that they would not fall victim to the ethnic oppression that had haunted their forebears; many were sympathetic to broad Irish nationalist ambitions; but most wanted an acknowledgement of their right to share power and resources in Newfoundland. In the nineteenth and early twentieth centuries in Newfoundland, ethnic tensions went beyond knee-jerk sectarianism. Although they tapped into understandings of centuries of colonial encounters in Ireland itself, these Irish Catholic and English Protestant settlers imagined this newfound space (mistakenly, as we now know) as unclaimed. And they were staking a claim in a context that was informed by similarly contested space in Ireland. It was in this environment that the shade of Fenianism continued to walk, even after the movement had had its day.[72]

Notes

1. European settlers in Newfoundland were primarily English Protestants from the West of England and Irish Catholics from the southern counties of Ireland. Irish Catholics tended to settle in St John's and areas to the south and south-west of the capital. English Protestants also settled in St John's or clustered to the north-west of the capital. Conception Bay had a mixed population.
2. I have discussed this phenomenon in Keough, 'Ethnicity as Intercultural Dialogue in Eighteenth- and Nineteenth-Century Newfoundland', *Canadian Journal of Irish Studies/Revue canadienne d'études irlandaises*, 31:1 (Spring 2005), pp. 18–28.
3. Such orders are peppered throughout governors' correspondence of the period. See, for example, Provincial Archives of Newfoundland and Labrador (PANL), GN 2/1/A: vol. 2, 236, Proclamation, Governor Richard Dorrill, 22 September 1755; vol. 3, pp. 232, 272–3; Orders (2), Governor Hugh Palliser, 2 July and 31 October 1764; vol. 4: pp. 2–3, 9, 19, 41–4, 79; Orders (5), Palliser, 31 July, 16 August, and 15 September 1766, and 2 June and 23 October 1767; vol. 4, pp. 201, 285; Orders (2), Governor Jonathon Byron, 29 September 1769 and 31 October 1770; vol. 5, pp. 60, 102, 143; Orders (3), Governor Molynoux Shuldham, 24 June and 13 July 1772 and 12 October 1773; vol. 6, pp. 17, 100–1; Orders (3), Governor Robert Duff, 12 July and 16 October 1775; vol. 7, pp. 33–6, 70; Circular Letter to Magistrates and Orders (2), Governor John Montagu, 6 and 20 October 1777 and 3 October 1778; vol. 12, pp. 38–41; Proclamation and Public Notice, Governor Mark Milbanke, 13 October 1789; vol. 12, p. 157; Public Notice, Governor Richard King, 19 September 1792; vol. 14, pp. 282–7; Proclamation, Governor William Waldegrave, and covering correspondence to the Magistrates of Newfoundland, 27 September 1798; and vol. 16, pp. 282–7; Proclamations (2), Governor John Gambier, 18 September 1802. For a broader discussion of the concerns of British authorities on Irish fishing servants, see Willeen Keough, *The Slender Thread: Irish*

Women on the Southern Avalon, 1750–1860 (New York: Columbia University Press, 2006, 2008), chapter 2.
4. PANL, GN 2/1/A, vol. 2, pp. 251, 256–64; various deportation orders by Dorrill and Surrogate Thomas Burnett, 15 August to the end of September 1755.
5. Five were executed on gallows erected at the site where they had congregated. The remaining eight were sent in Halifax in irons to be dealt with by the Duke of Kent. Three of them were executed, and the others were transported from the colonies.
6. PANL, CO 194, vol. 42, fols. 305–6; Thomas Tremlett, Jr., to William Adams, MP, 30 April 1800; and fols. 307–8; Thomas Tremlett, Jr., to Thomas Tremlett, Sr., 30 April 1800.
7. CO 194, vol. 42, fols. 167–9, Ogden to Governor Waldegrave, 2 July 1800.
8. Keough, *The Slender Thread*.
9. See: M. R. Beames, 'Rural Conflict in Pre-Famine Ireland: Peasant Assassinations in Tipperary, 1837–1847', *Past and Present*, 81 (November 1978), pp. 75–91; Beames, 'The Ribbon Societies: Lower-Class Nationalism in Pre-Famine Ireland', *Past and Present*, 97 (November 1982), pp. 128–43; Tom Garvin, 'Defenders, Ribbonmen and Others: Underground Political Networks in Pre-Famine Ireland', *Past and Present*, 96 (August 1982), pp. 133–55; and John William Knott, 'Land, Kinship and Identity: The Cultural Roots of Agrarian Agitation in Eighteenth- and Nineteenth-Century Ireland', *Journal of Peasant Studies*, 12:1 (1984), pp. 93–108.
10. *Newfoundland Patriot*, 10 February 1835.
11. *Public Ledger*, 11 November 1834.
12. *Public Ledger*, 2 June 1835.
13. *Newfoundland Patriot*, 26 May 1835.
14. For an excellent analysis of collective actions in Conception Bay more broadly, see Linda Little, 'Plebeian Collective Action in Harbour Grace and Carbonear, Newfoundland, 1830–1840' (master's thesis, Memorial University, 1984).
15. PANL, GN 5/3/B/19, file 30, box 11, Harbour Grace, information and complaint, Henry Winton, 19 May 1835, and deposition, William Churchward, 19 May 1935; PANL, GN 2/2, Harbour Grace Magistrates to Colonial Secretary James Crowdy, 20 May 1835, enclosure.
16. The Irish harp suggested republican sympathies; it had been incorporated into the flag flown by Irish republicans during the United Irish rebellion (1798) and would also be adopted by Young Ireland (1840s), the Fenians (1860s), the Land League (1870 –80s) and the Irish Volunteer Force in the years leading up to the 1916 rebellion.
17. See accounts in the *Public Ledger*, *Newfoundlander* and *Newfoundland Patriot* of the period.
18. PANL, GN 2/2, Harbour Grace Magistrate Stabb to James Crowdy, 10 June 1835.
19. CO 194, vol. 90, Governor Henry Prescott to Earl of Aberdeen, 30 May 1835, enclosure.
20. Herman Lott, deposition, 15 February 1840, reported in *Public Ledger*, 22 May 1840.
21. *Star and Conception Bay Journal*, 20 May 1840.
22. Ibid.
23. PANL, GN 5/3/B/19, box 11, file 30; *Newfoundlander*, 21 May 1840 (quoting the *Harbour Grace Mercury*, 15 May 1840); *Public Ledger*, 22 May 1840; *Star and Conception Bay Journal*, 20 May, 3, 10, and 24 June, and 8 July 1840.
24. *Newfoundlander*, 21 May 1840, p. 2 (quoting the *Harbour Grace Mercury*, 15 May 1840); *Star and Conception Bay Journal*, 3, 10, and 24 June, and 8 July 1840.
25. Examinations described in this section appear in PANL, GN 5/3/B/19, Harbour Grace, box 11, file 30.
26. See various depositions in PANL, GN 5/3/B/19, box 11, file 30.
27. See accounts in the *Newfoundlander*, *Public Ledger*, *Star and Conception Bay Advertiser* and *Newfoundland Patriot*.
28. See correspondence in PANL, GN 1/3/A, file 7/1866, box 4, 'The Fenians'; see also the *Newfoundlander*, 12, 16 and 19 January 1865; the *Public Ledger*, 10, 13 and 20 January 1865; the *Patriot*, 17 January 1865; and the *Daily News*, 14 and 17 January 1865.

29. *Harbour Grace Standard*, 25 January 1865.
30. Quotations from *Newfoundlander*, 16 January 1865, and *Patriot*, 17 January 1865. Similar sentiments were expressed in the *Newfoundlander* on 19 January 1865.
31. *Public Ledger*, 17 and 20 January 1865, and *Daily News*, 17 January 1865.
32. 'Port-de-Grave' to the *Harbour Grace Standard*, 8 February 1865, responding to 'Gamma', *Day-Book*, 24 January 1865, no longer extant; 'Gamma' to the *Harbour Grace Standard*, 15 February 1865; 'J.C.F.', to the *Public Ledger*, 3 February 1865; and 'Philo-Gamma', Conception Bay, to the *Patriot*, 14 February 1865.
33. Constable M. Rielly to John Wilcox, JP, Brigus, 20 January 1865, reported in the *Harbour Grace Standard*, 22 February 1865.
34. *Harbour Grace Standard*, 22 February 1865. Copies of these depositions were forwarded to authorities in St John's, but neither the originals nor the copies are extant.
35. 'Vox Populi in Una', Harbour Grace, to the *Patriot*, 24 January 1865.
36. Evidence from the oral tradition is based upon extensive interviews conducted by the author with sixteen residents or former residents of the area in 2003-4. See also an account of the episode retold from the oral tradition by Gerald Andrews in *Heritage of a Newfoundland Outport: The Story of Port de Grave* (St John's: Jesperson Publishing, 1997), pp. 123-5.
37. James S. Donnelly, Jr, *The Land and People of Nineteenth-Century Cork: The Rural Economy and the Land Question* (London: Routledge & Kegan Paul, 1975). These struggles provoked various land acts that ultimately led to a peasant proprietorship in Ireland.
38. See, for example: *Harbour Grace Standard*, 19 January 1878; *Patriot and Terra-Nova Herald*, 24 June 1878; *Evening Telegram*, 23 October 1979; *Terra Nova Advocate*, 20 November 1880.
39. The Orange Order existed in other parts of the island as well, but these communities were not ethnically mixed, so tensions did not flare during their marches.
40. James Hiller, 'Confederation Defeated: The Newfoundland Election of 1869', in James Hiller and Peter Neary (eds), *Newfoundland in the Nineteenth and Twentieth Centuries: Essays in Interpretation* (Toronto: University of Toronto Press, 1980), pp. 67-94. The issue of Confederation had been hard-fought in the election of 1869. Confederates rallied the Orange vote, but an alliance of anti-Confederates and Liberals (predominantly representing Irish Catholic districts) formed a new government under C. F. Bennett.
41. By the early 1880s, there were twenty-one lodges on the island; by 1889, the number had mushroomed to fifty-four. For an overview of Orangeism in Newfoundland, see Elinor Senior, 'The Origin and Political Activities of the Orange Order in Newfoundland, 1863-1890' (master's thesis, Memorial University of Newfoundland, 1960).
42. For details of this incident, see the various reports, depositions, minutes and correspondence contained in PANL, GN 1/3/A, file 19/1878, and GN 9/1, vol. 6, 1878, pp. 158-70. Orange lodges in the outports held the traditional 12 July march, although they rescheduled it outside the height of the fishing season to the Christmas period or January.
43. PANL, file 19/1878, no. 4, deposition of Maria Moyse, 23 January 1878, and no. 6, deposition of William Tulk, 26 January 1878; and PANL, GN 9/1, vol. 6, 1878, pp. 158-60; Bishop Thomas Power to Governor John Glover, 22 January 1878, pp. 164-9; F. B. T. Carter, Attorney General, to Glover, 4 February 1878.
44. PANL, GN 9/1, vol. 6, 1878, p. 161; Glover to Power, 23 January 1878; and PANL, GN 1/3/A, file 19/1878, no. 7, and GN 9/1, vol. 6, 1878, pp. 164-9; Carter to Glover, 4 February 1878. Actually, the governor had not initially been advised of the incident by the executive council, who had hoped to dampen its significance. However, in his response to Power, Glover strongly endorsed the council's policy of non-intervention.
45. *Harbour Grace Standard*, 4 September 1880, 6 November 1880, 11 December 1880, 6 January 1881, 22 October 1881, 3 November 1881, 26 February 1882 and 28 October 1882; *Carbonear Herald and Outport Telephone*, 28 October 1881; *Terra Nova Advocate*, 3 November 1880; *Evening Telegram*, 4 June 1881, 16 June 1881, 27 June 1881, 8 May 1883, 19 September

1881, 18 December 1883 and 10 July 1884; *Patriot and Terra-Nova Herald*, 6 June 1881, 27 June 1881 and 14 and 25 July 1881.
46. *Evening Telegram*, 9 and 15 May 1883. Halifax authorities swore in special policemen, but no attack materialised.
47. *Evening Telegram*, 18 December 1883.
48. The main sources for the following discussion of the 'Harbour Grace Affray' were: Mildred Howard, 'The Harbour Grace Affray', typescript of evidence at the ensuing trials in May/June 1884, and November 1884–January 1885, housed at the Centre for Newfoundland Studies [CNS], Memorial University; various government correspondence and reports in PANL, GN 2/2, box 61, GN 1/3/A, box 17, file 20/1883; GN 9/1, vol. 7 (1883–5); and CO 194, vol. 207; and local newspapers such as the *Harbour Grace Standard*, *Evening Telegram*, *Evening Mercury*, *Newfoundlander* and *Patriot*. See also Willeen Keough, 'Contested Terrains: Ethnic and Gendered Spaces in the Harbour Grace Affray', *Canadian Historical Review*, 90:1 (2009), pp. 29–70.
49. In 1755 Governor Dorrill and his Surrogate, Thomas Burnett, took measures against Irish Catholics who were caught flying the Irish colours on vessels, harbouring a priest and celebrating Mass in the Harbour Grace area. Fines were imposed, houses burned and deportations ordered in Harbour Grace, Carbonear, Harbour Main, Crockers Cove and Mosquito Cove from 15 August to the end of September 1755. See various orders in PANL, GN 2/1/A, vol. 2, pp. 202, 251–64, August–September 1755.
50. See evidence in Howard, typescript, particularly the testimonies of: Pierce Murphy, p. 75; Edward Lee, p. 63; John Shea, pp. 93–4; Alfred Shedwick, pp. 94–5; John Shoughrue, pp. 97–8; Robert Courage, p. 31; Pierce Wade, p. 109; and Edward Noseworthy, pp. 78–9.
51. PANL, GN 9/1, vol. 7, Executive Council minute re: telegram from Judge Thomas Bennett to Attorney General, 27 December 1883; PANL, GN 1/3/A, box 17, file 20/1883, draft of despatch, Carter to Colonial Office, 29 December 1883; and final version of the despatch, CO 194, vol. 207, fols., 5–8, 1 January 1884; PANL, GN 1/3/A box 17, file 20/1883, draft of despatch, Carter to Colonial Office, 14 January 1884. It is worth noting that administrator, chief justice and former premier F. B. T. Carter as well as current premier William Whiteway were indebted to the society for rallying the Orange vote and contributing to their recent election successes. Also, there were several prominent Orangemen in the predominantly Protestant governments of the last quarter of the century, including two grand masters: A. J. W. McNeilly, who served under Carter and Whiteway, and J. S. Winter, solicitor general under Whiteway. See Senior, 'Orange Order'.
52. Various police constables testified that they had been assigned that day to protect the Orange procession. Some were actually brought in from neighbouring communities for this purpose. See Howard, typescript, and proceedings of the preliminary enquiry in *Harbour Grace Standard*, 12 January 1884.
53. Doyle was a Protestant from Ulster, and although he seemed to act as a neutral party in the incident, a number of Irish Catholics from Riverhead suggested that it was he who was responsible for the one Catholic corpse among the dead.
54. Two of the three justices of the Supreme Court were Protestant, including Chief Justice F. B. T. Carter; the attorney general was Sir William Whiteway; the solicitor general was James S. Winter. See n. 56 above re: Orange connections/sympathies. The grand jury was a mixture of Protestants and Catholics.
55. Meetings at Carbonear, 23 January 1885, and Harbour Grace, 24 January 1885, reported in the *Evening Mercury*, 27 January 1885, and *Harbour Grace Standard*, 26 and 31 January 1885. The *Standard* concurred that the all-Catholic juries had 'succeeded in robbing Protestants of their birth rights, and of overthrowing the very foundations of Justice, Law and order'.
56. See evidence in Howard, typescript, of the following: William Ash, pp. 11–12; Martha Butt, p. 21; Archibald French, pp. 47–8; Deborah Marshall, p. 68; Priscilla Shute, p. 98; Pierce Wade, p. 109; Margaret Wiseman, p. 116; and Roseanne Wiseman, p. 116.

57. Papers such as the *St John's Daily Star*, the *Evening Telegram*, and the *Daily News* provided extensive coverage of these events in Ireland throughout the spring and summer.
58. For an excellent discussion of the development of the SDIL and FOIF in Newfoundland, see Patrick Mannion, *A Land of Dreams: Ethnicity, Nationalism, and the Irish in Newfoundland, Nova Scotia, and Maine, 1880–1923* (Montreal and Kingston: McGill-Queen's University Press, 2018). For further discussion of the SDIL within a biography about one of its chief organisers, Katherine Hughes, see Pádraig Ó Siadhail, *Katherine Hughes: A Life and a Journey* (Newcastle, ON: Penumbra Press, 2014). For a discussion of the broader FOIF movement, see Michael Doorley, *Irish-American Diaspora Nationalism: The Friends of Irish Freedom, 1916–1935* (Dublin: Four Courts Press, 2005).
59. *St John's Daily Star*, 22 September 1917.
60. Mannion, *Land of Dreams*, pp. 202–3.
61. *St John's Daily Star*, 8 and 16 April 1920; *Evening Telegram*, 9 and 16 April 1920.
62. PANL, GN 1/3/A, Box 111, 1920–1, Despatch No. 277, memo, 24 April 1920, draft despatch, Harris to Milner, 8 May 1920; and CO 194, fol., 298, Despatch No. 277, Harris to Milner, 8 May 1920.
63. *St John's Daily Star*, 8 and 12 July 1920.
64. *St John's Daily Star*, 28 October 1920, reporting on a joint meeting held the previous night.
65. 'Democrat' to *St John's Daily Star*, 9 and 13 October 1920.
66. Mannion, *Land of Dreams*, pp. 206, 210.
67. Ibid. pp. 201–14.
68. *St John's Daily Star*, 28 October 1920.
69. *St John's Daily Star*, 4 December 1920; *Evening Telegram*, 4 December 1920.
70. The reference to an epitaph harks to the dying words of Robert Emmett, a young United Irishman who led an aborted rebellion in 1803. In his speech from the dock, just before execution, he urged the Irish people not to write his epitaph until Ireland had gained independence and taken its place among the nations of the earth. He has since featured prominently in the pantheon of Irish republican saints and martyrs.
71. PANL, MG 612, records of the Benevolent Irish Society (BIS), 1822–1979.
72. Additional research might reveal that there is even a connection between the overwhelmingly anti-Confederate voting among the Irish Catholic population in 1869 and 1948 – that rather than being 'priest-led', Irish Catholics in Newfoundland were articulating their desire to remain free of an Anglo-Protestant oligarchy in Ottawa. The spectre of Fenian ghosts can also help us to understand the frantic mustering of the 'Protestant vote' to counter the 'Catholic vote' in the referenda of the late 1940s. And it is interesting to note that Michael Cashin, who would later lead the anti-Confederate forces of the National Convention and two national referenda, was reported by Katherine Hughes to de Valera in 1920 as 'developing from Redmondite status [constitutional nationalist; Home Rule supporter] to republican' (Hughes, quoted in Mannion, *Land of Dreams*, p. 206).

TEN

Cosmopolitan Engagements: Class, Place and Diplomacy in the Gulf of St Lawrence Fisheries, 1815–1854

Kurt Korneski

Politicians, civil servants and other government officials, men such as Lorenzo Sabine, George Brown Goode, Phillip Tocque, Matthew Warren and Moses Perley, all wrote early histories of the fisheries of the Gulf of St Lawrence. Their studies partly grew out of international disputes over that region and the waters lying off of north-eastern North America more generally. Indeed, in some cases discussions among politicians and diplomats engaged in negotiations over the fisheries led to the studies themselves.[1] In other instances, a more passive, but nevertheless partisan position is detectable in the general interpretation of detailed accounts of the timing and methods of different fisheries, and of the terms of treaties governing who could fish where, often with attention to fuzzy treaty language that might provide diplomats and politicians with leverage as they manoeuvred to maximise the extent to which crews from their respective countries and kingdoms could exploit different marine species.[2] Since the publication of these early analyses, historians, generally university-trained and employed, have added a steady stream of contributions. Some of the earliest of these scholars continued to focus on formal politics, political economy and diplomacy, mainly as a part of imperial history.[3] Subsequently, others turned their attention more squarely to economic matters, focusing on marketing, distribution and the causes of 'underdevelopment'.[4] In the last several decades, social historians have added much to our understanding of family life, the history of women and gender, the history of environmental change, the credit system and myriad other aspects of social relations of production in the fisheries.[5]

Taken together, these scholars have provided a valuable contribution to our understanding of an array of topics. Most, however, have tended to take as given a determining relationship between diplomatic and other agreements pertaining to the fisheries, and the personnel, employment and other relations among residents of the colonies and countries to which those agreements pertained.[6] Thus, it has been widely assumed that American vessels were crewed by American sailors who represented the aims and interests of the United States fishing sector as set out in formal agreements and policies. The same for the French, the Newfoundlanders, Nova Scotians and others. This assumption was often more the product of disinterest than serious consideration. Most scholars of imperial diplomacy wrote before history 'from the bottom up' was much a part of the intellectual landscape. Thus, as with a large number of historians before them, they kept their attention on matters of state, with little interest in the lives of 'ordinary people' and 'life on the ground'. For their part, many social historians were cognisant that residents of coastal colonies were subjects of empires and that their lives were in some ways shaped by imperial connections. However, they were mainly preoccupied by important debates and topics – class relations, gender, race, family production, among others – that they tended to conceptualise separately from imperial relations per se, a topic that some equated with the 'dry as dustism' of an earlier era. In this regard, historians of fisheries and coastal communities were not outliers. As scholars ranging from Phillip Buckner to Antoinette Burton have commented, this was part of a wider tendency in the post-1960 surge in social history, much of which was driven by projects of reframing nationalist histories in a setting where imperialism had become a 'bad word'.[7]

My point is not to criticise others for addressing the pressing questions of their day, for such shifting preoccupations are generative and necessary. Rather, it is to suggest, along with a many recent historians of Canada, the US, Britain, the Antipodes and elsewhere, that there is much insight to be gained from analysing how formal politics and high diplomacy and the history of social life are intertwined and mutually structuring.[8] Examining the Gulf fisheries from the close of the Napoleonic wars to the advent of the Reciprocity Treaty (1854) from such a perspective suggests that an informal set of relations, in which nation and metropole figured indirectly and unexpectedly, existed alongside the rights of access granted under treaty agreements and other formal arrangements. Though shaped by formal agreements and associated enforcement efforts, diverse social and geographic locations within a shifting set of transnational, trans-local political-economic conditions and ecological changes, rather than the homologous relations often assumed in histories of the fisheries, were central to developments in this informal realm. The crews of many vessels consisted of a mix of people from different nations and colonies, most of whom signed on with whichever master could, under prevailing national policies and treaty agreements, provide the most remunerative terms. Such crews, in turn, sought out the richest fishing areas, often with little regard for whether their endeavours honoured the terms of agreements negotiated on high. In short, employment and trading relations in the Gulf fisheries reflected the distinct, even conflicting, aims of differently situated merchants and outfitters and working people, rather than the dictates of the treaties of high imperialism, with working people and those who traded with and employed them deploying cosmopolitan strategies in their commercial and working lives.

Beyond providing insights into the history of employment and trading relations in the fisheries, examining these informal arrangements also reveals important aspects of colonial relations more broadly conceived. Particularly since the 1960s, historians have emphasised that coercion and the assertion of hegemonic rule from the metropolitan centre were important to British imperialism. More recently, scholars have revived and reconceived concepts – the notion of a 'British world', for example – that had been central to early twentieth-century thinking about the empire, their point being to highlight that cooperation between metropole and differently situated colonists was also important to the durability and stability of the Empire.[9] In this view, even though colonial subjects, and these scholars emphasise elite views, had interests that diverged from their metropolitan counterparts, on balance the benefits (primarily emotional and economic) to be had in remaining within Britain's orbit outweighed the benefits of severing ties with the 'mother country'. The case of the Gulf fisheries exemplifies some of the tendencies these historians have emphasised. As metropolitan groups sought to secure resources and strategic advantage throughout a wide range of locales around the world, they made tradeoffs with rival states to secure stability and looked for cost-effective modes of governing imperial spaces. In the Gulf, such tradeoffs and cost-saving measures resulted in the admission of rival fishing fleets into waters off British colonies with a minimum of surveillance to ensure that foreign vessels operated according to treaty arrangements. The presence of such vessels irritated colonial merchants and politicians. They believed that a monopoly over marine spaces would translate into increased profits and tax revenues that would, in turn, undergird vibrant businesses and robust, self-sufficient colonial states. Nevertheless, they remained within the empire. Without the backing of Britain, colonial states and businesses were no match for the US and France. This case also suggests, however, that the divergences between the interests of colonial and metropolitan elites themselves incidentally helped to strengthen and stabilise the Empire. For the many working people who were important participants in the improvised trading and employment relations in the gulf, participating in and defending those relations and transactions helped to preserve the indeterminacy and improvisation that made the Empire liveable for them.

Treaties and tensions

The disputes and negotiations that inspired early histories of the Gulf fisheries had a long pedigree. The fisheries of the north-west Atlantic were among the earliest industries that Europeans pursued in North America in the era of sustained contact that began some 500 years ago. For much of that time, Europeans negotiated with one another and with Indigenous people formally and otherwise as they sought to access or monopolise fishing grounds and shore spaces essential to processing their catch and to sustaining crews, vessels and equipment.[10] Formal agreements germane to the fisheries of the Gulf in the early nineteenth century had their roots in peace treaties and conventions that concluded conflicts between Britain and France and the United States. With the French, the British agreed, as parts of the Treaties of Paris (1814 and 1815) that ended the Napoleonic wars, to reinstate those rights to the fishery in place before the outbreak of war between the two powers in 1793. This effectively reinstated the terms and conditions of the 1783 Treaty of Paris. In essence, the French regained control over St Pierre and Miquelon, two islands located a short distance from Newfoundland's south coast, as a base for their offshore (also called the 'bank') fishery. Additionally, they secured rights to fish, and to use terrestrial resources essential to their fishery, on the coast of Newfoundland from Cape St John to Cape Ray during the fishing season. American fishermen operated under the Convention of 1818, an agreement negotiated in the wake of the War of 1812. The Convention restricted American fishing crews' access to waters within three miles of the shore, and to the shore itself, to three specific areas – the south and west coasts of Newfoundland from Ramea to Quirpon Islands, portions of the coast of Labrador north of Mount Joly, and the Magdalen Islands in the Gulf of St Lawrence. It also allowed such crews to fish in the Gulf outside of the three-mile limit, and to seek shelter near shore if necessary at any time.[11]

In meeting rooms in Paris, London and Philadelphia, where representatives of different governments hammered out agreements, there were few British colonists. Instead, British officials, members of the metropolitan government's diplomatic corps, met their counterparts from France and the United States.[12] Details trickled out as the negotiations were ongoing. However, decisions about how the fisheries would operate mostly reached those invested and working in these industries in the weeks and months after they were signed. Not surprisingly, officials and merchants based in the colonies and oriented to their fisheries sometimes found the agreements wanting, for their interests were not identical to the leading lights in the British state. Diplomats were concerned with a broad collection of localities essential to Britain's economic and strategic wellbeing. In conceding fishing areas to nations with which Britain had recently been embroiled in war, diplomats hoped to put in place at least partial foundations for a peaceful co-existence in future. By contrast, merchants, who held much sway in colonial political institutions, fixated on the resources and spaces in their immediate localities, and especially on securing exclusive rights to them.[13] Such control was important. Many of those invested in the fisheries had established, or vastly expanded, their fortunes because they had enjoyed a quasi-monopoly over the Gulf and other fishing grounds during the late eighteenth-century period of war and strife that the above-mentioned treaties brought to an end. Reasonably enough, these colonial elites believed that the loss of exclusive access to fishing grounds threatened the vibrancy of their concerns, and the stability of local colonial economies more generally.[14]

Even before the different peace treaties and conventions had been signed, many Newfoundland-based merchants expressed concern as rumours circulated that the British might readmit French and American fleets to the north-west Atlantic as part of a strategy to build a stable postwar peace.[15] Following the signing of agreements, Nova Scotia-based traders joined their Newfoundland counterparts in expressing dismay over what they saw as the British government's willingness to sacrifice the welfare of those who had stood by the 'mother country' in her time of need in favour of some skewed idea of the 'national interest'.[16] In the months and years that followed, dismay turned to indignation, with the increasingly intense nature of complaints reflecting two key developments. The first grew out of the postwar fisheries policies of the French and American governments. Both governments offered subsidies (also called bounties) to would-be investors in the fisheries.[17] Such incentives encouraged American and French traders to invest in the fisheries, and enabled them to build significant fortunes quickly, parts of which they invested in larger ships and expensive, more intensive gear that enabled them to catch larger quantities of fish in the Gulf, on the Grand Banks and elsewhere, which they, in turn, sold on international markets, on the likes of which merchants based in British colonies also depended.[18] Colonial merchants, then, not only faced increased competition, but, in their view, massively unfair competition, and in an era of increasing emphasis on free trade within the British Empire, they found little assistance as they tried to maintain profitable operations.[19] The second source of complaint grew out of the conduct of crews that Americans and French outfitters (also called 'armateurs') employed in the Gulf. Particularly concerning were reports, increasingly frequent by the 1830s, from colonial merchants based in areas outside of colonial capitals that the crews of foreign vessels regularly fished outside of waters allotted to them under treaty agreements. Such concerns reflected the continued desire of colonial merchants to limit the access of rival fishing crews to colonial waters. Just as merchants of St John's and Halifax had protested against the re-entry of rivals into the fisheries after the end of the Napoleonic wars, in the 1830s the same groups demanded that the British government ensure that foreign fishing vessels remain in waters allotted to them, thereby ensuring that whatever fish or other marine species happened to be in British areas were reserved for colonial operations.[20]

British officials met calls for increased vigilance in policing the Gulf unenthusiastically, as they did not want to shoulder the considerable financial burden that would have been required to police the area more effectively. In 1830, as in 1815, the British had interests in a wide range of localities, many of which were more commercially and strategically important than the northern North American fisheries. Moreover, at about the same time that colonial merchants made their plea, tensions over North Africa and the Netherlands were already straining relations between the French and British governments. Imperial officials, then, were unwilling to risk provoking another war over the over the matter of the North American fisheries.[21] Though disappointed, merchants based in the Atlantic region saw little advantage in dispensing with the British connection. Even though British officials did not pursue the course colonial merchants would have liked, in the early nineteenth century colonial states and commercial sectors were weak by comparison with those of France and the United States. There is little chance that colonial elites would have fared better in either realm without the backing of the metropolitan government. Thus, rather than sever the British connection, colonial statesmen enjoyed the protections it offered, while continuing to lobby the imperial state for further advantages.

Investigations into the 'actually existing' conditions in the fisheries were often the result of such lobbying. Indeed, colonial officials surveyed the regions under their jurisdiction to amass evidence they could use as they pressed for changes to imperial policy. The British government, often in response to such calls, conducted their own investigations. Rather than assuage colonial concerns, such inquiries produced further grounds for complaint, for they revealed that just as the captains of foreign vessels did not respect the spheres of activity prescribed in treaty agreements, a wide range of Gulf residents did not pay attention to imperial, colonial and national boundaries as they conducted employment and trading relations. Indeed, many American and French firms depended heavily on British colonists for their workforces. Working people from British colonies regularly hired on as crew members on American vessels. As Commander Cochrane of H.M.S. *Sappho* noted, in many instances 'seventeen or eighteen hands' were 'hired to make up a complement of 25 in some of the large mackerel schooners'. At times, vessels showed up with only three or four hands on board, hiring the remainder from such places as Shelburne, Bay Chaleur, Gaspe, Tignish, Burin and elsewhere.[22] British subjects facilitated foreign operations, especially in areas where the French had rights, by staffing and protecting shore-based facilities.[23] Throughout the Gulf, British fishers also provided large quantities of bait essential to the increasingly capital-intensive offshore operations that American and French outfitters developed with the assistance of subsidies from their respective governments. Finally, the inquiries revealed that British subjects employed in the bait trade and otherwise conspired with the masters of foreign vessels in a large-scale illicit traffic in tobacco, flour, spirits and a variety of other items essential to the survival and comfort of coastal residents.[24]

Colonial officials

For colonial officials, these practices were intolerable. The encroachment of foreign vessels onto grounds allotted to British colonists was a problem for obvious reasons. Any fish or other species that French and American vessels took from areas assigned exclusively to British colonists could not then fill the holds of colonial vessels, nor contribute to the profits of a colonial firm. With the crewing of foreign, primarily American-based vessels with British labour and illegal trading, commercial men such as Halifax-based John Starr and James Uniacke also raised alarm bells. According to them, these arrangements were abysmal and grew out of the predatory nature of Americans and unpatriotic disposition of some colonists, with the latter group supposedly being plied with inexpensive liquor. The resulting loss of British labour to foreign fleets was a matter of national concern (meaning the concern of the British government), for the lost value-producing potential of such labour affected the profitability of colonial firms. Moreover, if colonial labour went to foreign firms and if colonial subjects traded illegally with foreign capitalists, there were fewer workers available to catch fish for colonial operations, and fewer fish, and fewer goods, passed through customs houses, thereby starving colonial states of revenue. In short, the employment of British workers in foreign firms made it difficult for colonial businessmen to build up the strong, competitive enterprises and large tax bases essential to the independent, self-sufficient governments and businesses they imagined as being central to 'British civilisation'.[25]

The illegal trade imperilled merchants' profit margins, mainly because it undermined the system of clientage – often called the 'truck system' – in which colonial merchants engaged extensively. In that system, merchants extended on credit, food and necessary supplies to sustain fishermen and their families. At the end of a fishing season, the fisherman would turn over the product of the family's labour to the merchant, who paid the fisherman for his catch, minus the cost of any items advanced earlier in the year. In theory, merchant and fisher met as equals. In reality, the merchant set the price both for fish and for imported goods, charging high prices for the latter and paying a low price for the former. Fishing families often ended up in a cycle of debt that kept them beholden to whichever merchant supplied them.[26] Merchants could only maximally benefit, however, if they had something approaching a monopoly over the catch of fishing families and firm control over access to imported goods. The illicit trade undermined those conditions. The direct employment of colonists, therefore, represented the wholesale theft of labour. Illicit trading had the same effect, though it stole the hours of labour embodied in goods rather than the more general labouring potential of bodies themselves. Given that the illicit trade bypassed customs houses, it diminished colonial revenue, increasing the likelihood that colonial governments would require assistance from the imperial state.²⁷ As Starr put it, the illegal trade deprived 'the merchant, who has supplied those people with their outfits, of his payment – the earnings of the Fishermen are squandered in this useless traffic, his credit is destroyed, and his time is completely lost to the country'.²⁸

Working people, foreign capitalists and trading and working in the Gulf

There was some truth in the arguments and representations that colonial politicians made to the metropolitan government. The loss of British labour to American and French employers represented a loss of value-creating potential that ultimately underlay profits and tax revenue. Moreover, colonial merchants rightly pointed out that massive American and French fishing operations depended on British colonists for bait, and that British colonists thus helped to undermine colonial revenues through enabling that industry.²⁹ They were also correct in their estimation of the deleterious effects of this and other illegal trading on colonial businesses and governments. Yet it is not clear that the improvised trading and employment relations were the product of disloyal subjects, predatory French and American fishing captains, or that they were entirely inimical to the imperial interests. There is, for example, much evidence that many coastal residents who traded with, or took employment from, French and American outfitters still saw themselves, and articulated demands on their governments, as loyal 'free born Englishmen'.³⁰ Further suggesting a widespread attachment to Crown and Empire is the tendency for many of those who signed on to American vessels to return to their homes in British colonies at the end of the fishing season. There was no reason that such people could not have migrated to the US or elsewhere, and in fact a large number of residents, presumably with different sentiments, did exactly that.

It is, however, difficult to determine the motives of the thousands of people who hired on or traded with the French and British. After all, in the Gulf, as in many other localities, working people left few records. More certain is that large numbers of working men strove to secure independence, the definition of which paralleled the ideals central to the political institutions and commercial concerns that colonial elites sought to establish. For working men, as for elites, independence was the preserve of men. For them, it involved heading and organising the labour of a household. In combination with some manner of productive property – whether nets, wharves and boats for fishing, ploughs and seed for farming, traps for furring or some combination of all of these and other implements and facilities – those collective exertions ideally produced for subsistence and trade to a great enough extent to meet the needs of all family members. Indeed, as other scholars have shown, one of the features of the truck system that made it appealing to working people, and tenable as a system of trade, was that it provided some semblance of independence for those steeped in nineteenth-century ideas about the appropriate life of 'freeborn Englishmen'. Rather than depend on the patronage of a mercantile firm for wages, a man could become the patriarchal head of a fishing family. As the owner of productive property – boats, outbuildings, cordage, wharves, gear, nets – necessary to the conduct of his fisheries, he could organise the labour of his household, trading the produce of his family supposedly as an independent contractor.[31]

It is also clear that the modes of spatial governance conducive to independence for colonial merchants and working people in Britain's Atlantic colonies were different and often incompatible. The monopolisation of labour, trade and marine spaces reserved for British colonists, for example, may have enriched and empowered local governments and the commercial elites that dominated them. But the success of elite efforts to 'surround' and 'take hold' of spaces and people had very different consequences for working people.[32] The logic of the truck system, for example, tended to the extremes, with the highest prices charged for imports and the lowest prices paid for produce. If truly 'surrounded', a fishing household could likely expect little more than subsistence, and that did not much resemble the prosperous life they imagined as central to the life of independent men. The widespread tendency for working people to labour for and trade with foreign capitalists, then, did not indicate that they had been duped by predatory outsiders. Rather, it reflected calculated decisions to take advantage of, and through their cooperation with American and French businessmen, bolster, an informal set of relations that buttressed working people's independence even as it served the interests of American and French outfitters. Embracing such opportunities enabled British colonists and foreign capitalists to confront or to circumvent the designs of colonial merchants, which, if enacted, would have limited the prospects of colonists and foreign outfitters alike.

That such an informal set of relations existed is central to understanding the history of the Gulf fisheries. But we should not assume that treaties and national policies were unimportant simply because they did not determine the rhythm of social life in the Gulf in a straightforward way. Treaty agreements gave American and French outfitters the right to use resources in the first place, and they made access to some areas, both by colonial and foreign merchants, easier than others. Moreover, national policies shaped conditions on board vessels and the strategies that outfitters of different nations pursued. Social and trading relations in the Gulf, then, were often the unintended results of conditions underwritten by formal agreements combined with the improvisation of people of different social ranks all driving to maximise their advantages and live out the lives of independence in light of, but without rigid restrictions imposed by, different national, imperial and colonial governments.

With employment relations, for example, the different roles that Britons played in American and French operations reflected the distinctive commercial strategies that the French and the Americans developed, and the different kinds of opportunities and challenges British subjects faced because of how treaty arrangements shaped commercial and other arrangements in different locales. French and American fleets received subsidies. Yet, the two national governments dispensed their subsidies in different ways. The US government generally paid subsidies according to the size of the vessels deployed in a particular industry.[33] Consequently, there was no disincentive to hiring British subjects as crew. Indeed, for US vessel owners the prospect of securing experienced hands intimately familiar with the coves and shoals of the Gulf was enticing, as it made it more likely that crews would realise a good catch and that expensive vessels would return unscathed at the end of the fishing season. For British colonists, work on American vessels was also appealing. The American government's subsidies underwrote more remunerative wages and better working conditions. Such conditions and wages appealed tremendously to British subjects seeking prosperity and independence.[34]

By contrast, the French state rewarded their armateurs for employing their countrymen by paying bounties for each French sailor employed and for each quintal (112 pounds) of fish landed. Accordingly, the French tended not to hire British subjects as crew. Treaty arrangements, however, made hiring shore-based workers in places like the west coast of Newfoundland highly appealing. Most significant were clauses that limited French occupation of coastal parts of the island to the fishing season. This restriction meant that French captains risked losing the boats, gear, surplus salt, and other supplies and materials that they had brought to Newfoundland coast, either through foul weather or theft or acts of vandalism by sealing crews and others who happened upon the coast in winter. While they could have packed up their equipment and supplies, and hauled them back to France, such items took up space, which could not then be used to transport fish. Rather than lose cargo space or supplies, the French offered wages and supplies to British settlers as caretakers, also called 'guardians', of French fishing stations.[35]

Employment by the French appealed to some Britons operating in the Gulf at least partly because treaty arrangements limited their options. The Treaties of Paris (1814 and 1815) provided the French with rights to Newfoundland, though the exact nature of these rights was somewhat ambiguous and British negotiators had refused to grant exclusive rights to parts of Newfoundland. They did, however, forbid British subjects to interfere with French fisheries. In essence, this meant that British fishermen had the right to fish on the treaty coast provided they did not interfere with French operations.[36] The non-interference measures had led the imperial government to refuse to allow the establishment of electoral districts on the west coast of Newfoundland when representative institutions were set up on the island in 1832. It also undermined security of property on parts of the Newfoundland coast, for if French captains could show that a particular wharf or building interfered with their fishery, they could, and did at times, demand the structure's removal.[37] The tenuousness of any establishment on the French shore discouraged colonial merchants from investment in premises necessary for the conduct of a substantial trade. Uncertainties linked to the treaties themselves meant that the French offered some of the few employment opportunities that might undergird the independence of colonists on this coast.

A similar combination of inter and intra class division, international treaties and national policies encouraged and shaped illicit trading in the region. In a general sense, this trade flourished because the interests of foreign capitalists and working people in British colonies often aligned. American and French merchants and outfitters hoped to maximise profits. Procuring and selling a catch was one way of doing so. The fact that international treaties gave foreign merchants access to the coastal areas of British colonies, most of which were patrolled infrequently, provided added commercial opportunities. If merchants could carry significant quantities of trade goods, avoid customs duties and, therefore, offer British subjects imported items at a lower cost than British traders while still making a profit, they were happy to do so. For British subjects in Nova Scotia, PEI, New Brunswick or Newfoundland the source of lower-priced goods stretched the income they earned from their operations and provided an escape from exploitative relations of truck.

If these general motives were important for a range of coastal residents, the content, form and participants in the trade varied depending on how specific localities and actors fit into international agreements. The French and Americans did not trade evenly throughout the entire Gulf region. Instead, they occupied distinct, if overlapping, spheres. The Americans were most heavily involved in trading off Nova Scotia, Prince Edward Island and New Brunswick, and the French most active on the south and west coasts of Newfoundland, with these general orientations reflecting the fishing locations of the two fleets. After all, the bulk of American vessels engaged in the cod and mackerel fisheries off the Maritime colonies, while the French had rights to St Pierre (in close proximity to Newfoundland's south coast) and on the west coast and eastern side of the Great Northern Peninsula.[38] Moreover, on Newfoundland's west coast, the treaty stipulations that discouraged British colonial investment and limited employment opportunities also provided incentives for British colonists to trade with foreign capitalists. Indeed, if British settlers in this region had insufficient capital to build schooners or other long-range vessels, they had little choice but to trade with French and American traders who frequented the shore, as stable sources of essential items were otherwise few and far between.

While French and American traders took any of a variety of fish or other products in exchange for goods, residents of Newfoundland remarked that the

French were especially interested in British-caught cod. Again, this tendency stemmed from the French government's policy regarding bounties, for the French government paid bounties for crew members employed *and* for each quintal of fish that a ship brought home. French armateurs realised very soon after the peace of 1815 that they could earn substantial returns by adding British-caught fish to their cargoes. From the perspective of the armateurs of Bayonne, Brieux and other French ports, they would ideally profit both from the trade with British settlers and from the added bounties they received from the French government.[39]

Conclusion

Throughout the nineteenth century, colonial statesmen often diverged significantly from their metropolitan counterparts in their aims. Metropolitan officials focused on a global network of diverse locales, many of which differed significantly in their composition and in their relations with Britain, with the goal of maintaining access to areas of strategic and economic interest without bankrupting the British treasury. Colonial elites often operated on a more limited scale, with their attention primarily on spaces and resources adjacent to the legislatures and commercial hubs in which they exerted much influence. This configuration of interests was clearly on display in the Gulf fisheries. Colonial merchants built significant fortunes and capacity in the fisheries, especially during the period of war and international strife in the late eighteenth and early nineteenth centuries. Such men chafed as the imperial state readmitted rival fishing fleets following the end of those conflicts. Readmitting rival fleets might cultivate goodwill and promote stability that would make war less likely, a move calculated to strengthen Britain's position in the world generally speaking. It meant competition and reduced profits for colonial businessmen. Moreover, in refusing to patrol the Gulf and the coast to police fishing vessels once they entered the region, the British government had effectively helped to put in place an extensive illegal trade. That exchange undermined mercantile control over the produce of British colonists. It also diminished customs returns, and, from the perspective of colonial politicians, thereby robbed them of the means to establish robust independent states.

Historians have long noted that despite these perceived abuses, colonial statesmen persisted in the 'British connection' because the emotional, pecuniary and political benefits of the link outweighed the advantages of leaving. The case of the Gulf fisheries suggests that the divergences between the two ruling groups also likely helped to stabilise imperial relations, although for reasons that neither those in colonial or imperial capitals probably understood. The divergences of metropolitan and colonial interests produced an indeterminate set of relationships in which colonists could develop improvised trading and employment relations as they sought to secure independence. Something of the importance of these improvised relationships is suggested by popular reactions to instances when colonial states came close to asserting control over territories technically under their domain. Working people could, and did, defend alternative ideas about how spaces, resources and transactions should be governed, sometimes violently.[40] The case of the Gulf fisheries suggests, then, the importance of taking heed of the costs and benefits of the imperial connection for merchants and political elites at different scales to understand the stability and vibrancy of the British world order. It highlights that such stability also depended on the will of a wide range of other social groups. The starting point for their calculations could be quite different.

Notes

1. Lorenzo Sabine, *Report on the Principal Fisheries of the American Seas* (Washington, DC: Robert Armstrong, 1853); Charles Isham, *The Fishery Question: Its Origin, History, and Present Situation* (New York: Putnam, 1887); Joseph Doran, *Our Fishery Rights in the North Atlantic* (Philadelphia: Allen, Lane, and Scott, 1888).
2. Moses Perley, *Report on the Sea and River Fisheries of New Brunswick* (Fredericton: J. Simpson, 1852); Matthew Warren, *Lecture on Newfoundland and Its Fisheries* (St John's: Office of the Morning Post, 1853); Philip Tocque, *Newfoundland: As it was, and as it is in 1877* (Toronto: Hunter Rose and Company, 1878), pp. 182–33, 287–32, 333–64.
3. For instance, Harold Innis, *The Cod Fisheries: The History of an International Economy* (New Haven: Yale University Press, 1940); Frederic Thompson, *The French Shore Problem in Newfoundland: An Imperial Study* (Toronto: University of Toronto Press, 1961); Charles de la Morandière, *Histoire de la pêche francaise de la morue dans l'Amerique septentrionale*, 3 vols (Paris: G.P. Maisonneuve et Larose, 1962-6).
4. David Alexander, *The Decay of Trade: An Economic History of the Newfoundland Saltfish Trade, 1935–65* (St John's: ISER, 1977); Shannon Ryan, *Fish Out of Water: The Newfoundland Saltfish Trade, 1814–1914* (St John's: Breakwater, 1986); Rosemary Ommer, *From Outpost to Outport: A Structural Analysis of the Jersey-Gaspe Cod Fishery, 1767–1886* (Montreal and Kingston: McGill-Queen's University Press, 1991).
5. Daniel Vickers, *Farmers and Fishermen: Two Centuries of Work in Essex Country, Massachusetts, 1630–1830* (Chapel Hill: University of North Carolina Press, 1994); Sean Cadigan, *Hope and Deception in Conception Bay: Merchant Settler Relations in Newfoundland, 1785–1855* (Toronto: University of Toronto Press, 1995); Miriam Wright, *A Fishery for Modern Times: The State and the Industrialization of the Newfoundland Fishery, 1934–68* (Don Mills: Oxford University Press, 2001); David Starkey et al. (eds), *A History of the North Atlantic Fisheries* vol. 1, *From Early Times to the Mid-Nineteenth Century* (Bremen: Verlag H. M. Hauschild, 2009); Jeffrey Bolster, *The Moral Sea: Fishing the Atlantic in the Age of Sail* (Cambridge, MA: Harvard University Press, 2012).
6. I include here my own work, which sometimes echoes these broader historiographical tendencies. See, for example, *Conflicted Colony: Critical Episodes in Nineteenth Century Newfoundland and Labrador* (Montreal and Kingston: McGill-Queen's University Press, 2016), pp. 31–3. Other examples include Sean Cadigan, *Newfoundland and Labrador: A History* (Toronto: University of Toronto Press, 2009), pp. 138–40; Peter Neary, 'The French and American Shore Questions As Factors in Newfoundland History', in James Hiller and Peter Neary (eds), *Newfoundland in the Nineteenth and Twentieth Centuries: Essays in Interpretation* (Toronto: University of Toronto

Press, 1980), pp. 95–122. Amateur historians tend toward the same interpretative practices. See, James Candow, 'Migrants and Residents: The Interplay between European and Domestic Fisheries in Northeast North America, 1502–1854', in David Starkey et al. (eds), *A History of the North Atlantic Fisheries Volume I: From Early Times to the Mid-Nineteenth Century* (Verlag H. M. Hauschild GmbH, Premen, 2009), pp. 416–52. The main exception is Bryan Payne's *Fishing a Borderless Sea: Environmental Territorialism in the North Atlantic, 1818–1910* (East Lansing: Michigan State University Press, 2010).

7. Antoinette Burton, 'Rules of Thumb: British History and "Imperial Culture" in Nineteenth and Twentieth Century Britain', *Women's History Review*, 3:4, pp. 483–501; and Burton, 'Who Needs the Nation? Interrogating "British" History', in Catherine Hall (ed.), *Culture of Empire: A Reader* (New York: Routledge, 2000); Phillip Buckner, 'Whatever Happened to the British Empire', *Journal of the Canadian Historical Association*, 4.1 (1993), pp. 3–32.

8. For examples see Tony Ballantyne, *Webs of Empire: Locating New Zealand's Colonial Past* (Wellington: Bridget Williams Books, 2012), pp. 124–36; Marilyn Lake and Henry Reynolds, *Drawing the Global Colour Line: White Men's Countries and the International Challenge of Racial Equality* (Cambridge: Cambridge University Press, 2008); Catherine Hall and Sonya O. Rose, 'Introduction: Being at Home With the Empire', in Hall and Rose (eds), *At Home With the Empire: Metropolitan Culture and the Imperial World* (Cambridge: Cambridge University Press, 2006).

9. Recent examples include John Darwin, *The Empire Project: The Rise and Fall of the British World System, 1830–1970* (Cambridge: Cambridge University Press, 2009); James Belich, *Replenishing the Earth: The Settler Revolution and the Rise of the Anglo-World, 1783–1929* (Oxford: Oxford University Press, 2009).

10. Jean Pierre Proulx, *Basque Whaling in Labrador in the 16th Century* (Ottawa: Parks Canada, 1993); James Tuck and Robert Grenier, *Red Bay, Labrador: Whaling Capital of the World, 1550–1600* (St John's: Atlantic Archaeology, 1989); Sean Cadigan, *Newfoundland and Labrador: A History* (Toronto: University of Toronto Press, 2009), pp. 26–44; Harold Innis, *The Cod Fisheries*, p. 15.

11. Neary, 'The French and American Shore Questions as Factors in Newfoundland History', p. 115.

12. Rainer Baehre, 'Diplomacy, International Law, and Foreign Fishing in Newfoundland, 1814–30: Revising the 1815 Treaty of Paris and the 1818 Convention', in Jim Phillips, R. Roy McMurtry and John T. Saywell (eds), *Essays in the History of Canadian Law: A Tribute to Peter N. Oliver* (Toronto: University of Toronto Press, 2008), pp. 353–87.

13. Nova Scotia, Prince Edward Island and New Brunswick all were granted representative assemblies in the eighteenth century (1758, 1773 and 1784 respectively). Newfoundland did not have an assembly of this type until 1832. There were, however, different combinations of judicial officials, merchants and others who acted to administer justice locally, and who lobbied the imperial government.

14. Shannon Ryan, 'Fishery to Colony: A Newfoundland Watershed, 1793–1815', *Acadiensis*, XII, 2 (Spring 1983), pp. 34–52.

15. The Rooms: Provincial Archives Division [hereafter TRPAD], Office of the Colonial Secretary Fonds, Series 2/1: Outgoing Correspondence, vol. 25, Memorial of the Merchants and Principle Residents in the Trade and Fisheries of Newfoundland Assembled in the Merchants' Hall in St John's to Richard Godwin Keats, 27 October 1813, pp. 109–16.

16. Report from the Select Committee on Newfoundland Trade: With Minutes of Evidence Taken Before the Committee and an Appendix (London: Parliament of Great Britain, 1817); 'Address of His Majesty's Council and House of Assembly on the Subject of the Fisheries', 26 March 1818, in *Journal of the House of Assembly of Nova Scotia* [hereafter JHANS], *1819*, pp. 94–5; 'Address of His Majesty's Council and the House of Assembly', 27 March 1820, in *JHANS 1820*, p. 226.

17. Korneski, *Conflicted Colony*, p. 28.
18. Alexander Milne, 'Report on the Protection of the Gulf of St Lawrence Fisheries', 2 October 1841, in John Beeler (ed.), *The Milne Papers* (Aldershot: Ashgate, 2004), pp. 128-41; 'Report of Captain Decourcy of H.M.S. *Helena* on the Fisheries of Newfoundland, Address to Vice-Admiral, Right Hon. Thomas, Earl of Dundonald', in *Journal of the House of Assembly of Newfoundland* [hereafter *JHANL*] *1851* (St John's: E. D. Shea, 1851), Appendix p. 151.
19. Darwin, *The Empire Project*, pp. 25-9.
20. A key source of early information were petitions from traders and owners of large vessels from areas adjacent to fishing grounds. At times, petitioners themselves appear to have encouraged such encroachment, with their petitions reflecting a desire to see the arrangements between themselves and foreign capitalists altered rather than ended. See, for example, discussion of a petition of 'John Taylor and others interested in the Mackerel Fishery', in *JHANS 1834*, 734; 'A Petition of Richard McHeffey and others, of the County of Hants', in *JHANS 1834*, p. 776; Petition of John Smith, 30 November 1835, Nova Scotia Archives, Department of the Provincial Secretary, RG 7, vol. 8, petition 118; 'Report of the Select Committee to Whom was Referred the Petition of George Lake and others, Inhabitants of Fortune Bay', *Journal of the House of Assembly of Newfoundland* [hereafter *JHANL*], *1835*, 108.
21. Darwin, *The Empire Project*, pp. 25-9.
22. 'Report of H.M. Sappho', 3 October 1851, The National Archives United Kingdom [hereafter TNA], Colonial Office Fonds [hereafter CO] 194/135, pp. 53-6. Report of the Committee on the Fisheries and the Infringement of Existing Treaties by Other Nations [hereafter CIET], in *JHANS 1837*, Evidence: William Crichton, Little Arichat, NS, 20 May 1837; CIET, *JHANS 1837*, Evidence: Francis Cook, Guysborough, NS, 17 March 1831; CIET, *JHANS 1837*, Evidence: Elisha Payson, Brier's Island, NS, 13 May 1837; *Halifax Commission, 1877: Documents and Proceedings* vol. I (Washington: Government Printing Office, 1878) [hereafter HC], Evidence: Captain Simon Chivarie, Souris, PEI, 31 July 1877, p. 1. This paper draws on evidence from the Halifax Commission (1877) [hereafter HC] and the Report of Anglo-French Commission on the Newfoundland fisheries (1859) [hereafter RCNL]. Though these investigations occurred after the end of the study period of this paper, they include reminiscences of the era under consideration.
23. The French entered into such arrangements not long after the peace of 1815, mainly with a scattering of fishing families who had established themselves on the west coast and on the eastern side of the Great Northern Peninsula during the war years, when the French had been absent from the island. RCNL, Evidence: Captain Laignet, New Port au Choix, NL, 5 July 1859, pp. 13-16, in TNA CO 194/160, p. 292; RCNL, Evidence: William Plowman, Port Saunders, NL, 9 July 1859, p. 19, in TNA, CO 194/160, p. 296; RCNL, Evidence: Captain D. M. Eveillard, Quirpon, NL, 15 July 1859, p. 6, in TNA, CO 194/160, p. 312.
24. An 1838 investigation into smuggling indicated that vessels registered to both countries traded widely throughout the coast of Newfoundland. R. B. Dean, H. Richmond, and J. G. Lushington (customs officers) to James Stephen, 26 May 1838, TNA, CO 194/102, pp. 138-41. On the different trades and their orientations see TRPAD, Office of the Colonial Secretary Fonds. Series 2: Incoming Correspondence [hereafter GN 2/2], box 22, vol. 34, Stephen Lushington to Henry Prescott, 13 September 1839; TRPAD, GN 2/2, box 32, vol. 53, James Winter to Honourable Collector of Customs, 10 November 1845, 4-6; Dundonald to the Secretary of the Admiralty, 5 November 1849, TNA, CO 194/132, p. 179; 'Report of H.M. Sappho', 3 October 1851, TNA, CO 194/135, pp. 41-5, 54-5; 'Reports Made by Alexander Milne of Her Majesty's Ship *Crocodile* Relative to the Fisheries of Newfoundland', in *JLCNL 1841* (St John's Ryan and Withers 1841), Appendix p. 30; Milne, 'Report', in Beeler (ed.), *The Milne Papers*, pp. 128-412.
25. CIET, *JHANS 1837*, Evidence: John Starr, Halifax, NS, undated; James Uniacke, et al., 'Report of the Committee of the Fisheries', in *JHANS 1841*, pp. 163-4; TRPAD, MG 633, box 1, Records

of the Chamber of Commerce [hereafter RCC], 20 November 1834 to 5 August 1841,William Thomas, Annual Report of the St John's Chamber of Commerce, 1835; TRPAD, GN 2/2, box 28, RCC, Memorial from Kenneth McLea (on behalf of the Chamber of Commerce) to Governor Harvey, 7 August 1843. The *JHANS 1838* contains copies of depositions and letters of complaint from New Brunswick merchants and politicians. See J. Harvey to Sir Colin Campbell, 27 January 1837, Appendix 17; 'Deposition of Duncan Hay of Carraquette in the Country of Gloucester in the Province of New Brunswick', 24 January 1838, Appendix 17.

26. Jacob Price, 'Conclusion', in Rosemary Ommer (ed.), *Merchant Credit and Labour Strategies in Historical Perspective* (Fredericton: Acadiensis Press, 1990), pp. 360–73; Patricia Thornton, 'The Transition from the Migratory to the Resident Fishery in the Strait of Belle Isle', *Acadiensis*, 19 (Spring, 1990), pp. 92–120; Ommer, *From Outpost to Outport*; Cadigan, *Hope and Deception*.

27. Such concerns are clear in the discussion surrounding the presentation of a petition 'from John Flemming and others engaged in the Nova Scotia fisheries'. See, *JHANS 1837*, pp. 186; 'An Address to His Excellency Henry Prescott', *JHANL 1835* (St John's: John Shea, 1835), p. 114; CIET, *JHANS 1837*, 'Report of the Committee Appointed to take into consideration the Fisheries and the infringement of existing treaties by Citizens of other Nations', 10 April 1837.

28. CIET, *JHANS 1837*, Evidence: John Starr, Halifax, NS, undated; for similar observations see CIET, *JHANS 1837*, Evidence: Joseph Allison and Co., New Glasgow, NS, 11 March 1837; CIET, *JHANS 1837*, Evidence: William McLean, Pictou, NS, 11 March 1837; J. W. Johnson to Viscount Falkland, 16 June 1845, in *JHANS 1846*, Appendix 11.

29. Payne has made this point effectively in his *Fishing a Borderless Sea*.

30. Daniel Maudlin, 'Politics and Place-Making on the Edge of Empire: Loyalists, Highlanders, and the Early Farm Houses of British Canada', in Daniel Maudlin and Bernard Herman (eds), *Building the British Atlantic World: Space, Place, and Material Culture, 1600–1850* (Chapel Hill: University of North Carolina Press, 2016), pp. 290–312; Gail Campbell, 'New Brunswick Women Travellers and the British Connection, 1845–1905', in Phillip Buckner and R. Douglas Francis (eds), *Canada and the British World: Culture, Migration, and Identity* (Vancouver: University of British Columbia Press, 2006), pp. 76–91.

31. .On ideas of independence and settlement see Garfield Fizzard, *Unto the Sea: A History of Grand Bank* (St John's: Dick's and Company, 1987), pp. 93–5; Thornton, 'The Transition', Cadigan, *Hope and Deception*, pp. 37–50; Ommer, *From Outpost to Outport*; Cadigan, 'The Moral Economy of the Commons: Ecology and Equity in the Newfoundland Cod Fishery, 1815–1855', *Labour/Le Travail*, 43 (Spring 1999), pp. 9–42.

32. Here I am drawing on John Torpey's discussion of sovereign states and free labour. See *The Invention of the Passport: Surveillance, Citizenship, and the State* (Cambridge: Cambridge University Press, 2000), p. 11.

33. Korneski, *Conflicted Colony*, p. 28.

34. Payne is sensitive to the American elements of this swirl of transactions and interactions. See *Fishing a Borderless Sea*. On the French see Korneski, *Conflicted Colony*; and Korneski, 'A great want of loyalty to themselves'.

35. The French entered into such arrangements not long after the peace of 1815, mainly with a scattering of fishing families who had established themselves on the west coast and on the eastern side of the Great Northern Peninsula during the war years when the French had been absent from the island. RCNL, Evidence: Captain Laignet, New Port au Choix, NL, 5 July 1859, pp. 13–16, in TNA CO 194/160, p. 292; RCNL, Evidence: William Plowman, Port Saunders, NL, 9 July 1859, p. 19, in TNA, CO 194/160, p. 296; RCNL, Evidence: Captain D. M. Eveillard, Quirpon, NL, 15 July 1859, p. 6, in TNA, CO 194/160, p. 312.

36. Frederic Thompson, *The French Shore Problem*, pp. 15–20.

37. Olaf Janzen, 'The French Shore Dispute', in Hiller and English (eds), *Newfoundland and the Entente Cordiale*, pp. 45–6.

38. TRPAD, GN 2/2, box 22, vol. 34, Stephen Lushington to Henry Prescott, 13 September 1839; TRPAD, GN 2/2, box 32, vol. 53, James Winter to Collector of Customs, 10 November 1845, pp. 4-6; Dundonald to the Secretary of the Admiralty, 5 November 1849, TNA, CO 194/132, p. 179; 'Report of H.M. Sappho', 3 October 1851, TNA, CO 194/135, pp. 41-5, pp. 54-5; 'Reports Made by Alexander Milne of Her Majesty's Ship *Crocodile* Relative to the Fisheries of Newfoundland', in *JLCNL 1841* (St John's: Ryan and Withers, 1841), Appendix 30; Alexander Milne, 'Report on the Protection of the Gulf of St Lawrence Fisheries', 2 October 1841, in John Beeler (ed.), *The Milne Papers: The Papers of Admiral of the Fleet Sir Alexander Milne, Bt., K.C.B. (1806-1896)* (Aldershot: Ashgate, 2004), pp. 128-41; *Halifax Commission, 1877: Documents and Proceedings* vol. I (Washington: Government Printing Office 1878) [hereafter HC], Evidence: William McLeod, Gaspe, 8 August 1877, p. 11; HC, Evidence: John F. Taylor, Isaacs Harbour, NS, 27 August 1877, p. 42.
39. Richard Penney to Lord Viscount Goodrich, 24 February 1831, TNA, CO 194/82, pp. 298-9; hereafter RCNL, Evidence: H. H. Forrest, St George's Bay, NL, 18 June 1859, 16 in TNA, CO 194/160, p. 229; RCNL, Evidence: John Messervey, St George's Bay, NL, 20 June 1859, in TNA, CO 194/160, p. 241.
40. Korneski, 'A great want of loyalty to themselves', pp. 145-83.

ELEVEN

The Mi'kmaq, the Pattersons and Remembering the Scottish Colonisation of Nova Scotia

Michael E. Vance

On a cloudless day in July 1923, Harris H. Reid set up his circuit camera on the outskirts of the town of Pictou, Nova Scotia – levelling it with his tripod on the uneven ground of Norway Point in order to take a collective portrait of the assembled gathering. The year before, he had taken panoramic photographs of the dedication ceremony for the Acadian Memorial Church at Grand Pré in the Annapolis Valley, helping to promote the 'Land of Evangeline' as one of the central tourist draws in Nova Scotia.[1] These images likely assisted him in securing the role of official photographer the following summer in Pictou for the *Hector* celebration, which had been organised to commemorate the 150th anniversary of the arrival of the emigrant vessel from the Highlands of Scotland. The *Hector* celebration, which was advertised throughout North America, aimed to attract both descendants of the original settlers and others wishing to celebrate Scottish heritage. As with the creation of the Acadian Memorial Church on the Grand Pré site of the original building that had witnessed the notorious expulsions of the eighteenth century, the Pictou event sought to combine a pride in heritage with a broader appeal to tourists. For the Pictou gathering, Reid, himself of Scottish descent, took panoramic shots of the town as well as the open-air church service at Loch Broom on East River, where the *Hector* passengers had erected their Presbyterian church after arriving in the colony.[2] Nevertheless, Reid's Norway Point photograph was the most striking image taken that day. It captured a large number of settler descendants, some dressed in what purports to be period costume, alongside a group of approximately forty Mi'kmaw men, women and children in traditional dress. The Mi'kmaw men appear in feathered headdress and embroidered jackets, while several of the women and girls are wearing traditional hoods and beaded dresses.[3]

Reid's photograph clearly documents the presence of Indigenous peoples prior to European colonisation, but in this regard it was exceptional. The Mi'kmaw participation in the *Hector* celebrations, which stretched over the week of 15–22 July, was barely mentioned in the press reports of the events.

Figure 11.1 Detail of H. H. Reid's Norway Point photograph showing the Mi'kmaw participants at the *Hector* celebration. Elizabeth Paul, the Maliseet wife of Chief Lonecloud, is seated at the far left of the photograph. [Image courtesy of the McCulloch House Museum and Genealogy Centre, Pictou, Nova Scotia.]

The *Pictou Advocate* devoted five pages to the celebrations in their 20 July issue, but merely stated that during the re-enactment of the landing of the *Hector* passengers at Norway Point, '[in] the background [had] stood a group of seventy-five Indians in their costumes, their stoic, swarthy faces kindling with the smile of friendship which greeted the pioneers in the days that now seem so far away'.[4] In contrast to the extensive lists of dignitaries and visitors named in the *Advocate*, not a single Mi'kmaw participant was identified.[5] The celebration's official programme, which was prefaced by Judge George Geddes Patterson (1864–1951), chairman of the celebration committee and great-grandson of the *Hector* passenger John Patterson, failed to mention either Mi'kmaw participation in the ceremonies or the presence of Indigenous peoples at the time of the *Hector*'s arrival in 1773.[6]

While the significance of the 1923 *Hector* celebrations for the development of tourism and the branding of Nova Scotia as 'Scottish' has been well established, Harris Reid's photograph hints at the broader relationship between the public commemoration of colonisation from the British Isles and the marginalisation of Indigenous peoples in Mi'kma'ki.[7] This chapter explores this theme further by first identifying several Indigenous participants visible in Reid's photograph and suggests that their participation in the celebrations was part of a long-standing assertion of Mi'kmaw rights in the face of settler colonialism. By examining the role of Judge Patterson's father, Rev. George Patterson (1824–97), in characterising the relationship between the *Hector* colonists and the Mi'kmaq with both his antiquarian studies and his *History of the County of Pictou*,[8] the chapter then provides an explanation for the Mi'kmaw presence at the gathering from a settler perspective. Finally, Judge Patterson's own activities and writing are examined in order to illustrate how he succeeded in excluding discussion of the Mi'kmaq altogether during the event, in part by developing the idea that the *Hector* was Canada's *Mayflower*. I argue that despite the resilience demonstrated by the Mi'kmaq in insisting on their right to their homeland and traditions, it was Judge Patterson's exclusion of them from the *Hector* settler narrative that had the greatest impact in the years that followed.

Asserting Mi'kmaw claims

The appearance of Mi'kmaw men, women and children wearing traditional dress in Harris Reid's staged Norway Point photograph served to naturalise both the Scottish settlement of Pictou and the dispossession of the Indigenous inhabitants. The photograph, however, also provides some insight into the Mi'kmaw motives for participating in the 1923 *Hector* celebration. Several of the traditional headdresses adorned with turkey feathers worn by the Mi'kmaw men in Reid's image are still preserved in the collections of the Nova Scotia Museum. Indeed, it appears that Mi'kmaw participants at official events were often provided with turkey feathers and paid for their appearances.[9] That such sponsorship could lead to clear distortions of traditional culture can be seen in the images of Indigenous 'war' dancers at the 1914 provincial fair who are dressed as the native depicted on the Nova Scotia coat of arms, a figure depicting a Brazilian Indigenous person rather than a Mi'kmaw 'warrior'. Other early twentieth-century images from Nova Scotia depict Mi'kmaw men wearing the full headdresses belonging to the peoples of North America's Western Plains rather than the Mi'kmaq – suggesting that the Indigenous people of Nova Scotia were expected to conform to dominant 'Indian' stereotypes.[10] At first glance, the presence of figures like the seated Jerry Lonecloud, holding a moose bone knife and wearing a turkey feather headdress, near the centre of Reid's photograph could indicate a similar case of performed *Indian-ness*. Born Germain Bartlett Alexis in Maine, Jerry Lonecloud (1854–1930) had acquired the name he would use for the rest of his life while touring with the Healey and Bigelow Wild West Show in the 1880s. Using techniques learned in the United States, Lonecloud developed his own touring show to promote his 'Indian' medicines; nevertheless, Lonecloud was a much more complex figure than a performing 'Indian', and his commitment to his Mi'kmaw culture and advocacy on behalf of his people were noted by many of his contemporaries.[11]

Lonecloud's Mi'kmaw parents were from Nova Scotia, and he had gained from them knowledge of traditional medicines as well as hunting and tracking skills, while the family moved along the St Lawrence Valley and the Great Lakes selling medicines and working as hunting guides. As a consequence, the young Lonecloud was exposed to a range of Indigenous practices in addition

Figure 11.2 Detail of H. H. Reid's photo showing: standing, Grand Chief John Sark in an elaborately embroidered chief's coat and black hat; standing to the left, his wife in a traditional peaked cap; standing to the right, Isaac Sack in a captain's coat and bowler hat, wearing a medal; seated below, Chief Lonecloud wearing a turkey feather headdress and holding a moose bone knife; to the left, Chief Peter Wilmot with his hands on one knee; and further left, Chief Matthew Francis, looking out from behind another elder. [Image courtesy of the McCulloch House Museum and Genealogy Centre, Pictou, Nova Scotia.]

to the Mi'kmaw knowledge transmitted by his parents – this diverse experience was reinforced by his marriage to Elizabeth Paul, a Maliseet woman he met while working in New Brunswick. After settling permanently in Nova Scotia in the late 1880s, Lonecloud became the principal informant on Mi'kmaw culture for Harry Piers, the first director of the Nova Scotia Museum of Natural History,[12] and in Harris Reid's photograph Elizabeth Paul is wearing a traditional Mi'kmaw peaked cap and dress borrowed from the Museum's collection – reflecting the closeness of the association between the two men. Mi'kmaw elder Don Julian has noted, however, that Lonecloud not only acted as a significant intermediary between Indigenous and settler culture, he also had an important role in the political life of the Mi'kmaw community after settling at Tufts Cove on the Dartmouth side of Halifax harbour. Julian has found Lonecloud's name on hundreds of Department of Indian Affairs documents in which he pushed for the recognition of Mi'kmaw hunting rights and title to long-standing settlements. In doing so, Lonecloud provided one of the clearest early twentieth-century assertions of Indigenous sovereignty: 'we consider the whole lands of the Province were once our own'.[13] His advocacy on behalf of Mi'kmaw communities in Halifax County, especially after the destruction of the Tufts Cove settlement during the Halifax Explosion in 1917, which took the lives of two of his daughters, was recognised in his elevation from Captain to Sub-Chief and then to Chief of Halifax County.[14]

The high status granted Lonecloud by the Mi'kmaq of Halifax County is echoed by that of others found in Reid's Norway Point photograph. Seated directly in front of Lonecloud is Peter Wilmot (c.1824–1932), elder and former Chief of the Pictou Landing Reserve. Like Lonecloud, Wilmot was acknowledged as an important keeper of traditional knowledge and as a significant political leader whose own lifetime stretched from the colonial period through Canadian Confederation and past the First World War.[15] Also in the group is Mathew Francis, the contemporary Chief at Pictou Landing, as well as John Sark, the Grand Chief of Prince Edward Island. At the same time as Reid's photograph was taken, an unofficial souvenir-postcard booklet containing portraits of Chief Sark, Chief Francis and Agnes Francis, as well as images of the Pictou Landing Reserve, was also produced. In addition, a studio portrait taken by Pictou photographer John Muir during the *Hector* celebrations also included Chiefs Sark, Francis and Lonecloud, along with other family members, revealing a close relationship between all of these individuals.[16]

According to Roger Lewis, curator of ethnology at the Nova Scotia Museum, Prince Edward Island and the lowland area along the Northumberland Strait, including Pictou, comprised one of the seven traditional Mi'kmaw districts in Mi'kma'ki, and the closeness between the districts is reflected in Chief Sark's appearance along with Chief Francis at the 1923 celebrations as well as in John Muir's collective portrait. Lewis has also identified political groupings that overlaid these traditional districts, with each one being governed by a Grand Council and a Grand Chief. These arrangements predated the governance system imposed on First Nations by the Canadian federal government with the Indian Act in 1876 and, according to Lewis, reflected the traditional use of the land's river systems. By comparing historical accounts of Mi'kmaw governance with the watersheds, Lewis has identified three political groupings in Nova Scotia in addition to the Grand Council on Prince Edward Island.[17] On mainland Nova Scotia, one of those Grand Councils made up of 'captains' from each of the river systems in the watershed comprising the present Halifax, Lunenburg, Hants, Kings, Colchester and Cumberland Counties was centred on the Catholic mission at Shubenacadie. Since the Pictou Landing Reserve was also associated with this broader Shubenacadie Grand Council, the presence of other Mi'kmaw council members, such as Lonecloud, at the *Hector* celebrations was warranted. Another member, Chief Isaac Sack (1855–1930), who had served as Grand Chief of the Shubenacadie Council, is standing to the right of Grand Chief Sark in Harris Reid's photograph. Like Lonecloud and Peter Wilmot, Sack was a well-regarded hunting guide who continued to make his living off the land using traditional practices.[18]

As with most of the other Mi'kmaw men in Reid's image, Isaac Sack is dressed in a traditional beaded captain's coat which only headmen in the Grand Council were permitted to wear. While less elaborate than the chief's coat worn by Grand Chief Sark, the captain's coats clearly identified the wearer's importance in the Mi'kmaw community, and the practice of adorning the dress went well back into the colonial period and, indeed, predated the British presence in Nova Scotia. In 1847 the *Acadian Recorder* provided a description of the Shubenacadie Grand Council members who had come to Halifax to address the Legislative Assembly that could easily have been applied to the Mi'kmaw men in Harris Reid's photograph:

> The appearance of ten Chiefs and Captains, dressed in their gay and ancient costume, and decorated with medals received by the tribe from different ancestors of Her Majesty [Queen Victoria] – in former times when Indians outnumbered the British inhabitants of the country – was at once novel and interesting.[19]

In Reid's photograph, both Chief Sark and Chief Sack appear to be wearing medals. Lonecloud was photographed wearing a George III medal while serving as Chief of Halifax County, and John Muir's studio portraits clearly show Chief Mathew Francis wearing a Louis medal that the Mi'kmaq of Merigomish had received from the French.[20] Since these medals were granted by the representatives of the French and British monarchs, they represented to the Mi'kmaq both a recognition of their chief's status and the relationship between themselves and the Crown. The Shubenacadie Council had sought to reinforce this relationship several times during the nineteenth century with petitions to Victoria on her accession and by officially welcoming her son, the Prince of Wales, during his Royal Tour in 1860, and at various times had the election of their Grand Chiefs recognised by the Queen's representatives. The Shubenacadie Council had even sent a delegation to London during Confederation to try to ensure that their hunting and fishing rights, guaranteed by earlier treaties, were protected in any new arrangement between the former colonies.[21]

For the Mi'kmaw participants, the *Hector* celebration provided the opportunity to once again assert the claim for recognition of their treaty rights and to remind the gathering that these had been guaranteed by the British monarchy. By 1923, the traditional governing structure of the Grand Council and Grand Chiefs had been undermined by the provisions of Canada's Indian Act and, according to Roger Lewis, were in serious disarray after 1906. Nevertheless, Grand Chiefs continued to be elected at Shubenacadie, and the memory of the long relationship with the Crown was maintained. Given the presence of Lord Byng, the Governor General of Canada, the attendance of the Mi'kmaw chiefs and captains at the *Hector* celebrations was a reassertion of that relationship. Byng had been asked to unveil the statue of a male Highland figure commemorating the arrival of the *Hector* settlers in Pictou's renamed Pioneer Square, and photographs taken at the ceremony clearly show the Mi'kmaw leadership in attendance – even if the local press failed to acknowledge their presence. Margaret MacDonald, the daughter of a prominent Pictou barrister, included photographs of the event in her carefully maintained scrapbook, and was perhaps typical with her caption alongside her photographs of two Indigenous groups that read 'Our own Micmac Indians'.[22] As with Reid's Norway Point photograph, the Mi'kmaw presence at the unveiling normalised the colonisation undertaken by the *Hector* passengers and their descendants; for them, it was not a recognition of any kind of ongoing obligation or debt owed to the Indigenous peoples.

Reverend Patterson's Mi'kmaq

The specific obligation owed by the Patterson family to the Mi'kmaq, however, had been openly acknowledged by Rev. George Patterson in his *History of the County of Pictou*, where he reported that his grandfather, John Patterson, had been rescued by Chief John Lulan, a local Mi'kmaw elder, after falling through the ice. As a consequence, Lulan was 'freely entertained' at the Patterson home for the rest of his days, although Patterson implied that the chief's expectations for continuing hospitality, which extended to John Patterson's widow and sons, were excessive.[23] Unlike most of the *Hector's* other passengers, who were drawn from Sutherland, Ross and Inverness-shire in the Scottish Highlands, John Patterson (1748–1808) had joined the vessel in Greenock. He had grown up in the Lowland village of Linwood in Renfrewshire, where he had apprenticed as a carpenter. His companions, who boarded the *Hector* at Loch Broom in 1773, were rejecting the transformations occurring in the Highland economy and looking to Nova Scotia for improved prospects that included the acquisition of land. John Patterson, however, already had capital earned from the leasing of miners' cottages he had built in Quarrelton near Linwood. The money earned from those rents enabled him to acquire the 250-acre site in 1788 that would become Pictou, an English corruption of a local Mi'kmaw name,[24] after a brief period of being called New Paisley. At his new settlement, Patterson established a successful lumbering, construction and trading business which connected with both Scotland and the West Indies.[25] His earliest land sales at the Pictou town site were also to other Lowland entrepreneurs like himself, and these Lowland connections were maintained by his descendants.[26]

His grandson, George Patterson, travelled to Edinburgh to study divinity and follow the vocation of his maternal grandfather, Pictou's first Presbyterian minister, Rev. John Drummond MacGregor. His education, both in Lowland Scotland and in Pictou, influenced his view of the Indigenous people of Nova Scotia in fundamental ways.[27] Prior to studying in Edinburgh, Rev. Patterson began his schooling at Rev. Thomas McCulloch's Pictou Academy, and he later followed his headmaster to Dalhousie College in Halifax. McCulloch, a graduate of the University of Glasgow, imbued both Nova Scotian institutions with the spirit of the Scottish Enlightenment and its emphasis on practical knowledge and the application of reason to all aspects of society. Enlightenment scholars and antiquarians believed in the importance of collecting and classifying the world's 'primitive' cultures as part of the 'scientific' demonstration of the progress of 'civilisation' and, as historian John Reid argues, early Presbyterian ministers in the colony, like McCulloch and MacGregor, were influential in encouraging antiquarian interest in the Mi'kmaq. Intriguingly, while both men relied on Chief Lulan, John Patterson's rescuer, as their informant for Mi'kmaw culture, they also subscribed to the generally accepted idea that Indigenous communities were in decline and inevitably fated to disappear in the face of the 'civilisation' introduced by the settlers.[28]

The commonplace trope of the 'disappearing Indian' provided the stimulus for both the collection of Indigenous artefacts and the development of ethnography in North America. Rev. Patterson engaged in both. Following his old school master, who also collected stories and artefacts, George Patterson was involved in some of the earliest archaeological investigations in Nova Scotia. As archaeologist Michael Deal shows, as an early member of the Nova Scotia Institute of Science, Patterson assembled an extensive collection of pre-contact material culture drawn from his archaeological investigations of a Mi'kmaw burial site on Big Island in Merigomish Harbour and from the various shell midden sites he had visited around the province. Patterson published the results of what he called his 'stone age' investigations in an article for the 1883 *Annual Report of the Smithsonian Institution* and an 1890 essay for the *Proceedings and Transactions of the Nova Scotian Institute of Science* before donating his collection to Dalhousie College.[29] Rev. Patterson also highlighted his archaeological findings in his *History of the County of Pictou*, which devoted an entire second chapter to the 'prehistoric period' where he described the discoveries at Big Island and recorded the Mi'kmaw names for key places in the county including 'Espakumegek' or Green Hill, where Patterson was minister for twenty-five years. For Patterson, both archaeological and place-name evidence reflected the time when the Mi'kmaq 'held undisputed possession of all these regions', but he saw the contemporary informants who provided him with much of his ethnographic material as part of the 'decaying remnant of the Micmac tribe'.[30]

When he came to describe the early encounters between the local Mi'kmaw and the early settlers, Rev. Patterson relied on community and family lore which added the hostile image of the troublesome 'savage' to his own 'disappearing Indian' trope. In the edited memoirs of his maternal grandfather, Rev. James MacGregor, Patterson retold a tale that came from his great-grandmother, *Hector* passenger Christiana McKay (1753–1818), whom Patterson described as a 'woman of great firmness'.[31] While the 'Indians were very bold' when the *Hector* colonists arrived and 'the whites were afraid of them', his great-grandmother 'never yielded to them, and when they came into her house she feared not even to scold them if they took undue liberties'.[32] In his *History of the County of Pictou*, Patterson relayed similar tales passed down from the *Betsy* passengers who had arrived from Philadelphia, six years earlier than the *Hector*. The original group sent by the colonisation company that later recruited the *Hector* passengers were initially reluctant to land since the fires on shore set by settlers from Truro, who had come to greet the vessel, were misinterpreted as being made 'by savages, of whom they naturally stood in terror'.[33] Rev. Patterson connected the source of those fears with the experience of the colonists during the Seven Years War, who had published widely circulated narratives recounting their trials and tribulations at the hands of Indigenous captors. But the difficulties encountered in Nova Scotia appear to have consisted of the 'Indians' entering 'the houses of the settlers, and help[ing] themselves to the cakes that the women might be baking on the hearth, or [to] other provisions, with threatening gestures'.[34] Patterson claimed that the Mi'kmaq were aware of the settler fears and deliberately played upon them, but by retelling community folklore he also created the impression that the 'Indians' were both 'savage' and easy to control. In an episode that continues to be widely retold, Patterson claimed that when William McKay, a piper from Loch Broom on board the *Hector*, began playing as the vessel dropped its anchor '[a]ll the Micmacs fled in terror and were not seen for some time'. This stereotypical, and likely apocryphal, tale was reinforced by Christiana McKay's story that she had removed the Mi'kmaw visitors from her house by informing them that a 'regiment of soldiers had arrived in Halifax' and that they 'must now behave'.[35]

Rev. Patterson, however, also relied on named and unnamed Mi'kmaw informants for his *History*, and occasionally the episodes he relates give some insight into the Mi'kmaw perspective of the settlers' arrival.[36] In recalling the 'trouble' that the Indigenous inhabitants gave the early colonists, Patterson reported hearing 'of a white man taking a fish from the river, and an Indian taking it from him, saying it was not his'.[37] From a settler perspective, the fish belonged to the individual who caught it, but from an Indigenous perspective it was part of the communal resources in Mi'kmaw territory.[38] Patterson's account reveals that the Mi'kmaw endeavoured to instruct the settlers on the appropriate manner in which to exploit the natural environment as well as the importance of sharing what was obtained. As he put it, from the 'Indians' they 'learned to make and use snow-shoes, to call moose, and other arts of forest life. From them they often received supplies of provisions. One old man used to say that the sweetest meal he ever ate was provided and prepared by them.'[39] What Patterson reported as the 'frightening' practice of entering settler homes when the men were away, and demanding food from the women left behind, could also be seen as a more assertive effort to communicate the idea of communal resources. In retelling Christiana McKay's story, Patterson suggested that his great-grandmother's actions resulted in the Mi'kmaq making a 'peace offering':

> ... shortly after there came an invitation to all the whites to attend a great feast provided for them by the red brethren. The invitation was accepted, and going on to a place appointed they found provided every variety of provision, which sea or forest afforded, fish, flesh, and fowl, which they allowed the whites to cook in their own way.[40]

The overture, however, can be viewed as another attempt to educate the settlers in Indigenous values. Other conflicts reported by Patterson might also be seen as a consequence of the clash between Mi'kmaw communal practice and settler ideas of private property.

A similar incident to the one related by his great-grandmother occurred in Merigomish at the home of the *Hector* settler George Morrison who, according to Patterson, responded to the intrusion with violence. This attack happened despite the fact that the children of the first settler in the area, Barnabas McGee, had played with those of their Mi'kmaw neighbours.[41] While Patterson noted an awareness among the colonists that the Mi'kmaq had several places in the Pictou region where they grew 'beans and Indian corn' on a seasonal basis, 'the Government, in granting the land, made no reserves of such rights'. At least two settlers paid the Mi'kmaq 'to relinquish all claims' to traditional arable plots on the grants they had settled, but at Middle River Point, across the harbour from

Pictou, the Mi'kmaq where not willing to give up control of their communally farmed territory. At this seasonal gathering place, later called McKay's Grant by the settlers, they 'drove off' all settlement attempts. According to Patterson's informants '[o]n one occasion, a person came and built a house in their absence. Having left to bring his family, the Indians returned, and when they saw the intrusive dwelling, they gathered bush round it, which they set on fire, causing a great conflagration, around which they danced and yelled as long as it lasted.'[42] But even here, the Mi'kmaq were eventually dispossessed by the settlers.

Rev. Patterson acknowledged that the 'trouble' given to the settlers by Indigenous peoples was far outweighed by the support they had provided them and stated that '. . . from the time of the arrival of the Hector, [the Mi'kmaq] never gave the settlers any serious molestation, and generally showed them real kindness, which, when the tables were turned, so that the whites had plenty and they were needy, has not always been reciprocated'.[43] Although he demonstrated such sympathy, Patterson still tended to place Indigenous people in a secondary and largely supportive role in the central story of settlement. As historian M. Brook Taylor notes, the *History of the County of Pictou* has an underlying narrative that highlights an 'antagonistic relationship between moral strength and material progress', and, as a consequence, Rev. Patterson tended to view the early history of pioneer settlement with nostalgia – a sentiment that was extended to relations with the Mi'kmaq.[44] The widespread circulation of his account, along with the central role that it gave to early Indigenous assistance, helps to explain why the Mi'kmaw leaders seen in Harris Reid's photograph would have been welcome at the *Hector* celebrations, but it does not account for their absence from contemporary publications.

Canada's *Mayflower*

Typical of the exclusion was the Montreal *Standard*, which failed to note the presence of Mi'kmaw chiefs at the statue unveiling in Pioneer Square and instead highlighted the address given by Sir Robert Falconer, a *Hector* descendant and the president of the University of Toronto. The *Pictou Advocate* also ignored the Indigenous presence at the ceremony, while paying particular attention to Governor Channing Harris Cox of Massachusetts' speech which claimed that the *Hector* had laid the foundation for 'a new civilization'.[45] As chairman of the Hector celebration committee, Rev. Patterson's son, Judge George Geddes Patterson, had a significant influence on the shaping of the events, and an analysis of his preoccupations can help to explain why the Mi'kmaq presence was largely ignored by the press. It was Judge Patterson who had helped to ensure that, in addition to Governor Cox, prominent Canadian political figures such as the prime minister, William Lyon Mackenzie King, the leader of the opposition, Arthur Meighan, as well as the premier of Nova Scotia, George

Henry Murray, were in attendance. Other attendees were leading military men, such as Lord Byng and J. H. MacBrien, the Chief of Staff in Ottawa, as well as the influential churchmen Bishop Alexander MacDonald, the Roman Catholic Bishop of Victoria, British Columbia, and Rev. John P. MacPhie, the author of a popular celebratory history *Pictonians at Home and Abroad: Sketches of Professional Men and Women of Pictou County – Its History and Institutions*. Indeed, Judge Patterson's organising committee had even recruited the New Brunswick-born prime minister of Great Britain, Andrew Bonar Law, as the honorary chairman of the celebrations.[46] The presence of such notable men reflected Patterson's own social circle. Like his father, Patterson had attended Dalhousie College, where he studied and later taught law. After representing Pictou County in the Nova Scotia legislature from 1901 until 1906, Patterson was appointed county court district judge in New Glasgow – a position he held until his retirement in 1939, when he subsequently served on the Nova Scotia Rationing Board during the Second World War.[47]

Judge Patterson's career not only placed him among the Nova Scotian legal and political elite, it also brought him into contact with prominent men in other parts of Canada as well as in Britain. Indeed, prior to the *Hector* celebrations, Patterson had reinforced these links by serving as captain of the Canadian curling team competing in Scotland in 1921 for the Strathcona Cup, which had been established by Lord Strathcona with the goal of maintaining links between Scotland and Canada.[48] When he came to publish his own historical writing, Judge Patterson further indicated his connection to the larger transatlantic political establishment by dedicating his first volume, *Studies in Nova Scotia History*, to Max Aitken, Lord Beaverbrook, who was photographed with the judge in the 1940s.[49] Patterson's Rationing Board work had likely involved contact with Britain's wartime Minister of Supply and, later, War Production, while his political and professional life undoubtedly placed him in contact with the dedicatee of his second volume, *More Studies in Nova Scotia History*, the influential Nova Scotian-born banker and 14th lieutenant governor of Ontario, William Donald Ross (1869–1947).[50] The majority of the 'studies' contained in both volumes focused on leading Nova Scotian politicians and judges, many of whom Patterson had known personally, but his first volume opened with 'The Coming of the *Hector*'.

Judge Patterson's essay on the *Hector* drew heavily on his three-page 'Historical Statement' in the *Official Souvenir Programme of Celebration* produced for the Pictou event. In both documents, Patterson made the argument that while the *Hector* settlers were not the first Scots to settle in Nova Scotia, they had paved the way for more substantial immigration into the province both before and immediately after the American Revolution. In making his case he also drew heavily on his father's writing, expanding on the elder Patterson's claim that the young men on the *Hector* donned their kilts 'with *skein dhu*, and some with broadswords', as the *Hector* dropped anchor, to include all the Highlanders coming ashore in kilts and weapons 'from Ancient trunks'.[51] Both father and son alluded to the disarming acts introduced in the wake to the Jacobite Rebellion that had forbidden the wearing of tartan, but Judge Patterson went further, making the claim that there were men on the *Hector* who had been '"out" with Prince Charlie' twenty-eight years earlier.[52] Both men thus linked the arrival of the *Hector* to the Victorian 'Highlandism' that sentimentalised the Jacobites and elevated the tartan and the bagpipes as emblems for all Scots, including Lowlanders like the Pattersons.[53] Judge Patterson, however, went further, arguing that the martial qualities exhibited by the settlers were subsequently applied to transforming and 'upbuilding' the Maritime Provinces of Canada, particularly in the field of education, with the founding of the Pictou Academy. In the paragraph that concluded both of his essays, Judge Patterson, an Academy graduate, argued that it was in the struggle to create the non-denominational institution 'that the reformers bared their arms and fleshed their swords for the battle for Responsible Government. We do not exaggerate if we say that Free Schools and Responsible Government came to Nova Scotia with the coming of the immigrants in the cabin of the *Hector*.'[54] Such sentiments were echoed on the plaque placed on the base of the statue in Pioneer Square, which claimed that the passengers on board the *Hector* represented 'the vanguard of that array of Scottish Immigrants whose intellectual ideals, moral worth and material achievements have contributed greatly to the good government and upbuilding of Canada'. As with Patterson's 'Historical Statement' in the official program, no mention was made of the Mi'kmaq.[55]

In assessing the significance of the *Hector*'s arrival 150 years later, Judge Patterson claimed that 'Her arrival mark[ed] the beginning of Scottish Immigration to Canada.' In doing so, he downplayed the significance of earlier Scottish colonists, particularly the Highland settlers of Prince Edward Island, who had arrived a year earlier, since they were still tenants at the mercy of their landlords on their island farms.[56] For Patterson it was the *Hector* passengers who had encouraged the large-scale Scottish migration to the Maritime provinces and beyond to Ontario:

> As quickly as the indifferent means of communication of those days would permit they spread the gospel of land rent free among their kinsmen at home who made haste to join them. The 'Hector' was thus the pioneer ship of great movement – She was the 'Mayflower' of Canada.[57]

Since one of the goals of the 1923 celebrations was to attract American tourists to Pictou, Judge Patterson's parallel with the more famous New England vessel had obvious utility, and the *Boston Herald* followed suit with its own article on the 'Nova Scotia *Mayflower*'.[58] The analogy would have appeared natural to Governor Cox and other attendees from Massachusetts, since the state had celebrated the tercentenary of the arrival of the vessel's arrival only three years earlier;[59] however, Patterson repeated his *Mayflower* claim in his *Studies* essay seventeen years later. By invoking the 'Pilgrim Fathers' of New England, the *Mayflower* label served to reinforce the 'moral' and 'intellectual' virtues that Judge Patterson and the Pictou celebrants wished to attach to the *Hector* settlers. In addition, casting the arrival of the *Hector* as a foundational moment in the history of Nova Scotia and, by extension, the rest of what would become Canada, placed emphasis clearly on the activities of the settlers and their descendants. As a consequence, and unlike his father's account, there was no need to discuss in Judge Patterson's assessment of the *Hector* contribution to the 'upbuilding' of Canada the assistance provided by the Mi'kmaq to the Scottish colonists, or the Indigenous people's dispossession.[60]

Legacies

Five years after chairing the organising committee of the *Hector* celebration, Judge Patterson was asked to preside over an appeal launched by the Grand Chief of Cape Breton, Gabriel Sylliboy (1875–1963). Sylliboy, who had been convicted of hunting muskrat out of season, appealed on the basis of Mi'kmaw traditional hunting rights enshrined in the Peace and Friendship Treaty concluded with representatives of the British Crown in 1752. In upholding the conviction in the King vs Sylliboy [1928] case, Judge Patterson provided a precedent that was used as a model to deny Indigenous treaty rights up to the establishment of the Canadian Charter of Rights and Freedoms in 1982 and revealed how little he valued the Mi'kmaw contribution to his own community. By 1928 it was clear that the Mi'kmaq were not dying out, as Rev. Patterson had believed, and in his posthumously published *History of Victoria County*, Judge Patterson indicated as much.[61] This fact, combined with the reassertion of traditional hunting and fishing rights by Chiefs such as Lonecloud and Sylliboy, can help account for Patterson's decision, but in his written judgement the judge dismissed the treaties altogether, stating that:

> A civilized nation first discovering a country of uncivilized people or savages held such country as its own mark until such time as by treaty it was transferred to some other civilized nation. The savages' right of sovereignty even of owner-ship were never recognized. [62]

Judge Patterson's dismissal of Mi'kmaw rights in the landmark case was matched by the removal of any reference to the Indigenous peoples in later celebrations of the *Hector*. No mention was made of the Mi'kmaq in the programme of events celebrating the 200th anniversary of the ship's arrival in 1973, and the accompanying illustration of the kilted Highlanders wading ashore shows them being greeted by a colonial hunter in a 'coon' skin cap rather than the Mi'kmaw representatives in Harris Reid's 1923 photograph.[63] Similarly, the programme of events at the *Hector* replica launch in Pictou in 2000 made no mention of the original inhabitants. As recently as 2016, the *National Post* ran an article in its travel section aimed at encouraging visits to the *Hector* replica that not only failed to acknowledge the presence of Indigenous people, but reasserted instead the claim that passengers had provided the foundation for further Scottish immigration to Canada – leading John Meir, vice-chairman of the Hector Quay Society, to assert that '[T]his is our *Mayflower*'. Indeed, Judge Patterson's analogy has proved persistent, with a BBC Scotland documentary released in 2017 entitled *The* Hector: *Canada's Mayflower*.[64]

Thanks in large part to Judge George G. Patterson's efforts, the official memory of the *Hector* has moved away from Rev. Patterson's settler and native encounter and naturalised the Scottish presence in Nova Scotia with a foundation analogy that has ultimately made Scottishness synonymous with the province itself.[65] Still, the interviews in the BBC Scotland documentary revealed that the memory of the importance of the initial contact has not been entirely lost. According to one descendant, Genevieve Oliver, the settlers were only able to get through the initial years because they had the 'Indians to help them', while Lindsay Marshall, former Chief of the Potlotek First Nation in Cape Breton, speaks eloquently of the loss endured by the Mi'kmaq as a consequence of colonisation. The recent recognition of Mi'kmaw treaty rights in a series of Supreme Court decisions, along with the revelations on the disastrous impact of residential schools on Canada's First Nations through the report of the Truth and Reconciliation Commission, has opened up a new opportunity to reassess the long neglected role of Scottish colonisation in dispossessing the land's original inhabitants or, in the case of the *Hector* commemoration, erasing their presence altogether.

Notes

1. The negatives for the photographs are in private hands, but the images have been posted online at https://vimeo.com/122578030 (last accessed 20 October 2019). For the development of the Grand Pré site as a tourist destination and the associations with Henry Wordsworth Longfellow's fictional 'Evangeline', see Ian McKay and Robin Bates, *In the Province of History: The Making of the Public Past in Twentieth-Century Nova Scotia* (Montreal: McGill-Queen's University Press, 2010), pp. 71–129. The cultural significance of the Acadian Memorial Church is explored in Michael Gagné, '"Memorial Constructions": Representations of Identity in the Design of the Grand-Pré National Historic Site, 1907–Present', *Acadiensis*, 62:1 (Winter/Spring 2013), pp. 67–98.
2. Harris Harding Reid (b. 1891) was born into a farming family in Avonport, Nova Scotia, and his photography business was located in Windsor, Nova Scotia. His Pictou images can be found online at: http://novastory.ca/cdm/ref/collection/phps/id/348 and http://haggis.mccullochcentre.ca/document/100 (last accessed 20 October 2019).

3. The image can also been found at: http://haggis.mccullochcentre.ca/document/99 (last accessed 20 October 2019).
4. *Pictou Advocate*, 20 July 1923, p. 1.
5. Only one subsequent report named a Mi'kmaw individual – Chief Francis of the local Pictou Landing Reserve. *Pictou Advocate*, 27 July 1923, p. 3.
6. *Official Souvenir Programme of Celebration*, <http://haggis.mccullochcentre.ca/document/2847> (last accessed 20 October 2019).
7. Michael Boudreau, 'A 'Rare and Unusual Treat of Historical Significance': The 1923 Hector Celebration and the Political Economy of the Past', *Journal of Canadian Studies*, 28:4 (Winter 1993), pp. 28–48; McKay and Bates, *In the Province of History*, pp. 270–5; John G. Reid, 'Scots in Mi'kma'ki, 1760–1820', *The Nashwaak Review*, 22/23:1 (Spring/Summer 2009), pp. 541–6.
8. Rev. George Patterson, *A History of the County of Pictou, Nova Scotia* (Montreal: Dawson Brothers, 1877).
9. Author's communication with Roger Lewis, Nova Scotia Museum. See Nova Scotia Museum: Mi'kmaq Portraits MP0625 and MP0626 <https://novascotia.ca/museum/mikmaq/default.asp> (last accessed 20 October 2019).
10. Nova Scotia Museum: Mi'kmaq Portraits MP0528, MP0529, MP0928 and MP1208. Ruth Holmes Whitehead, 'A Brief Glimpse of Micmac Life: Objects from the McCord Collection', in *Wrapped in the Colours of the Earth* (Montréal: McCord Museum of Canadian History, 1992), pp. 75–9. For 'Indian' stereotyping, see Daniel Francis, *The Imaginary Indian: The Image of the Indian in Canadian Culture* (Vancouver: Arsenal Pulp Press, 1992).
11. Ruth Holmes Whitehead, *Tracking Doctor Lonecloud: Showman to Legend Keeper* (Halifax, NS: Nova Scotia Museum, 2002), pp. 27–47.
12. Whitehead, *Tracking Doctor Lonecloud*, pp. 32–5, 41–3.
13. Lonecloud to the Department of Indian Affairs, 17 July 1916, cited in Whitehead, *Tracking Doctor Lonecloud*, p. 37. For Don Julien's comments, see pp. 9–11. See also Jacob Remes, 'Mi'kmaq in the Halifax Explosion of 1917: Leadership, Transience, and the Struggle for Land Rights', *Ethnohistory*, 61:3 (Summer 2014), pp. 445–66.
14. Lonecloud's knowledge of traditional medicine was also recognised with the title Chief Medicine Man for Halifax County. Whitehead, *Tracking Doctor Lonecloud*, p. 302.
15. Ruth Holmes Whitehead, 'Wilmot, Peter', in *Dictionary of Canadian Biography*, <http://www.biographi.ca/en/bio/wilmot_peter_16E.html> (last accessed 20 October 2019).
16. Mi'kmaq Portraits MP0596, MP 0597, MP0607–0609.
17. Author's communication with Roger Lewis. See also Trudy Sable and Bernie Francis; with William Jones, Roger Lewis, *The Language of this Land, Mi'kma'ki* (Sydney, NS: Cape Breton University Press, 2012), pp. 19–23.
18. Mi'kmaq Portraits MP 0572, MP0592, MP0597 and MP0598; Ruth Holmes Whitehead, *The Old Man Told Us: Excerpts from Micmac History, 1500–1950* (Halifax, NS: Nimbus, 1991), pp. 315–16.
19. *Acadian Recorder*, 24 February 1849, cited in Whitehead, *The Old Man Told Us*, p. 239.
20. Mi'kmaq Portraits, MP 0597. Merigomish was the site of the mainland Catholic mission during the French regime but the mission had moved to Shubenacadie by the nineteenth century. The medals worn by Lonecloud and Francis are now in the Nova Scotia Museum Collection along with the Chief's coat associated with the Shubenacadie Grand Council.
21. Whitehead, *The Old Man Told Us*, pp. 218–19, 259, 260–2, 271–2.
22. Mi'kmaq Portraits MP 0594 0595; Margaret MacDonald Scrapbook, http://haggis.mccullochcentre.ca/document/4781 (last accessed 20 October 2019). Margaret MacDonald was the daughter of William MacDonald. The author is grateful to Teresa MacKenzie at the McCulloch House Museum and Genealogy Centre for providing background on Margaret MacDonald.
23. John Lulan, Chief at Boat Harbour, died in 1827 at the apparent age of ninety-seven. Patterson, *A History of the County of Pictou*, p. 190. The Boat Harbour lands are part of an ongoing dispute

between the Pictou Landing First Nation and the Canadian government concerning their inappropriate transfer to a pulp mill that continues to pollute the waters near Pictou.
24. According to *Ta'n Weji-sqalia'tiek: Mi'kmaw Place Names Digital Atlas* [http://mikmawplacenames.ca], Pictou was derived from 'Piktuk' or 'Piwktuk', Mi'kmaw for 'explosion', an apparent reference to the naturally occurring sulfur gas in the area.
25. Frank H. Patterson, *John Patterson the Founder of Pictou Town* (Truro, NS: Truro Printing, 1955), pp. 1, 14–21, 80, 93–4.
26. John Patterson's sons, John Jr and Abraham, followed him into the timber and fish trade. Abraham journeyed to Scotland to dispose of the Quarrelton leaseholds after his father's death. For other Lowland connections, see Patterson, *John Patterson*, pp. 15, 26, 33, 41, 75, 90, 97–8.
27. George Patterson was studying in Edinburgh from 1846 to 1848. See Patterson, *John Patterson*, p. 26, and Allan C. Dunlop, 'Patterson, George', in *Dictionary of Canadian Biography*, <http://www.biographi.ca/en/bio/patterson_george_12E.html> (last accessed 20 October 2019).
28. John G. Reid, 'Scots, Settler Colonization and Indigenous Displacement: Mi'kma'ki, 1770–1820, in Comparative Context', *Journal of Scottish Historical Studies*, 38:1 (2018), pp. 189–93. See also Alan Wilson, *Highland Shepard: James Macgregor, Father of the Scottish Enlightenment in Nova Scotia* (Toronto: University of Toronto Press, 2015), pp. 50, 182, 185; Susan Buggey and Gwendolyn Davies, 'McCulloch, Thomas', in *Dictionary of Canadian Biography*, <http://www.biographi.ca/en/bio/mcculloch_thomas_7E.html> (last accessed 20 October 2019); and Holly Ritchie, 'For Christ and Covenant', this volume.
29. Patterson's collection, comprising 250 objects obtained in Nova Scotia, was put in storage and then 'lost' sometime in the 1940s. Michael Deal, 'George Patterson: Nova Scotia's First Archaeologist', paper presented at the Annual Meeting of the Canadian Archaeological Society, Ottawa (2017). The author is grateful to Prof. Deal for providing him with a copy of his unpublished paper.
30. Patterson, *History*, pp. 28–32.
31. George Patterson, *Memoir of the Rev. James MacGregor, D.D., missionary of the General Associate Synod of Scotland to Pictou, Nova Scotia: with notices of the colonization of the lower provinces of British America, and of the social and religious condition of the early settlers* (Philadelphia: Joseph M. Wilson, 1859), pp. 300–1. See also Patterson, *History*, pp. 183–4. Christiana McKay, nee Grant, was the wife of Roderick MacKay (1746–1818). Their daughter Ann married Rev. James MacGregor: <http://www.shiphectordescendants.ca/> (last accessed 20 October 2019).
32. Patterson, *Memoir*, p. 301.
33. The Philadelphia Company, which arranged the *Betsy* and *Hector* voyages, was headed by Dr John Witherspoon, the founder of Princeton College. See Bernard Bailyn, *Voyages to the West: A Passage in the Peopling of America on the Eve of the Revolution* (New York: Knopf, 1986). For other early colonisation projects in Nova Scotia, see Alexandra L. Montgomery, 'Barren Icy Rocks or a Nursery for Seamen?', this volume.
34. Patterson, *History*, pp. 57, 58, 63. For the widely popular 'captivity narratives', see Linda Colley, *Captives: Britain, Empire, and the World, 1600–1830* (New York: 2002).
35. Patterson, *History*, p. 82; Patterson, *Memoir*, p. 301.
36. For his Mi'kmaw informants, see Patterson, *History*, pp. 23–4, 29, 43, 188, 190–1, 290.
37. Patterson, *History*, p. 63.
38. See Andrew Parnaby, 'The Cultural Economy of Survival: The Mi'kmaq of Cape Breton in the Mid-19th Century', *Labour/Le Travail*, 61 (Spring, 2008), pp. 69–98; Patterson, *History*, p. 205.
39. Patterson, *History*, p. 92.
40. Patterson, *Memoir*, p. 301.
41. Patterson, *History*, pp. 108–9.
42. By ending his account with the dancing scene, Patterson associated the First Nation's traditional use of the land with 'savage' behaviour. *History*, p. 187.

43. Patterson, *History*, p. 92.
44. M. Brook Taylor, 'Nova Scotia's Nineteenth-Century County Histories', *Acadiensis*, 10:2 (Spring 1981), pp. 159–66.
45. The *Standard* article can be viewed at <http://haggis.mccullochcentre.ca/document/1530> (last accessed 20 October 2019); *Pictou Advocate*, 20 July 1923.
46. Bonar Law was too ill with throat cancer to attend. He had resigned as prime minister on 22 May 1923 and died on 30 October 1923. E. H. H. Green, 'Law, Andrew Bonar (1858–1923)', *Dictionary of National Biography*.
47. Dalhousie University Archives, MS-2-196, SF Box 32, Folder 2–3 <https://memoryns.ca/george-geddie-patterson> (last accessed 20 October 2019).
48. Alan Stanfield, 'Srathcona Cup History', <https://www.scottishcurling.org/about-us/tours/strathcona-cup-history/>. A photograph of the 1921 team has been posted online at <http://www.doftw.com/curling1921/start1921curlers.html> (last accessed 20 October 2019).
49. George Geddie Patterson, *Studies in Nova Scotia History* (Halifax, NS: Imperial Pub. Co., 1940). The photograph can be found at <http://haggis.mccullochcentre.ca/document/4111> (last accessed 20 October 2019). See also D. George Boyce, 'Aitken, William Maxwell, first Baron Beaverbrook (1879–1964)', *Dictionary of National Biography*.
50. George Geddie Patterson, *More Studies in Nova Scotia History* (Halifax, NS: Imperial Publishing Co., 1941). *Globe and Mail*, 26 June 1947, p. 3.
51. Patterson, *Studies*, p. 13.
52. Judge Patterson provided no evidence for his claim, while his father merely mentions two men who witnessed the Battle of Culloden as boys.
53. See John Coull Morrison, 'Highlandism and Scottish Identity', in *A Shared Legacy: Essays on Irish and Scottish Art and Visual Culture* (New York: Ashgate, 2005), pp. 97–111; and Murray Pittock, *Celtic Identity and the British Image* (Manchester: Manchester University Press, 1999).
54. Patterson, *Studies*, p. 16; Judge Patterson 'Historical Statement', *Official Souvenir Programme of Celebration*, p. 3.
55. The statue's sculptor was John Albert Wilson (1877–1954), a New Glasgow-born professor of architecture at Harvard, whose Waban Studio at Chestnut Hill, Massachusetts was responsible for the creation of several turn of the century Civil War monuments that have recently been the focus of considerable controversy in the United States. Unlike his Civil War monument *Silent Sam*, commissioned by the Daughters of the Confederacy to commemorate the fallen at the University of North Carolina and which ignored the slaveholding foundation of Southern secession, Wilson's Highlander in Pictou has not produced a similar re-evaluation despite its erasure of the presence of the Mi'kmaq.
56. See S. Karly Kehoe, 'Catholic Highland Scots and the Colonisation of Prince Edward Island and Cape Breton Island', this volume.
57. 'Historical Statement', p. 3.
58. *Boston Herald*, 11 July 1923. Reproduced in the *Pictou Advocate*, 27 July 1923, p. 2.
59. Christine Arnold-Lourie, 'Baby Pilgrims, Sturdy Forefathers, and One Hundred Percent Americanism: The *Mayflower* Tercentenary of 1920', *Massachusetts Historical Review*, 17 (2015), pp. 35–66.
60. The Wampanoag had been similarly sidelined in the *Mayflower* celebrations. See Arnold-Lourie, 'Baby Pilgrims', p. 56. The Thanksgiving holiday representation that features Native American participation was a later development. James W. Baker, *Thanksgiving: The Biography of an American Holiday* (Durham: University of New Hampshire Press, 2009).
61. George Geddes Patterson, *Patterson's History of Victoria County, Cape Breton, Nova Scotia; with related papers*, compiled and edited by W. James MacDonald (Sydney, NS: College of Cape Breton Press, 1978), pp. 11–13.
62. Patterson had a range of, often contradictory, rationales for his decision. See William C.

Wicken, *The Colonization of Mi'kmaw Memory and History, 1794–1928: The King v. Gabriel Sylliboy* (Toronto: University of Toronto Press, 2012).
63. See <http://haggis.mccullochcentre.ca/document/3599> (last accessed 20 October 2019).
64. *National Post*, 13 May 2016. Intriguingly, the documentary was simply titled *The Hector: From Scotland to Nova Scotia* in its UK release, but given the *Mayflower* descriptor for the History Channel broadcasts in North America, Australia and New Zealand.
65. See Michael E. Vance, 'Powerful Pathos: The Triumph of Scottishness in Nova Scotia', in Celeste Ray (ed.), *Transatlantic Scots* (Tuscaloosa: University of Alabama Press, 2005), pp. 156–9.

Index

abolitionism, 45, 46, 52
Acadian Recorder, 124, 176
Acadie, Acadians, 12, 28, 95
African-descended people *see* Black Loyalists; Jamaican Maroons
Afzelius, Adam, 46-7
Aitken, Roger, 97, 105-6
American Revolution, 27, 30, 31, 45
  loyalist and other migrants, 14, 50, 95-6, 116, 182
Anglicanism, 16-17, 93-112, 114, 123, 133
Anglo-American migration, hostility towards, 28-9
archaeological investigations, on the Mi'kmaq, 178-9
aristocracy, British, and manorial schemes, 32-3
Atlantic Canada, definition, 11

Bailyn, Bernard, 26, 31
bait trade, 159
BBC Scotland documentary, on the *Hector*, 185
Beothuk, 11, 13, 19
bishops, 82, 85, 86, 104
  Anglican, 93, 94, 96, 99, 106-7
Black and Tans, 145, 146
Black Loyalists, 16, 41, 43-7, 95
  arrival in Sierra Leone, 46-7
  and the British Empire, 42, 53, 96
  fatalities, 50, 51
Blanchard, Jotham, 122
Board of Trade, 29, 30, 34, 80
Bonnie Prince Charlie, 82, 183
Book of Common Prayer, 93, 94, 97, 103-6
Boulton, Henry, 136, 137
bounties *see* subsidies, fisheries
Brandy Election, 124
Bras d'Or Lakes, 80, 87
British Empire
  black allegiance to, 42, 53, 96
  and free trade, 158

  and the Gulf fisheries, 156
  ideology, 27, 31-2
  and the Irish Newfoundlanders, 18
  and Scottish identity, 116
British fishers, and foreign trade operations, 159-62
British Parliament
  funding of settlements, 27, 28, 35, 96
  on the Maroons, 52-3
  and PEI land purchase act, 64
Burke, Edmund, 118
Byng, Lord, 177, 182

Calvin, John, 114-15
Campbell, William, 32, 34
Canadian Atlantic Provinces, 26
Canadian Charter of Rights and Freedoms, 1982, 20, 184
Canadian Confederation, 14, 68
Cape Breton, 12, 14, 16, 43, 77, 78, 79-80, 83, 84, 85, 86
Catholicism
  Irish, Newfoundland, 133-49
  in Scotland, 115
  and Scottish anti-Catholicism, 77, 82-3
  see also Highland Catholics
Charles Edward Stuart, 82, 183
Charles II, 114
Church of England *see* Anglicanism
Clan na Gael, 140, 142
Clarkson, John, 44, 46
Clarkson, Thomas, 44, 45
climate, and the Maroons, 49-51
colonial elites, and the Gulf fisheries, 156, 160-5
colonial merchants, and the Gulf fisheries, 156, 157-9, 160-1, 165-6
Colonial Patriot, 122, 124
  commercial policy, 28-9; *see also* Board of Trade; fisheries
Conception Bay, 134-7, 142-3

INDEX

Confederation *see* Canadian Confederation
Continental Congress, 31
Convention of 1818, 157
Cornwallis, Edward
  policy toward the Mi'kmaq, 3-4
  statue, 3-5, 8
Covenanters, Covenanting, 17, 114, 122
Cox, Channing Harris, 181, 184
cultural genocide, 4
Curry family, 77, 80

deBerdt, Dennys, 35
Dickinson, John, 27
  Letters from a Farmer in Pennsylvania, 26, 35-6
dissenters, 98, 100, 103; *see also* Presbyterian
Dufferin, Governor General Lord, 15, 59-74
  and Irish land purchase, 63, 64-7
  and PEI land rights controversy and reform, 62-9
  promotion of Canada and the empire, 61-2, 68

Easter Rising, 145, 146
Edward, Duke of Kent, 48
Edwards, Bryan, 52
Egmont, John Perceval, 2nd Earl of, 33-4
Ellis, Henry, 28
Empire, ideology of *see* British Empire
environmental change, 12, 19

Fenianism, 18, 144
  fears of, 138-40, 142, 149
fisheries, fishing communities, 11, 12, 13
  and Britishness, 18
  illegal trading, 159-61, 165
  Newfoundland, 93-4, 95, 97, 134-5, 140-1
  Nova Scotia, 29
  seasonal vs residential, 15
  treaties and tensions, 156-9, 164
forced migration, African, 16
France, French
  Acadie, 12, 28, 95
  collapse of power in Atlantic colonies, 27, 78, 95
  and the Gulf fisheries, 157-65
  Nova Scotia, 25, 27, 47-8, 97, 104, 105
Francklin, Michael, 32, 34
Franklin, Benjamin, 25, 29, 30, 35
free trade, 158
Friends of Irish Freedom (FOIF), 145-6, 147, 148
fur trading, 12

Gaelic, 84, 104
Gauvreau, Michael, 93, 96-7, 98, 106
George III, 29
Georgia, 28-9, 35
German settlers, 17, 95, 97, 98, 100, 105
Glasgow Society, 121

Glenaladale settlers, 77, 79, 81-2, 86; *see also* Highland Catholics
Gregory, Jeremy, 94, 101, 104

Halifax, 2nd Earl of, 27-8
Halifax, Nova Scotia, 8, 13, 17, 53, 119, 120
  anglicisation, 95, 97, 98-9, 101-2, 117
  and episcopal authority, 107
  founding and settlement, 3-4, 9, 14, 41, 43, 47-9, 53
  merchants, 158
  religious literature, 104, 105
  see also Nova Scotia
Harbour Grace Affray, 142-3
Hardwick, Joseph, 16-17
Hector settlers, 171-85
  anniversary celebrations (1923), 171-7, 181-3
  later anniversary celebrations, 184-5
  and the *Mayflower*, portrayal, 19, 183-5
Highland Catholics, settlers, 16, 77-92, 183
historians on the Gulf fisheries, 154-5
Hollett, Calvin, 93-4, 99
Howe, Joseph, 124
Hughes, Katherine, 145, 146
humanitarians, 49-50

Independence *see* American Revolution; Irish War of Independence (1919-21)
Indian Act (1876), 176, 177
Indigenous peoples
  archaeological investigations on, 178-9
  treaty rights, 20, 184
  see also Mi'kma'ki, Mi'kmaw
Inglis, Charles, 96, 99, 101, 116-17, 123
Inglis, John, 120
Ireland, Irish, land agitation and reform, 63, 64-9, 142
Irish Catholics, Newfoundland, 133-49
Irish Land Act (1881), 67, 69
Irish migrants, 13, 14, 17-18, 84
Irish Republican Brotherhood (IRB), 138, 142, 145; *see also* Fenianism, fears of
Irish War of Independence (1919-21), 145, 146, 148

Jacobitism, Jacobites, 81-2, 183
Jamaican Maroons, 16, 41, 47-53, 104, 105
  and the British Empire, 42, 53
Jefferson, Thomas, 30
Julian, Don, 175

Keough, Willeen, 17-18
Kimberley, Lord, 60, 61, 63, 68
King v. *Sylliboy* (1928) case, 19-20, 184
King's College, Nova Scotia, 93, 113, 117-19, 121, 123
Kirk, 115-16, 120, 121, 123, 125; *see also* Presbyterianism
Korneski, Kurt, 7, 18

_# INDEX

land granting/boom, Nova Scotia, 25–9, 30–6
land ownership
   and absenteeism, 28, 34, 63, 64, 72n
   divisions over, 14–15
   Highlands, 81
   see also Ireland, Irish; Prince Edward Island (PEI)
Land Purchase Act, 15, 63–4
land tenancies, 30, 63–4
laypersons and preaching, 94, 97, 99, 102, 106
Lewis, Peter, 175–6
Lonecloud, Chief Jerry, 174–5, 176, 184
Lott, Herman, 137–8
Louisbourg, 12–13, 28
Lulan, Chief John, 177, 178
Lunenburg, 28, 97, 100, 105
Lutherans, 95, 98, 100, 105

McCulloch, Thomas, 17, 19, 113–25, 178
Macdonald, Alexander, 84
Macdonald, Angus, 84–5
MacDonald, John A. (Canadian prime minister), 4, 142
Macdonald of Boisedale, Colin, 82
Macdonald of Glenaladale, John, 81–2
MacEachern, Angus, 84–5, 86
MacGregor, James, 113, 118, 129n
MacGregor, John, 78
MacGregor, John Drummond, 178
McKay, Christiana, 179–80
McLaughlin, Beverley, 4
McNutt, Alexander, 30–2, 34–5
McPhaggan, Archibald, 86–7
MacPhie, John P., 182
manorial schemes, 32–4
Maroons *see* Jamaican Maroons
Mayflower analogy, 119, 183–5
Meaney, John, 146
merchants *see* colonial merchants
Mi'kma'ki, Mi'kmaw, 11, 12, 13–14, 58n
   absence from contemporary publications, 181, 183, 184–5
   and Anglicanism, 104
   archaeological investigations on, 178–9
   assertion of treaty rights, 177, 184
   colonial treaties/policies with, 4, 6–7, 14
   Cornwallis' policy toward, 3–4
   exclusion from settler narratives, 173
   governance and districts, 175–7
   Hector celebrations, 19–20, 171–7
   and the Highland settlers, 16, 77, 79–88
   and 'Indian' stereotypes, 174
   land, dispossession of, 180–1
   Nova Scotia, 19, 25, 27–8, 48, 56n, 171–85
   and the Patterson family, 177–85
military service, blacks in, 46, 48
missionaries, 16–17, 84
   Anglican, 95–107
   Kirk, 119, 120
monarchy, British, and the Church, 97

Montagu-Dunk, George *see* Halifax, 2nd Earl of
Moreau, Jean-Baptiste, 104, 105
Morgan, Cecilia, 6
Mortimer, Edward, 113, 119
Muir, John, 175, 176
Munro, George, 83

Napoleonic wars, 157
national identity, Canadian *see* Canadian Confederation
   nationalism, Irish Catholic, 136, 143–8; *see also* Fenianism; Ribbonism
natural resources, exploitation of, 80
New Brunswick, 83, 86, 93, 96, 107
   Anglicanism, 99, 104
   Irish in, 14
New England
   dissenters, 98
   Planters, 14, 41–2
New England Company, 104
New Scotland, 12
Newfoundland, 14, 17–18
   Anglican missionaries and dissent in, 95–8, 99, 100–1, 102
   English settlement, 13
   ethno-religious tensions, 133, 135–49
   fisheries/fishing communities, 18, 93–4, 95, 97
   Indigenous people, 15, 19
   land issues, 15
   population, 14
newspapers *see* press
Nova Scotia, 25–40, 93
   Africans migrate from, 16
   Anglicanism, 95, 96, 97–8, 116–17
   as British province, 29
   church and state, 116
   Indigenous peoples, 19, 25, 27–8, 48, 56n, 171–85
   land boom, 25–9, 30–6
   Museum of Natural History, 175
   politico-religious divisions, 113–25
   raw materials and British manufacturing, 29–30
   Scottish settlers, 113–25, 171–85
   see also Halifax, Nova Scotia
Nova Scotia Archives (NSA), land petition documents, 86

Orange Order, Orangeism, 18, 141–4, 147
Owen, William, 32–3

Patterson, George Geddie, Judge, 173, 181–5
   dismissal of Indigenous treaty rights, 19–20, 184
Patterson, John, 173, 177–8
Patterson, Rev. George
   History of the County of Pictou, 19, 177, 179–81
   'stone age' investigations, 178–9

INDEX

Paul, Elizabeth, *172*, 175
Paul, Peter (indigene), 19
Peace and Friendship treaty/policy, 4, 6–7, 184
Philadelphia, Philadelphians, 25–6, 31, 32
Pictou, Nova Scotia, 26, 175, 178
Pictou Academy, 17, 113, 115, 118–25, 178, 183
Pictou Advocate, 173, 181
Port de Grave, 'Fenian scare,' 133, 138–40
Portland, Duke of, 50
  prayer books, 104; *see also* Book of Common Prayer
Presbyterianism, 82, 113–25, 178
press
  on blacks and climate concerns, 49, 50
  on Fenian/IRB activities, 142
  on the *Hector* celebrations, 171–3, 176, 177
  Irish republican sympathies, 145–6, 147–8
  on Newfoundland ethno-religious tensions, 136, 138–9
  on Nova Scotia's politico-religious issues, 122–3, 124
Pretyman-Tomline, George, 99
Prince Edward Island (PEI), 14, 15, 63
  Church propaganda, 99
  and confederation, 63, 64
  and Dufferin, 59–74
  Highland settlers, 77–92, 183
  Mi'kmaw governance/districts, 175–6
  transnational land issues, 62–9
  see also St John's Island
  print networks, Anglican, 98–103; *see also* Book of Common Prayer; press
private devotional manuals, 100
Protestantism, 31
  dissenters, 98
  German, 95
  Nova Scotia, 25, 27, 36
  see also Anglicanism; Orange Order; Presbyterianism

Quebec clergy, 85–6

railways, PEI project, 63, 67–8
Reciprocity Treaty (1854), 155
Reid, Harris H., Norway Point photograph, 171–6, 177, 181, 185
Reid, John G., 43, 58n, 79, 80, 86, 178
  religious literature, Anglican, 94, 98–103; *see also* Book of Common Prayer
religious toleration, 77, 81, 95, 117
rent strikes, 63–4
residential school system, 4, 185
Ribbonism, 135–8, 141, 143, 144
Roude, G., 147–8

Sack, Chief Isaac, 176
Sark, Chief John, 175, 176, 177

Scottish Enlightenment, 17, 178
Scottish settlers, Nova Scotia, 171–85; *see also* Highland Catholics; Presbyterianism
sectarianism, 113, 120
Self-Determination for Ireland League (SDIL, later SDILN), 145, 146, 147
settler folklore, Patterson's retelling, 179–80
Seven Years' War, 28, 179
Shanawdithit, 19
sharecroppers, 44, 47
Sharp, Granville, 45, 50
Shelburne, Nova Scotia, 26, 159
Shubenacadie Grand Council, 176–7
Sierra Leone, black migration to, 16, 45–7, 50, 53
Sierra Leone Company, 45–6
Sinclair, Murray (Justice), 4–5
slaves, freed *see* Black Loyalists; Jamaican Maroons
Society for the Promotion of Christian Knowledge (SPCK), 98–9, 102, 103–4
Society for the Propagation of the Gospel (SPG), 95, 96, 98, 103, 104, 107
South Uist, Inverness, emigration from, 77, 82–3
St John's Island, 13, 33, 77, 96, 134, 145, 148; *see also* Prince Edward Island (PEI)
Starr, John, 160, 161
Stuarts, 16, 115
subsidies, fisheries, 158, 159, 163
Sylliboy hunting case (1928), 19–20, 184

Taylor, Thomas, 103
Thornton, Henry, 46
tourism, Nova Scotia, 171, 173, 183
trade, 80, 81; *see also* Board of Trade; fisheries
Treaties of Paris
  (1763), 78
  (1814 and 1815), 157, 163
Treaty of Union (1707), 79
Treaty of Utrecht (1713), 12, 13, 42
truck system, 159, 161–2, 164
Truth and Reconciliation Commission (TRC), 4–5, 185

United Irishmen, 135, 139
United States of America
  and the Gulf fisheries, 157–65
  see also American Revolution
urban society, growth of, 13

Valera, Eamonn de, 145, 146
Vance, Michael, 19–20
Victoria, Queen, 62, 65, 177
voluntary societies, 94, 102, 104; *see also* Society for the Propagation of the Gospel (SPG)

Wallace, Michael, 123, 129n
Wallace, Valerie, 79, 114

Walpole, General, 48, 51–2, 54
War of the Austrian Succession, 14, 27
Wayne, Anthony, 25, 27
Wentworth, John, 47–9, 50–1
White Loyalists, 43–4
Wilberforce, William, 45, 46, 51–2
Wilmot, Peter, 175, 176

Winton, Henry, 136, 137
Wix, Edward, 98, 99
Wolastoqiyik, 12, 13–14, 18–19
Wood, Thomas, 95, 104
working people
   and the Gulf fisheries, 156, 159, 161–2, 166

EU representative:
Easy Access System Europe
Mustamäe tee 50, 10621 Tallinn, Estonia
Gpsr.requests@easproject.com

www.ingramcontent.com/pod-product-compliance
Lightning Source LLC
Chambersburg PA
CBHW070357240426
43671CB00013BA/2533